The Language of Inequality in the News

Why in the early 1970s does *The Times* reject the idea of a national lottery, as rewarding luck rather than merit and effort, but then warmly welcomes one by the 1990s? Why in the 1970s do the *Daily Mail*'s TV reviews address serious contemporary themes such as class and race relations, whereas forty years later the reviews are largely concerned with celebrities, talent shows, and nostalgia? Why does the Conservative Chancellor in the 2010s mention 'Britain' so very often, whereas the Conservative one in the 1970s scarcely did so at all? Covering news stories spanning forty-five years, Michael Toolan explores how wealth inequality has been presented in centre-right British newspapers, focusing on the way that changes in the representation may have helped present-day inequality seem justifiable. Toolan employs corpus linguistic and Critical Discourse Analytic methods to identify changing lexis and verbal patterns and gaps, all of which contribute to the way wealth inequality has been represented in each of the decades from the 1970s to the present.

MICHAEL TOOLAN is Professor of English Language at the University of Birmingham. He has been conducting research in literary linguistics and discourse analysis for many years, and has published extensively on stylistics and narrative. He is editor of the *Journal of Literary Semantics* and is currently Chair of the Poetics and Linguistics Association.

The Language of Inequality in the News

A Discourse Analytic Approach

Michael Toolan

University of Birmingham

Shaftesbury Road, Cambridge CB2 8EA, United Kingdom

One Liberty Plaza, 20th Floor, New York, NY 10006, USA

477 Williamstown Road, Port Melbourne, VIC 3207, Australia

314–321, 3rd Floor, Plot 3, Splendor Forum, Jasola District Centre, New Delhi – 110025, India

103 Penang Road, #05–06/07, Visioncrest Commercial, Singapore 238467

Cambridge University Press is part of Cambridge University Press & Assessment, a department of the University of Cambridge.

We share the University's mission to contribute to society through the pursuit of education, learning and research at the highest international levels of excellence.

www.cambridge.org
Information on this title: www.cambridge.org/9781108464208

DOI: 10.1017/9781108565172

First published 2018
First paperback edition 2024

A catalogue record for this publication is available from the British Library

ISBN   978-1-108-47433-7   Hardback
ISBN   978-1-108-46420-8   Paperback

Contents

Figures

Tables

Acknowledgements

I have presented versions of parts of the following chapters at a number of conferences and seminars over the past few years and under different linguistic associations' auspices, in diverse cities (Santiago de Compostela, Heidelberg, Delhi, Cardiff, Genoa, and Florianopolis). I am grateful for comments and suggestions from colleagues at all those meetings. I want particularly to thank Wolfgang Teubert for his continual advice and wisdom. Researchers with whom I have discussed this work and from whose responses I have also benefitted include Rukmini Bhaya Nair, John Douthwaite, Malcolm Coulthard and Carmen Rosa Caldas-Coulthard, Beatrix Busse, Viola Weigand, Michaela Mahlberg, Melvyn Westlake, Lesley Jeffries, Brian Walker, Ruth Page, Joe Bennett, Jai Mackenzie, Nicholas Groom, Chris Heffer, Eva Maria Gomez-Jimenez, Teun van Dijk, Sebastian Brun and Julianne Statham.

1 Analysing the Evolving Press Discourse of Contemporary UK Inequality

This study explores the discursive representation of wealth inequality in Britain in two centre-right newspapers – *The Times* and the *Daily Mail* – and possible changes in that representation over the past forty-five years (1971–2016). I seek to address two main questions: are British newspapers writing about wealth inequality differently in recent years than they did in the 1970s, and might those differences have helped present-day inequality seem reasonable and unavoidable? The study uses corpus linguistic and critical discourse analytic methods to help identify significant and changing lexis, multi-word phrases and clausal patterns that contribute to the implicit representation of wealth inequality in the early 1970s and the subsequent decades, attending to shifts in those representations. The project can be classified as corpus-assisted discourse studies (Partington et al. 2013), but there is a diachronic dimension and a critical motivation to the project also, which situate it in the critical discourse tradition of work by Fowler (1991), Van Dijk (e.g., van Dijk 1991, 2008a) and many others.

1.1   Increased Wealth Inequality in the United Kingdom

The United Kingdom has become one of the Organisation for Economic Co-operation and Development (OECD) countries with the highest levels of wealth inequality, and in recent decades this inequality has increased rather than declined: these facts are universally recognised. While wealth and income inequality gradually reduced throughout most of the twentieth century, from the late 1970s onwards this progressive trend reversed. That this entrenched and possibly still-growing inequality is a cause for concern is also widely acknowledged and discussed in academic and political circles.

Commentators, economists, historians and think tanks of all political persuasions acknowledge the problem of growing (not shrinking) inequality. Writing in 2012, even Ferdinand Mount, who once ran Prime Minister Thatcher's Policy Unit and was head of the right-wing Centre for Policy Studies in the 1980s, noted that 'over the past 30 years the share of national income going to the bottom half of earners in Britain has fallen steeply. Real wages nearly

1

doubled overall during those 30 years, but only 8% of that growth went to the bottom earners' (Mount 2012: 5, 7). Also reporting in 2012, Cribb et al. noted:

Up to 1977, income inequality had been on a long-term downward trend, a trend which, as it happens, turned around towards the end of the 1970s. The 1980s saw a historically unprecedented increase in inequality – an increase which has not been unwound since, despite the very substantial growth in the benefit and tax credit budget in the 2000s . . . The income share of the richest 1% has nearly trebled. Even after tax, the richest 1% of households took home nearly 9% of all income in 2009–10 compared with 3% in 1977. (p. 3)

The broad trends were summarized again by Zucman (2015):

Inequality in pre- and post-tax income has risen remarkably in the UK since the late 1970s. Inequality growth was strongest in the 1980s, but has continued steadily for those in the top half of the income distribution (especially the top 1%). Inequality of net income fell in the crisis as the welfare system 'did its job'. But there are signs that it is rising once again and the tax and benefit changes since 2010 have been largely regressive. Perhaps the main cleavage is between pensioners who have done relatively well compared with those of working age, especially the young and households with children.

The best-known way of measuring inequality (there are many) is the Gini coefficient, which aggregates the gaps between people's incomes into a single measure. If everyone in a group has the same income, the Gini coefficient is 0; if all income goes to one person in the group, it is 1. The Gini coefficient shows that the United Kingdom is one of the OECD countries with greater wealth inequality – and that it has grown more like the United States and less like the rest of Western Europe in this respect over the last forty years. According to the Equality Trust:

Most OECD countries have a coefficient lower than 0.32 with the lowest being 0.24. The UK, a fairly unequal society, scores 0.34 and the US, an even more unequal society, 0.38. In contrast, Denmark, a much more equal society, scores 0.25. [www.equalitytrust.org.uk/how-economic-inequality-defined]

The inequality is apparent when income alone is measured, but when personal wealth of all kinds is calculated, the United Kingdom is even more unequal. The richest 10% of households hold 45% of all wealth. The poorest 50%, by contrast, own just 8.7%. We can also measure relative (not absolute) poverty, nowadays commonly defined (e.g., throughout the European Union) as having a household income, adjusted for family size, that is less than 60% of the median income. The number of people in the United Kingdom living in relative poverty by this useful measure increased disturbingly in the 1980s, from 5% to 12%, and has moved only slightly since. By 2020 it is estimated that five million children in the United Kingdom (the per capita sixth richest nation in the world) will be growing up in relative poverty.

Another important measure is the 'wage share' of GDP: the proportion of GDP (gross domestic product: total national earnings) that returns to workers as wages. As a Trades Union Congress (TUC) position paper shows, between 1975 and 2008 the wage share fell from 63% to 53.5% (between 1948 and 1973 it rose, broadly, from 57% to 59%, surged to 64% in 1975, dropped rapidly to 52% in 1996, and has risen only slightly since). Think of this as a small business with profits (after non-salary costs) of £100,000: a few decades back, £64k of this would have gone to those who did the work, rather than the non-working investing owners. Now the workers get £53.5k: considerably less, while the owners get considerably more. When it is remembered that wages for top earners have risen disproportionately, the impact on the average-income worker is clearly worse: their wages have not kept pace with the GDP income that they have helped generate (if they had, actual UK average earnings in 2010 would have been £33k, and not £26k).

Although disparities of *income* (earned or unearned) may be easier to document, the background to my study is not merely income but all sources of *wealth*, all assets, since this gives a fuller picture of the financial basis of inequality of opportunity. Wealth is much more unequally distributed than income, with the top 10% owning 100 times more than the bottom 10% (Rowlingson 2012: 3).

The main long-term trend was for income and wealth inequality to fall during most of the 20th century until the 1980s when inequality began to grow. There is some suggestion that, since 1995, relative wealth inequality may have reduced due to those in the middle benefitting from house price inflation but those at the very top have seen huge absolute increases in wealth and there are still significant numbers of people with no or indeed negative net wealth. (Rowlingson 2012: 4)

In the five years since Rowlingson's report, wealth and wealth inequality have grown again. According to a June 2017 report from the Resolution Foundation (D'Arcy & Gardiner 2017), UK wealth inequality is almost twice as high as inequality of household incomes. The report finds that overall wealth inequality has risen slightly, both within and across age cohorts, for each successive cohort born since 1960. For that minority who have enjoyed growth in their wealth, this has largely come from 'unexpected wealth windfalls' (such as the house price boom in the South-East) and not 'active savings behaviour'.

While there have always been rich people and poor people, powerful people and powerless ones, the relatively steady 'direction of travel' in the United Kingdom for two centuries and more, in matters of wealth/income as in a host of related social 'goods' (suffrage, freedom of expression and belief, open access to education and employment, non-discriminatory treatment regardless of race or gender or sexual orientation, age-longevity, good health and health care) has been to reduce inequality and to reduce disadvantage or the access differential. Gender and sexuality discrimination are mostly in decline, albeit still evident in many contexts. Similarly, race and ethnicity inequality have generally been in decline, notwithstanding local pockets of backsliding. These reductions in unequal treatment are reflected in changes in the way people and institutions routinely talk about race, gender, and sexuality. The general trajectory of decline in discoursally enshrined inequality in areas such as gender and ethnicity is not hard to demonstrate. One significant reflection of these improvements is the change in ways of talking about women, or people from black or minority ethnic groups, or with a minority sexual orientation, in the national press (e.g., in *The Times* or the *Mail* in the 1960s). Ways of describing our neighbours and fellow citizens that were once seemingly acceptable are now quite 'unsayable' – unpublishable in contemporary newspaper references to gender, race/ethnicity and sexual orientation. In most of those parameters, inequality continues to decline, albeit now more slowly and not without local reversions. But with regard to wealth and income, a parameter that often powerfully enables several of the others, the progressive trajectory has not only been halted, it has been reversed.

1.2   Why Does Increasing Wealth Inequality Matter?

Is this of any great importance? Doesn't this just tell us what we have always known, namely that the rich are rich and the poor are poor? The answer is that it matters a great deal; the wider divide that has grown up in living memory between the rich and poor in the United Kingdom and is probably growing yet larger is causing and will continue to cause great harm, not only locally to individuals but collectively and nationally.

In *The Impact of Inequality* (2005), social epidemiologist Richard Wilkinson has shown with compendious statistics that in a country, however wealthy, where the gap between social classes grows too wide, there will be increases in kinds of dysfunctionality, crime and physical and mental illness. Even quite poor countries with a more equal wealth distribution are healthier and happier than richer but more unequal nations. The full title of Wilkinson and Pickett's 2009 follow-up book encapsulates their powerful thesis, again supported by authoritative graphs and statistics: *The Spirit Level: Why More Equal Societies Almost Always Do Better*. Wilkinson and Pickett show that inequality of wealth and income is by far the clearest correlation and explanation for the 'social failure' of the most materially affluent societies (such as the United States and the United Kingdom). Affluent but comparatively equal countries such as Scandinavia and Finland (income-equal, note, not wealth-equal) perform considerably better than unequal ones on a great many measures, including infant mortality, mental health, incarceration rates, educational attainment, and frequency of diabetes and obesity.

More recently, Danny Dorling's *A Better Politics: How Government Can Make Us Happier* (2016) has pointed to the very sharp rise in the UK mortality figures, most markedly for those over eighty, for the year mid-2014 to mid-2015, which are spread geographically and chronologically in ways that make increases in dementia, Alzheimer's or influenza unconvincing explanations. Why are the elderly dying markedly earlier (in effect prematurely)? Dorling suggests that the cause has been the austerity cuts and their effect on public health care for all, but especially for those elderly with long-term care needs. At the same time, statistics for recent years from the Office of National Statistics (ONS) show that the percentage of people at least somewhat satisfied with their own health (a good indicator of sense of well-being) is steadily declining – arguably in response to people's experience of growing austerity and inequality.

All *other* things being equal, acute wealth inequality leads to many negative outcomes for the population as a whole: higher infant mortality; lower life expectancy; higher likelihood of unemployment or low-paid work; lower educational attainment; higher incidence of chronic illness, addiction, service use and involvement in the Criminal Justice System. Here the phrase *for the population as a whole* is critical – and tempting to brush aside by the relatively affluent and well insured, who may not be aware of the evidence that *their* family wealth may lead to higher illness, unemployment or educational failure in other people, let alone have adverse consequences for themselves. But acute wealth inequality has been shown to have all these undesirable effects.

The consequences of the increased, US-style inequality emerging in the United Kingdom are many. In 2016, for example, the richest Americans lived up to fifteen years longer than the poorest, according to studies in *The Lancet* (Dickman et al. 2017). We now live in a country where three million children are at risk of hunger and malnourishment during school holidays, according to an All Party Parliamentary Group study headed by Frank Field (Forsey 2017). Highly unequal societies have less social mobility and lower aggregate educational attainment, but higher property crime and violent crime rates, than less unequal ones. Acute and preventable inequality is not only morally questionable, it is also enormously wasteful of the potential within a society as a whole, caused by disproportionate protection of a subsection of that society.

Acutely unequal economic relations can also lead to the kinds of morally or ethically dubious activities discussed in Michael Sandel's *What Money Can't Buy*, such as paying someone (perhaps a homeless person) to queue on your behalf for a place at some restricted-access event. In Sandel's view, in this and other practices (such as corporations' purchase of so-called dead peasant insurance to protect their own interests, and not those of the employee) the market approach has crossed a line and has developed in a direction that is damaging to democracy. We might also note the rise (return) of slavery in developed countries: in Britain this prompted the creation of a Minister for Modern Slavery and Organised Crime in the 2010–15 coalition government, and the Modern Slavery Act 2015, passed to facilitate the prosecution of traffickers. It is sobering to think that today in Britain the meaning of *slave driver* has regressed to the literal sense, in much usage.

What might a reduction in wealth inequality achieve? If the evidence from Wilkinson and Pickett (2009), Piketty (2014), Stieglitz (2012b), Atkinson (2015), Hills (2015), the Equality Trust (www.equalitytrust.org.uk) and many others is a guide, then it will usher in lower levels of suicide, imprisonment, mental illness, obesity, addiction, infant mortality, antisocial behaviour in the poor as well as the rich. Many other desiderata of living 'fully' are likely to flourish in a more equal, more Scandinavian-style economy, desiderata of the kind outlined in the 'Capabilities Approach' championed by Amartya Sen and Martha Nussbaum (Nussbaum & Sen 1993). Even greater economic produc- tivity is likely to ensue as a result of greater investment in developing the skills of those currently consigned to the 'gig', low-wage, low-skill economy.

1.3   Facts, Discourse, Myths

How did increased inequality become so 'normal' and accepted as reasonable? I believe it did so in part by changes in public discourses, changes in the discoursal representation of everything in the news, so that this state of affairs became understood to be normal, reasonable and ordinary. A naturalising and legitimising within public discourses of kinds and degrees of inequality, pre- viously much less generally accepted, took hold. This is the supposition the present study seeks to confirm.

Even if certain kinds of discoursal difference among newspapers in the 1970s and the 2010s can be uncovered, are these differences anything more than epiphenomenal? Surely any evidence of change in the discursive repre- sentations of inequality is simply an effect, rather than a cause, of increased inequality. Discourse simply names or describes whatever the facts are; it cannot create or alter those facts.

Declaring that facts are unalterable and outside language is itself a rhetorical claim, and a continually disproven one. Mostly the speaker who begins a statement by saying 'The fact of the matter is . . .' is adding some coercive stiffening to the expression of his or her own judgement. Facts are always (made) within language, and are therefore always susceptible to subtle reformulation (or, in Orwell's dystopian vision, not so subtle alteration). Rocks and trees and the oceans and the moon arguably exist outside language – but it is impossible to talk about them or make sense of them until we have clothed them in language, and have developed discourses around them.

In all domains of human activity and experience, language profoundly shapes the activity or experience itself; it is not a mere after-the-act labelling. Situations come about to a significant degree consequent upon the production and acceptance of a specific kind of enabling discourse. We see this in small ways with local promises and apologies and decisions, but we may struggle to see it in the larger ways, where a vast network of discourses represent the way things are, and this representation takes hold as valid, accurate, reasonable and normal. There is a long tradition of linguistic studies that underpin the present one, a tradition that understands a society's language habits and practices as shaping and influencing (but not straitjacketing) that society's customary and ordinary assumptions about everything. The tradition includes publications by Sapir (1983) and Whorf (1956), the exhortations of those who advise us to mind our language, much of the thinking in critical discourse analysis (surveyed in the following paragraphs), and studies like those of Cameron (1993) and Teubert (2010).

The shaping of thoughts, expectations and assumptions by language is not simply a matter of your saying *tomaydo* and my saying *tomahto*, of your calling a *tundish* what I call a *funnel*, or your saying *man and wife* when I say *husband and wife* or *partners*. Beyond the influence of habitual labels, there is the influence of habitual sentences, descriptions, metaphors, narratives and myths: extended discourse of one kind or another. Hills (2015) highlights how pernicious stories ('myths') are fed back into discussions of social security spending, seriously distorting ordinary people's political thinking. According to Hills' research, people imagine that nearly half the welfare budget is spent ('wasted') on unemployment benefits when the actual figure is approximately 1%; likewise they imagine that 50% of those on the jobseeker's allowance are chronically jobless and will still be unemployed after twelve months, when in fact fewer than 10% will be. The myths foster damagingly divisive misrepresentations, such as the imagined existence of a large cohort of 'work-shy' benefits claimants.

A myth of a different kind – often crucial to inequality apologists – is the idea that inequality is 'good for the economy', by inducing the ambitious to strive while handsomely rewarding the most successful, stimulating productivity and growth. The reality appears to be very different: too much inequality depresses economic activity, as the experience of the United States, with its similar pattern of affluence-cum-inequality to that now characterizing the United Kingdom, shows. In the quarter of a century or so from the end of World War II, the United States enjoyed an in-tandem improvement in both standard of living and equality, but this was followed by more than thirty years in which affluence and equality diverged, and in which, importantly, the increasing inequality depressed rather than stimulated the economy. As the economist Joseph Stiglitz commented in a widely disseminated article:

Defenders of America's inequality argue that the poor and those in the middle shouldn't complain. While they may be getting a smaller share of the pie than they did in the past, the pie is growing so much, thanks to the contributions of the rich and superrich, that the size of their slice is actually larger. The evidence, again, flatly contradicts this. Indeed, America grew far faster in the decades after the second world war, when it was growing together, than it has since 1980, when it began growing apart. (Stiglitz 2012a)

A highly unequal society (on any measure: gender, race, etc.) is inevitably also an undemocratic society. A society (increasingly a transnational society) where a whole class of families continues to have far greater wealth than the majority is one in which a wealth-based elite subsists. That elite inevitably wields far greater power and influence than everyone else, and that power inevitably extends to politics, undermining democracy.

The growth in UK wealth inequality is undisputed: the interesting question is how this happened. There are some 'grand narrative' explanations, such as the story of Western capitalism flourishing while Soviet bloc communism faltered and collapsed, leading to the reunification of Germany and 'the end of history', and the ever-growing reach of a neoliberal, capitalist, market-driven form of globalisation. I do not question this narrative, thus broadly drawn. But since the heady days of 1989–90 we have also seen 'history' refusing to end (contrary to predictions), with new ethnic- and religious-based wars arising, most notably from Islam-invoking terrorists, and equally 'globalised'. It is doubtful, also, that the state-shrinking, inequality-tolerant preference of Mrs Thatcher's brand of Conservatism was quite so 'inevitable' in the 1980s as it now seems (having been largely maintained by the Major and New Labour governments). If political developments had been only slightly different, and a Clarke-Heseltine Conservative government had ruled through the 1980s, a host of decisions, responses and policies might have cumulatively created a quite different effect. So whatever we say about the overarching story of increasingly entrenched neoliberalism, it is worth recognising that the larger outcomes emerged as a result of a vast network of choices that people made, or that others made and most people accepted or could not resist. These choices were of many kinds: about economic and financial arrangements, about jobs and working conditions; about pay, profits and taxes; and about political arrangements. But these choices were also language choices – including decisions about what one said was economically fair, reasonable, necessary or unavoidable.

1.4   'Ethical' Differentiation

Discriminating representation is not always contentious. Difference of representation and evaluation on the grounds of race, age or gender are automatically questionable. But differences of representation or evaluation on grounds such as hair colour, dietary preference or musical ability would not ordinarily be regarded as discriminatory or questionable. Short students will rarely make the basketball team; bald actors tend not to be hired to appear in TV shampoo commercials. In plenty of competitions many must lose for a few to win.

Where do economic inequalities and disparities fit, relative to the preceding distinction? Are the very poor and the enormously rich simply like the extremes in a sport such as professional football: the top teams, continually winning and richly rewarded, compared with bottom-of-the-league impecunious clubs that mostly lose their matches? In many respects they are not, and should not be conflated. To see this we need only to tweak the example, away from professional football, to, for example, a game of tennis in the park between your son and your daughter. Suppose your daughter wins: would you be sure to speak long and loud about her accomplishments, and criticise your son's 'failings' at equal length? Ice cream and a celebratory Pepsi for your daughter and just a glass of water for your son? Did I mention that the daughter is sixteen and has been expensively coached, the boy only half her age? These and similar factors are circumstantial details that would cause any reasonable parent to remember that tennis is only a game, and that you have more important connections to the two players, and they to each other, than this disproportionate focussing on who won and who lost would justify. Relations among people across society as a whole are (or should be) more like those within the family, where differences may be plentiful but episodes of winning and losing are of minor importance, and less like professional sport presented to a paying public, where the win/lose difference may be of great importance – but not, even for most professionals, to be pursued 'at any cost'.

1.5   Inequality as 'British' Once More

A sense of identity is important for any person's well-being, their sense of self; it is in part constructed or performed, especially through discourse, rather than simply given. Because we do so much identity performance through language, a large branch of linguistics, sociolinguistics, is devoted to its study, including how our acts of identity or identification are by the same token acts of distancing, exclusion and rejection, defining ourselves by our difference from various others. But every stating or performing of difference can turn into an assertion of an inequality, a hierarchy: 'we are different from you … and better or "higher" than you'. In our narrativising discourses, we tell or absorb stories about ourselves and how we are different from others. These include stories in the newspapers, among which are some that treat differential resources and opportunities, for different classes of Britons, as normal and reasonable.

Becoming again a more entrenched fact of life in modern Britain, wealth inequality is also becoming again a more central characteristic of British identity, of what it means to be British. If identity generally is 'performed' through the countless acts and communications an identity bearer engages in, national identity is performed in part through the content and assumptions of myriad public discourses about that nation which, at a given point in time, are accepted by that nation as indicative, a fair representation. Granted, identity is never monolithic and impregnable. It is likely in some places and at some times to be performed or represented as indeterminate, conflicted and variable. But if increased inequality is now a more pronounced part of the United Kingdom's identity, we should find this more prominently reflected in many of our social and cultural practices, including such powerful public discourses as the print and online national newspapers.

It is in this internalisation of inequality, as part of British identity, that a supplement can be made to the powerful argument of Benn Michaels (2006) concerning inequality and cultural diversity in the even-more-unequal United States. Benn Michaels argues that liberal America has become preoc-cupied with diversity of identity – combatting potential discrimination based on race, gender, or any other basis of cultural difference – to the absolute neglect of wealth inequality. Indeed, defenders of diversity, he argues, feed the illusion that rectification of diversity failings will in time solve the inequality or poverty problem. The situation in the United Kingdom at least is arguably more nuanced, or pernicious. If being wealth unequal has been renewed as an element in British identity (i.e., it is in the nature of being British that a few of us are rich, most of us manage, and some are poor), then a celebrating of diversity does not involve a neglecting of inequality. Instead it is folded into our conception of diversity.

1.6   Why *The Times* and the *Daily Mail*?

Two national newspapers – the *Daily Mail* and *The Times* – are the focus of attention. My interest was in moderately centrist or centre-right newspapers, which one might expect broadly to encourage rather than resist the political and economic developments that have led to greater wealth inequality (compare, e.g., the *Daily Mirror* and *The Guardian*).

The *Daily Mail* has been severally described as 'middle-market' and 'tabloid'; it is centre-right in politics and conservative in values generally, like *The Times*, but it is targeted at a lower-middle- and upper-working-class readership, who are more often women than men (55% to 45%). Far older than

The Sun or even the *Daily Express*, the *Daily Mail* has a long and sometimes chequered history. It was launched in 1896 by the recently ennobled Harmsworth brothers: Lord Northcliffe and Lord Rothermere (the present Viscount Rothermere is chairman and chief shareholder of its publisher, the Daily Mail and General Trust). The paper is distinguished by its editors' longevity of tenure: from 1971 to 1992 it was edited by David English, and since then by Paul Dacre – both redoubtable figures. The *Mail* remains the United Kingdom's second largest-selling newspaper, after *The Sun*, with 1.7 million copies in daily circulation and an estimated readership of the print version of more than double that number. Alongside the daily and Sunday printed newspaper, *MailOnline* is a free online newspaper, the content of which mostly duplicates the printed paper; in 2011 it was the second most visited English-language newspaper website worldwide. According to ABC, reporting in November 2015, *MailOnline* remains the United Kingdom's most popular newspaper website with an average of 13.2 million browsers visiting the site every day; the National Readership Survey estimates that the *Daily Mail* in 2014 was the most read newspaper brand – print and online – in the United Kingdom, with a monthly readership of 23.5 million.

Among the daily broadsheets or so-called quality newspapers in England (for the entire more-than-forty-year period, these comprise just *The Times, The Telegraph*, the *Financial Times*, and *The Guardian*), *The Times* stands out because it has always purported to be the 'newspaper of record' – more authoritative but also more moderate in its centre-right politics than the *Daily Telegraph* (*The Guardian* being centre-left in politics, mostly). *The Times* is the longest-established and most authoritative national daily in the United Kingdom, reputedly the newspaper of and for 'top people', with historically considerable influence on the thinking among people of property and influence (e.g., in regard to the National Strike of 1926 and King Edward VIII's abdication in 1936). In the 1970s it was owned by Canadian magnates the Thomson Organisation, with William Rees-Mogg as its editor from 1967 to 1981. The late 1970s and early 1980s were a period of deep industrial conflict at *The Times*. At first, unlike its Fleet Street rivals, it observed the Labour Government's pay restraint policy, which caused the pay of its printers and production workers to fall behind that of their fellow unionised workers. Thomson offered a pay deal that was contingent upon agreed improved productivity, which the print workers rejected, so the paper closed down from 1 December 1978 to 12 November 1979 (by which time Mrs Thatcher had already been in power for six months). The Thomson Organisation reportedly 'had enough' by this point, but finding a willing buyer of the loss-making *Times* proved difficult (its partner, the *Sunday Times*, was by contrast financially strong).

In 1981, in a surprise move, the Australian-born media magnate Rupert Murdoch bought both the *Times* and the *Sunday Times* (a rival bidder, interestingly, was Rothermere, owner of the *Mail*). The sale was quite controversial because, with his existing ownership of *The Sun* and the *News of the World*, Murdoch was acquiring control of a broad range of national titles, yet the government did not require Murdoch's bid to be referred for adjudication to the Monopolies and Mergers Commission. Had Murdoch's close relations with Mrs Thatcher and her government given him an improper advantage, people speculated?

In 1981 Murdoch appointed Harold Evans editor of *The Times*, moving him from the editorship of the *Sunday Times*, where he had overseen several successful campaigns (including one for adequate compensation for those damaged by the Thalidomide drug – the campaign led to considerable reform of press freedom to publish). While some regarded Evans as Murdoch's 'agent', *The Times*'s critical reporting on the Thatcher government suggested otherwise. In March 1982 Evans resigned (he was replaced by Charles Douglas-Home), perhaps under pressure from Murdoch but also after some *Times* journalists, dismayed at the more sensationalising tone of some articles, had called for him to go. The newspaper rapidly moved to the right, politically, after Evans's departure. Greenslade (2003) summarizes a widespread view in arguing that Murdoch expects his newspapers both to make profits and to propagandise on behalf of the neoliberal politics he espouses – the politics which allowed him to accumulate the wealth that enabled him to buy *The Times, The Sun*, and many other media outlets. The goals of the Daily Mail and General Trust, and of Dacre as *Mail* editor, are a similar combination of profitability with political interestedness.

In the study that follows, covering the years 1971 to 2016, I refer mostly to the print newspaper versions of the *Mail* and *Times* – at least until the most recent period from 2005 onwards, when access to the online versions became routine. As noted, online news facilitates an enormous amount of sharing on other social media platforms, meaning that stories are made available to a huge secondary readership (just how many recipients of such recommendations open these links and read the stories is less clear). A recent annual *Digital News Report* of the Reuters Institute for the Study of Journalism (Newman et al. 2016) confirms the dominance, for people in the United Kingdom under the age of forty, of online news sources (rather than print, television or radio), usually accessed by smartphone; it also notes, however, that for these users, the strongly preferred online sources are 'traditional' broadcast and print sources, such as the *BBC, Mail* and *Guardian* online. In those sources, the user may still encounter the longer, reflective item, in addition to instant 'hard' news.

1.7   Spreading the Word about the New Inequality: The News Media

It is sometimes argued now that with newsprint sales declining, any attention that discourse analysts pay to what print newspapers say borders on the irrelevant: young people especially get their news from social media, we are told; therefore critical analysts need to be looking at what is posted, retweeted or promoted on Twitter, Facebook, and similar social media outlets. Although powerful today, none of the latter existed in the 1970s, so this presents a comparability challenge for a diachronic discourse analysis. At the same time, younger people vote less, have little money and have less power/capital in society than their parents and grandparents. Newspapers such as *The Times* and the *Daily Mail* are digital and online, as well as available in print (*MailOnline* has a readership in the several millions). The best and most influential journalists still tend to write for the national newspapers. They are still *attended to* (and often recirculated/promoted in tweets). People use social media to stay informed, but it is likely they still turn to their newspaper and their preferred TV and radio channels for in-depth and considered views.

There is, besides, a symbiotic relationship between, for example, the broadsheet newspapers (now especially their online versions) and the main television/radio news or politics programmes – each recycling any fresh content found in the other, alongside the millions of users of Facebook and Twitter who are continually posting, linking and retweeting content from the mainstream and other sources. Despite the emergence of countless new digital sites carrying news and commentary (some visited by hundreds of thousands, others quite niche), it is no accident that newspapers are still a better expression and indicator of a person's broad political affiliation than the SMS channels are: it is informative of your assumed identity/values to say 'I'm a typical *Guardian/Telegraph* reader . . .', whereas it reveals nothing of your political preferences to say 'I'm a Facebook/Twitter user' (or, perhaps, 'I'm a *Huffington Post* reader').

The importance of President Trump's Twitter account is often cited as evidence that socio-political commentary has moved far away from the established newspapers, or even their online outlets. But how many of those who learn of Trumps' tweets do so as subscribers to his account? Rather, we learn of his tweets through the reporting of them on Sky, the BBC, and the (print or online) national newspapers. His tweets are like former presidents' ad hoc remarks to the press, or at public events. A tweet or a blog may be first with breaking news and political announcements, but it is the uptake of such news, by the established and still much-consulted outlets, that with far greater authority tell people what to think of that news. In short, there remain certain agents that are exceptionally powerfully placed to influence and shape the meaning of the news, as well as the content and background assumptions of the ongoing national conversation, which in turn continually updates the nation's narrative about itself.

1.8   Landmarks in the Politics of Language Tradition

Reflections on the politics of language in the Western tradition are traceable to Aristotle and Plato, but in the modern British era George Orwell's essay of 1946, 'Politics and the English Language', followed soon after by his dystopian novel of a totalitarian future Britain, *Nineteen Eighty-Four*, are key texts. In that novel, the language of Newspeak is portrayed as crucial to the state's efforts to manage the populus (Orwell 1949: 312–26). Newspeak is designed to restrict individual and potentially radical or dissenting thought by reducing the range of 'available vocabulary', and is aimed at controlling or at least *priming* the people over and over again with certain ways of speaking about matters (schools, the unemployed, entrepreneurs, etc.). This is done with a view to entrenching a preferred way of representing and by implication thinking about the world – 'reality' – so that when citizens share this understanding in talk with others, those ways of speaking and thinking are reinforced. The premise of Newspeak is that discourse control is the best kind of mind control; in fact it is the only kind of control you need – how someone speaks and writes about something are the best evidence as to what they think about it, so once you control the former you control the latter.

Jumping forward to the 1970s, a notable contribution to the study of language's political effects is Raymond Williams's important slim volume *Keywords* (1976). A keyword in the Williams sense (quite different from the use of this term in corpus linguistics) is one that gives you structured access to concepts of central value in (in this case) British culture; a keyword is a cultural resource, a way of thinking and a core cultural principle or value. For all 110 words selected for the first edition (the second edition of 1983 added twenty-one more, including *ecology, ethnic, racial, sex* and *western*), Williams sought to distinguish their different senses and by this means help to uncover the roots of what he saw as disturbing misunderstandings (mutual alienation, even) among different groups of English speakers who, after the catalytic maelstrom of the Second World War, no longer felt they were 'speaking the same language' (1976: 11).

Turning from the politics of language in general to the more particular study of language in the news media, a recurrent message has been that notional journalistic objectivity invariably masks dangerous bias and ideological framing. The Glasgow University Media Group have produced many sobering findings on this topic. From their earliest publications [*Bad News* (1976) and *More Bad News* (1980)] they have charged the UK television media with being sharply slanted in their explanations of economic problems such as recession, inflation and unemployment. Where not attributable to unions and excessive pay demands, they are represented as natural or inescapable developments – beyond human agency or control.

A final preliminary orientation point is the work on media bias by Stuart Hall and his colleagues. One of their most-cited publications (1978) was incisively titled 'The Social Production of News'. It argued that the media

do not simply and transparently report events which are 'naturally' newsworthy *in themselves*. 'News' is the end-product of a complex process which begins with a systematic sorting and selecting of events and topics according to a socially constructed set of categories. (p. 53)

Unexpected events are 'framed' or 'mapped' according to the dominant cultural values that the mass media reflect and adopt: the 'central value system' (Hall et al. 1978: 55). Since the central value system is integrated into what becomes news, '[t]he media define for the majority of the population *what* significant events are taking place, but, also, they offer powerful interpretations of *how* to understand these events' (Hall et al. 1978: 57).

1.9   Language-Oriented Critical Discourse Analysis: A Brief Survey

1.9.1   Fowler

Roger Fowler's *Language in the News* (1991) merits revisiting as the most developed linguistic critique of news discourse of that time. Like Hall and like Johan Galtung and Mari Holmboe Ruge, Fowler dispels any assumption of the intrinsic or automatic newsworthiness of events: events become 'news' when selected for press treatment (1991:11). One of his themes is the role of 'conflictual oppositions', which he claims the Thatcher governments of the 1980s particularly asserted and exploited, to create a polarised 'we' and 'they' opposition. This message of conflict and opposition operated alongside a theme of consensus, paradoxically. The Conservative governments and the rightward-leaning press that endorsed them constantly contrived to project the idea that 'we' were all in agreement about what was right, proper, desirable and, for that matter, undesirable or intolerable. Strikes were one of the things deemed intolerable, and as 'we' all knew, strikes were caused by unions. But as Fowler goes on to say,

[c]onsensus is the affirmation and the plea of all political parties, expressed in appeals for 'one nation', for people to 'pull together', and so on ... But ... [i]n order to place a fence around 'us', the popular papers of the Right are obsessed with stories which cast 'them' in a bad light: trades unionists, socialist council leaders, teachers, blacks, social workers, rapists, homosexuals, etc., all become stigmatized 'groups'. (1991: 16)

Fowler often invokes the concept of 'structure' or linguistic structure; news writers always have alternative choices of structure available to them, he says. These 'choices of structure' sometimes concern categorization and habitual naming tendencies, but Fowler also examines a discourse's transitivity options (e.g., those for encoding participants as Agents or Affected entities, using Halliday's systemic-linguistic grammar). Important to Fowler's method is the idea that a fluent user of a language has access to many varieties of that language, many alternative semantic grids for 'mapping' an event or situation and realises that anything described in one way can alternatively be described rather differently. In principle, or at least with the help of critical linguistics, any reader should be able to see 'through and around the settings of the semantic system of the language' (Fowler 1991: 31) used in news reports.

Like Hall, Fowler believes that articulating 'the ideology of consensus' is a crucial means by which a right-wing press negotiates its relations with government and capital (on one hand) and with its readers (on the other); he calls this articulating a 'linguistic practice' (49) and argues that media analysts have largely neglected it – hence the task for critical linguistics to perform. The point about such a constructed consensus is that it is by this means that *The Sun* or the *Mail* assumes 'and in times of crisis actually *affirms*' (49) that their readers agree with them on a whole set of beliefs. Strikingly, Fowler adds, 'The content of the consensual assumption could be spelt out as a long series of propositions about (in this case) contemporary Britain' (49). Fowler proceeds to give examples of these postulated propositions: 'that workers and factory-owners are equally benefited by productivity and economic growth; [that] class differences are a thing of the past ... [and that] everyone would like to buy their own house and live in a family life-style' (50) and so on. Because Fowler was writing in the days before extensive machine-readable corpora were available, his incisive observations could not be supported by an extensive body of textual evidence drawn from the newspapers' discourse. A crucial question is whether corpus and critical linguistic methods can furnish a great deal more in the way of an inspectable empirical basis for whatever 'series of propositions' are derived from a newspaper corpus.

For Fowler, consensus on these propositions underpins the Galtung and Ruge (1965: 49) news value of 'meaningfulness', which he renames 'homo-centrism': the journalist's calculation of the degree to which a story would seem relevant to the target readers, about them and their world (hence the idea of ethno- or homo-centrism) and distinct from others'. Thus the Galtung and Ruge 'meaningfulness' value has a lot to do with identity and the 'othering' of all those who are, in view of their assumed values and characteristics, not the target readership. Research on news values by Galtung and Ruge and by Colleen Cotter (2010) has recently been greatly supplemented by Monika Bednarek and Helen Caple (2014), who explore a number of news values (negativity, eliteness, novelty, superlativeness, proximity and timeliness) that seem to most affect newsworthiness decisions and who seek to understand why just these particular 'deeply ideological' values take priority in story selection. My study directs limited attention to news values as such (but see, e.g., Chapter 4), treating that interest as a focus mostly on the production side of stories. The stories readers are offered will clearly combine the general values in varied ways, but their connections to a changing narrative about inequality are likely to be complexly indirect – at least, less direct than the use in specific socioeconomic contexts of keywords and key phrases.

1.9.2   Van Dijk

Teun van Dijk has long advocated a rigorous critical analysis of discriminatory media representations of marginalised or subordinated groups in society. He contends that a critical discourse approach considers the relationship between language and society in order to understand 'the relations between discourse, power, dominance, [and] social inequality' (1993: 249). Like Fowler, van Dijk has been interested in the role of ideology and discrimination in press journalism. He was also (in van Dijk 1988) an early proponent of the idea of using a kind of editorial stripping and generalising of the sentences of a newspaper article in order to reduce it to a more concise set of what he called macropropositions. Macropropositional summary could be applied recursively, he suggested, perhaps reducing a ten-paragraph article to ten sentences (one per paragraph), and then further reducing those ten sentences to three or four by replacing particular named entities or processes by single superordinate terms or by deleting material judged to be secondary or 'background'. The point of undertaking such macropropositional reduction is that it is expected to encapsulate and highlight an article's core message and, by extension, some clear pointers to its core ideology.

Van Dijk also developed the idea of the 'ideological square' as a kind of covert structure shaping a writer's referential strategies when representing a politically contentious account of events. The four quadrants of the square relate to the representing of the Self, including those with whom the writer aligns him- or herself, and the representing of Others or 'the Other', whom the writer implicitly sets at a distance. The ideological square predicts that the Self's positive characteristics will tend to be foregrounded and the negative ones backgrounded, whereas the exact reverse tendency will apply to the positively and negatively evaluated qualities of the Other(s). The most striking thing about van Dijk's proposal is that, as with Fowler and several others commentaries, it is emphatically binary: it recognises and reflects the tendency for politically charged discourse to construct two sides and take one of them, simplifying policies, conditions and events to an either/or logic, where if one side is true, ethical or sensible, then the other must be false, immoral or nonsensical. Differences are discursively magnified to become oppositions. As van Dijk recognised, any identifications of macrostructure, macropropositions and 'core macropropositions' are subjective exercises (van Dijk 1988: 33), guided by the interpreter's interpretive preferences (Brown & Yule 1983: 110) and unlikely to be replicated identically by another analyst. In addition, the suspicious reading of newspaper discourse needs to notice also what is backgrounded or even given no textual mention. To capture the different degrees of explicitness of mention, Fairclough (1995: 106) proposed a four-level classification, ranging from foregrounded to backgrounded to presupposed to completely absent, whereas van Leeuwen (1996: 39), perhaps recognising that 'absent' is too broad a category (covering both strategic silences and unremarkable kinds of absence), proposed a distinction between suppression and backgrounding.

1.9.3   Fairclough

A third leading figure to emerge in the field by then usually called critical discourse analysis (CDA) was Norman Fairclough; over the past quarter century he and his co-researchers have published numerous works applying CDA; the discussion here will focus on what has perhaps been his most influential work, *Language and Power* (1989), which was updated in later editions of 2001 and 2014. [Were my interest confined to the New Labour years, 1997–2010, Fairclough (2000) would be a relevant volume to discuss, to which we should now add Jeffries and Walker (2017), a work very much in the spirit of the present study, which appeared too late for fuller attention here.] In its first edition *Language and Power* captured the spirit of an increasingly politically attuned critical discourse, which had emerged in the analysis of political language in the deregulatory 1980s of Reagan and Thatcher, but which was also apparent in the study of other kinds of often dyadic transactional talk, including doctor–patient, teacher–pupil, manager–employee, and police officer–interviewee interactions. In all these, discourse analysts accepted the need to explain the structure and content of talk as not only guided by a 'grammar' of talk, with its regularities and expectations, but also shaped by the wider context that included the power- and authority-relations inhering among participants.

For Fairclough the analysis begins with a description of the text or discourse event, and then proceeds to interpretation (of both the text and its situation or context), and finally explanation of it, as an instance of social practice, structured in part by the power relations among those involved. The initial description stage identifies those aspects of the vocabulary, grammar and text structure which are said to perform ideological functions in the discourse. These linguistic elements may enable one or another participant to control the content, or the relations between participants and the social roles they are filling. The second edition of *Language and Power* (2001) is substantially unchanged from the first, except for the addition of a final chapter on how the world that now needed addressing was more globalised than was apparent in 1989: globalised in the sense that political, economic and social language and discourse representations now operated in a global context rather than one mostly bounded by the nation-state. Now 'we need to look at social relations, structures and processes on an international scale', Fairclough writes (2001: 203), to understand the negative effects of capitalism in a number of areas [including, in Fairclough's list, 'the increasing gap between rich and poor' (p. 203)]. He notes that the new order involves 'winning acceptance for particular representations of change' and that critique will involve resisting the new ways of using language and the new representations (2001: 205).

In the third edition of *Language and Power* (2014), Fairclough adds a lengthy new introductory chapter, which situates his own conception of CDA in comparison to the work of historicist and corpus linguistic discourse analysts (Robinson 2016 is a useful review of the significance of this new chapter). Fairclough now summarises CDA as explanatory critique of discourse as a basis for changing 'existing reality': 'CDA combines *critique* of discourse and *explanation* of how it figures within and contributes to the existing social reality, as a basis for *action* to change that existing reality in particular respects' (2014: 6). In this third edition and other recent work, Fairclough also emphasises the importance of analysing the argumentation implicit within and underpinning a given discourse. If the consequences of a particular argumentative position are that certain aspects of social reality are maintained in conditions of inequality, exclusion or discrimination, then 'defeating' (in some sense) the argument is necessary to enable change in the social reality that the flawed arguments sponsor. He writes that CDA should prioritise the analysis of 'argumentation in political and policy-making discourse' (2014: 6) because this in his view is the most direct shaper of social change. It is hard to fault Fairclough's wish for CDA work, ultimately, to make a material social difference; it is something that many have called for it to attempt [see discussions in McKenna (2004), Billig (2002b), Jessop (2003), Meyer (2001) and Partington et al. (2013)].

There is no single method of CDA. It is conducted in noticeably different ways by, for example, Fairclough, van Dijk and Baker. Fairclough is primarily a social theorist, with a complex model of how discourse constitutes and reflects social relations, particularly those of power and marginalisation; but there is only very limited use of quantitative data regarding frequencies of semantic categories or structures. His usual method is to identify one or several broad political trends, such as conversationalisation and mediatisation or 'synthetic personalisation' and to demonstrate evidence of those phenomena in the language choices in a very few signal or indicative speeches or texts (such as a politician's speech or media interview, or a government health advisory leaflet).

A suitably brief 'worked example' is included in Fairclough et al. (2011), a contribution to a multidisciplinary introductory guide to many different traditions of discourse studies, edited by van Dijk. The worked example is Fairclough's well-known critical discourse analysis of one passage (a few minutes long) of a 1985 radio interview with the then UK prime minister, Margaret Thatcher (this analysis was also the lynchpin chapter 7 of Fairclough's *Language and Power*, discussed earlier). The condensed 2011 account demonstrates the links between Mrs Thatcher's linguistic choices and her political allegiances. Fairclough shows Mrs Thatcher's using her rhetorical power to 'police' the interview and give answers that suit her interests rather than the thrust of the interviewer's questions; he shows her adept use of the *you* and *we* pronouns, sometimes strategically ambiguous in reference, and of *people*. But there is no attempt to widen this study (e.g., to look at all the one-to-one political interviews given by Mrs Thatcher in 1985, or across the 1980s) nor any demonstration that Mrs Thatcher's use of *you* and *we* pronouns is significantly different from that of prime ministers in the 1970s, or that of Mr Kinnock, her opposite number in the Labour party from 1983 to 1992. Focussing at length on a few moments in just one interview, Fairclough can contextualise his critical reading of the language of that interview relatively fully. But for discourse analysts who believe that it is the steady accumulation of many instances over time that creates an ideological stance or is likely to habituate addressees to a particular shifted conception of the world, a different kind of context is missing: a description of each speech (or interview or editorial) in the context of all the other speeches of similar importance at that time or chronologically related.

1.9.4   Mulderrig

The CDA work of Jane Mulderrig (whose research is closely aligned with Fairclough's) is also relevant to the present study. In 'Enabling Participatory Governance in Education' (2015), Mulderrig notes how over the past thirty or more years, the burden on the individual to be directly responsible for his or her own well-being has grown markedly, alongside a decline in the sense of a collective responsibility, overseen by the state, for ensuring everyone should have access to good jobs, health care, schools, pensions and housing. In recent decades, the conviction has taken hold that the state 'cannot afford' to fund particular areas in ways once possible. Now, the state is 'enabling' its citizens rather than providing unconditional but allegedly competitiveness-sapping protection, and *competitiveness* itself has become a key term in contemporary governance discourse, and a key driver underpinning education policy in the race to create a globally successful 'knowledge economy' (Mulderrig, 2009).

One of the many reflexes of this change in the relations between state and citizen, Mulderrig notes, is the idea of 'workfare', a term to be understood as a rugged replacement for *welfare*. Workfare schemes require some form of social contribution from recipients in return for their benefit payment: 'In terms of the social relations of governance, this entails new forms of "active, participatory" citizenship coupled with a more devolved, "enabling" model of political leadership' (Mulderrig, 2015: 1). She finds this focus on 'enabling' reflected in a more restricted use of verbs such as *help* and *ensure* and a suitably circumscribed use of *provide* (e.g., government documents are more likely to speak of *providing the conditions in which people can do X* than of *providing people with specific goods/services*).

1.10   Corpus Linguistic Methods for Exploring the Ideology in Discourse

1.10.4   The Collocational Meaning of Elderly

Some kinds of CDA over the last two decades have increasingly turned to the study of large corpora of texts, and the use of corpus linguistic techniques of analysis, to underpin arguments. Hardt-Mautner (1995) and Stubbs (1996, 2001) were among the first to combine corpus linguistic and critical discourse methods in this way, and a paper by Mautner (2007) on patterns of use of the word *elderly* is a good example of what the alliance can achieve. Mautner searches a large corpus for lexico-grammatical evidence to help to decide whether *elderly* is a neutral or a stigmatizing label. The discursive or 'collocational profile' that emerges shows that *elderly* is associated with discourses of care, disability and vulnerability, arguably to a disproportionate degree. A premise of the study is one that is general in CDA: that important social and political categories such as age and ageing are not neutral, standing outside of culture, but socioculturally constructed and more particularly discursively constructed (constructed by being voiced and accepted, or challenged or amended). Her study of *elderly*, she notes, bears some resemblance to the kinds of cultural keywords such as *heritage* and *community*, which Stubbs explored: 'nodes around which ideological battles are fought' (Stubbs 2001: 188).

What is the rationale behind seeking guidance as to the meaning of *elderly* by collocational analysis (i.e., extracting from their fuller textual settings very many segments, approximately fourteen words in length, in which each actual use of the target word is positioned in the middle of the line and the patterns of wordings that surround it are sorted and examined)? The assumption is that the recurrent collocations of a word or phrase are a good guide to its meaning. In the famous declaration of Firth, 'You shall know a word by the company it keeps' (Firth 1957: 11); or, more guardedly, the most frequent meanings of an expression (this might be multiword or idiomatic, but still functioning in a unitary way) can be derived, by nonextravagant interpretive inference, from its most frequent collocates. In most forms of corpus-assisted CDA, collocational analysis carries a heavy explanatory burden.

1.10.1   Teubert's Paraphrase Principle

According to Wolfgang Teubert's theory of corpus linguistics, the motivation for such collocation analyses is the paraphrase principle (Teubert 2010). This is the idea that the meaning of an expression in discourse is best captured by seeing how else the expression has been used in a large corpus of discourse. The meaning of a lexical item can be identified roughly (the process is inevitably an approximation, Teubert argues) by looking at the paraphrases, the things people have said about that item in discourses. Occasionally an expression will be linked in the text to a gloss or paraphrase by a verb such as *means* or *is*, in a subject–complement relation, but degrees of paraphrastic relation are implicit in a word's collocates generally. With a critical mass of instances of contextualized uses, and in some respects like the child acquiring its native language, the linguist has good evidence with which to construct a semantic profile for any given expression.

A fundamental principle of critical discourse analysis is that a study of the words, phrases and propositions of a discourse can uncover its overt and covert meanings. There is no surprise in this – it is the assumption with which ordinary people read their newspaper and engage in linguistic communication generally. Unlike the ordinary reader, however, the corpus-using discourse analyst can undertake far more kinds of comparing and contrasting; identification of patterns of repetition, synonymy and locally crafted semantic opposition; role-attribution; semantic transitivity; conventional and creative metaphor; disproportionalities of use and the searching across innumerable instances, tracking a word's usual collocates and changing ones over time. Still, at its core the analysis is undertaken under the assumption that the words of a discourse index the text's representation of the topics directly or indirectly addressed and, more broadly, 'the world'. A newspaper that repeatedly, disproportionately, contains words such as *monarchy, crown, royal family,* and in which these regularly collocate with *archaic, unelected* and *undemocratic,* can reasonably be interpreted to be representing monarchy in general as antithetical to modern democratic governance. The basic contention is that particular choices of words and phrases used to describe and report inevitably convey one or another viewpoint and evaluation. And in the case of a professionally edited newspaper, it is reasonable to expect there to be a considerable degree of 'convergence' or coherence among the viewpoints and in the ideology, despite the diversity of journalists and editorial staff contributing.

1.10.2   Muslims and Foreign Doctors

Collocational analysis underpins research like that of Baker et al. (2013), which identifies patterns in the recent (1998 to 2009) uses of the word *Muslim* in a corpus of British newspapers (143 million words). The most frequently occurring categories of noun collocates of *Muslim* included words referring to ethnic or national identity, characterising or differentiating attributes, conflict, culture, religion or group or organization. The 'conflict' category was particularly lexically rich, instanced by such collocates as *extremist, fanatic, terrorist* and *fundamentalist*. The authors also propose that the contexts of use of the two most frequent collocate pairs – *Muslim world* and *Muslim community* – suggest that these were used to 'collectivise' Muslims, treating them as all one group, and different from 'the West'. None of these findings was surprising, but the methodology is so robust that the study rises well above the scepticism of those who might suspect use of selective evidence or researcher bias.

Can corpus methods like these, applied in arguably more complicated and interpretation-dependent cases than that of mainstream media presumptions about Muslims or the elderly, work as well and be as persuasive? To test this, Baker (2015) conducted a study of inter-rater consistency. To answer the question "How are foreign doctors represented in the British press 2000–10?' five experienced corpus/CDA analysts were set the task of examining uses of the phrase *foreign doctors* and similar terms in a 500,000-word corpus of British newspapers. Baker summarized their diverging findings or attributions, and found that only one feature of the newspapers' representations of the doctors – that they have 'poor language' – was reported by all five analysts. A further four characterisations (such as 'need to be regulated/tested', 'NHS shortages') were named by four of the five raters. Beyond that, there was considerable divergence in the raters' assessments of the representations of foreign doctors. So it seems that, despite starting with the same corpus and collocational evidence, no two (experienced) discourse analysts are likely to come to closely similar interpretive conclusions, even in the analysis of a relatively simple phrase.

1.10.3   Jeffries and Davies on Opposition in Discourse

A text-rhetorical feature of some importance, and supplementary to those derived from the Hallidayan system-linguistic grammar which most subsequent CDA practitioners have adopted, is textual opposition. As Jeffries and Davies have shown (Jeffries 2010a, Davies 2012), texts routinely effect kinds of relational evaluation in two ways that exploit opposition: first, by deploying established oppositions and equivalences, and second and more creatively, by constructing an opposition locally and opportunistically within the specific text and with special relevance to the present discourse. Opposition in discourse is a broader phenomenon than antonymy, just as equivalence is broader than synonymy (among the syntactic 'triggers' of the latter are noun phrase apposition and parallel structuring). Established oppositions – *war* and *peace; urban* versus *rural; collective* versus *individualist* – are part of the language: traditional, autonomous, conventionalised opposites or antonymic pairs, ratified by dictionary and thesaurus. Their familiarity makes them more predictable and less arresting (given one partner, the other is highly predictable). More ingenious and potentially effective are contextually generated opposites: pairings where, decontextualized, the phrases would not be recognized as opposites. If I say *Although Kim was rich, he was honest* I am implying that normally being rich and being honest are 'opposites' in the sense of being disjunct, and that the rich can be expected to be dishonest. An early example in Davies (2012: 2) comes from a political speech by the Labour politician Ed Miliband when he asks: 'Are you on the side of the wealth creators or the asset strippers?' Not only are wealth creators and asset strippers not conventional opposites in a notional, decontextualized abstract realm of English, they may even be interpreted as in a paraphrase relation.

So one challenge to the analyst is to identify reliably the second of two phrases or clauses in discourse as nonparaphrastic, as not elaborating or expanding but opposing the first. The subsequent challenge, for the CDA practitioner, is to show that this is usefully revealing about the text's ideology (e.g., that they are likely to have an influence on text consumers). In helping to demonstrate the difference that text-specific oppositions make, the analyst should be able to show that the 'same text/discourse' with the identified oppositions removed (or replaced by graded, nonpolar distinctions) would have a different and less pronounced effect.

One effect of textual oppositions is to make the description more vivid and memorable, the way a metaphor can. This in turn may magnify readers' emotional response; depending on the topic and context, they can add to the good humour or pity or fear or anger. The magnification comes from the fact that although the paired terms or processes are not intrinsic or logical opposites (they may not even be mutually incompatible), they are being presented as such. The creation of an opposition asserts fundamental difference, and with difference, as noted earlier, typically comes hierarchy (unmarked versus marked, better versus worse, reasonable versus unreasonable): in short, an inequality between the paired terms. Constructed or contextually created oppositions encourage the reader's alignment with the implicitly preferred of the two postulated closed-set alternatives. The group which the dispreferred description denotes tend to be discursively shunned or marginalised, treated as opponents, outlaws, other or foreign. An 'inner' preferred condition or group is thereby strengthened, but another one is necessarily set at a distance and outside this approved inner status. Oppositions, in socio-political discursive representations, thus tend to articulate an 'us versus them' narrative rather than a 'we all, whatever our differences' narrative.

1.10.4 Van Leeuwen

In his monograph of 2008, Theo van Leeuwen synthesizes his conception and model of critical discourse analysis, one that still uses systemic-linguistic grammatical categories where necessary but integrates this with his own descriptive system of multimodal and nonverbal semiosis. In particular, his work on the representation of social actors and social actions is set in a fuller context. Van Leeuwen follows the early sociologist Max Weber, who argued that under conditions of modernity (industrialisation, urbanisation, nation-state formations) social relations are no longer based on truth and meaningfulness, but pragmatics and efficiency – that is, functionality. Meaning is fragmented, while social action is regimented or 'proceduralized' (2008: 3).

In his analysis of how social actors are represented in discourse, van Leeuwen offers a 'sociosemantic inventory' of the main ways in which actors (participants) in practices are represented (e.g., whether an actor is identified by name in the discourse or by function or role, and whether the actor is an agent or affected/patient). He prioritizes the semantic choices that are involved, but also ties each type to a specific linguistic or rhetorical realisation. He also writes at length about legitimation (chapter 6) and identifies several strategies used in discourse to do this work: *authorisation, moral evaluation, rationalisation* and *mythopoesis* (2008: 92). For the purposes of the present study, the typology is particularly important for drawing attention to the most powerful ways in which social actors can be variably represented; but often the simpler labelling systems outlined by stylisticians (e.g., in Simpson 2004, Toolan 1998, and Jeffries 2010b) will be sufficient to underpin the discussion.

1.10.5 Metaphor

Metaphorical language in newspaper opinion-editorial discourse, especially unconventional metaphor, stands out from the general flow of the text, by characterising things in unexpected terms, which cannot be literally true. Where the metaphor is apt, readers may also feel (again surprisingly, and therefore memorably) that it explains the subject matter with out-of-the-ordinary insight. The paradoxicality of the situation adds to a metaphor's power: it cannot be valid, logically, but in all the circumstances it makes uncommon sense. The following chapters will consider metaphor in the news stories of interest, but on a selective basis.

Much has been written about metaphors in specifically nonliterary contexts, from many perspectives, and only a few contributions of greatest relevance are noted here: Goatly 1997 [2011] and 2007; Lakoff and Johnson 1980; Chilton 2004; Knowles and Moon 2006; Ferrari 2007; Deignan et al. 2013; Steen and Dorst 2010; Charteris-Black 2013; Kovecses 2010; Vessey 2016; Musolff 2016 and Semino et al. 2016. Sometimes the distinctiveness of metaphors in discourse has been overstated. For instance, conceptual metaphor theory declares that metaphors structure thinking and knowledge, are central to abstract language, are grounded in physical experience and are ideological, but all these claims could equally be made about naming in general, including literal meaning. Similarly it is rightly noted that metaphors construe a topic in a particular partial way – highlighting some aspects of the topic and backgrounding others – and are thereby evaluative, but again this is true of all naming and description. It is the vividness and surprising aptness of metaphors that make them important to the representational function in discourses.

Charteris-Black (2013) notes how metaphor is used by politicians striving to 'manage' socio-political change, often by conveying certainty and control (while discouraging dissent and disorder) where these may be in doubt and under threat. Metaphors can help legitimise particular courses of action and help make alternative representations of the political context of a situation seem outlandish or scarcely imaginable. The most powerful metaphors may induce the recipient to assume that 'there is no alternative' to seeing the situation in the way that the metaphor represents it [see, e.g., Cammaerts (2012) on metaphors of 'reasonableness' in North-Belgian (Flemish) news outlets during the 2007–11 Belgian constitutional crisis and Musolff (2012, 2015) on the 'othering' and demoting effects deployed in racist discourses].

In Musolff (2016) a 'scenario' approach to contemporary political discourse is proposed, combining critical discourse analysis and the cognitive metaphor theory of Lakoff and Johnson, for whom metaphor is 'among our principal vehicles of understanding' (1980: 159). Musolff identifies several core conceptual metaphors as instrumental in political argument, such as 'the nation is a human body' conceptual metaphor. This metaphor gives its user an 'argumentative advantage' when rebutting political opponents:

Instead of laboriously having to demonstrate and back up their claims with facts, which could be critically tested and challenged, the speaker/writer invites the hearer/reader to access knowledge about the undesirability of illness and the necessity for therapy by referring to generally known illnesses and agents of disease. (2012: 303)

The very clear source domain (infected body) makes it easier for the arguer simply to identify the shunned phenomenon (human rights, migrants, the European Union) as the target domain, a disease that must be treated and 'defeated'. Like slogans (e.g., 'Take back control!' 'Labour isn't working!'), metaphors can provide a crucial framework for the legitimising of questionable policies and responses. However, metaphor construal always involves a complex interaction of the vehicle (source) associations and those of the tenor or target, and cancellation of many of the former as irrelevant to the latter and nonsalient – and the grounds of those retentions and cancellations are themselves contentious. A closer look at the analogy underlying a metaphor such as 'the EU is an illness afflicting the UK body' can highlight the respects in which it could be judged incoherent or invalid. Creative metaphors are always risky.

How secure can our identifications of metaphors in discourse be? Can we make metaphor analysis of news discourse more useful by singling out just those expressions and constructions that ordinary readers might recognise as distinctly metaphorical? Various attempts have been made to devise a procedure for reliably identifying all the lexical units in a text that can be said to be used metaphorically, one being that of Steen and colleagues, known as the Pragglejaz Group. Their metaphor identification procedure (MIP), described in Pragglejaz Group (2007) and elsewhere, proposes that a word in a text is metaphorical if its contextual meaning *in situ* diverges from its 'basic meaning'. The 'basic meaning' is usually 'more concrete', related to the senses or bodily action, more precise or older, but not always the most frequent meaning; this cluster of prescriptions seems to substitute for a more 'mechanical' referral to a suitable dictionary, but dictionaries are also cited. On that basis, MIP identifies six words (here bolded) in the following sentence as being used metaphorically:

For years, Sonia Gandhi has **struggled** to convince Indians that she is **fit** to **wear** the **mantle** of the political **dynasty into** which she married, let alone to become premier. (Pragglejaz Group 2007: 4)

Many readers will judge that only *wear the mantle* is noticeably metaphorical here; for such readers, the MIP is overstating the metaphoricity, chiefly by denying to various non-physical senses the status of 'basic meaning'. It is unclear whether one dictionary was invariably consulted (both the Shorter Oxford and the Macmillan Advanced Learners' are mentioned) or exactly how they were used; by contrast Dorst (2015) systematically appeals to the Macmillan online dictionary for basic meanings. Where metaphors are of interest in the present study, only those words or phrases that are used in senses not recorded in the *Collins Cobuild English Dictionary for Advanced Learners* or the Macmillan online dictionary will be recognised as metaphorical, nor broadly synonymous with those recorded senses. Finally it is important to keep an interest in metaphor (or other figurative mechanisms, including metonymy, euphemism and irony) in perspective, relative to all the other powerful representative devices – and silences or aporia – that shape the verbal construal of the world in newspapers or anywhere else, including the uses of words in their basic or conventional dictionary-recorded meanings.

1.11   Theoretical and Methodological Assumptions of This Study

This chapter turns now to an outline of this study's key theoretical assumptions and methodological techniques; some of the latter are explained further, as relevant, in subsequent chapters.

Earlier I described how the CDA practiced by Fairclough tends to focus on a single moment or speech event, as exemplification of a trend that he has argued for independently of the presenting of discourse evidence. My own method here is different, surveying much larger extents of discourse comparatively, but also making arguments for a subsequent narrowing of focus to particular most relevant instances. I often use quantitative data derived from a corpus and make comparisons with relevant reference samples, in order to identify patterns and disproportionally frequent or infrequent uses; these are the bases of conservative interpretive commentary.

Much recent CDA that draws on corpus linguistics seeks broad collocational trends across perhaps thousands of instances of a word or phrase but clearly cannot say much about the contextual particularities of use of individual instances. In the work of Baker, Mautner, and others, the size of corpus used and therefore the number of instances of a particular word or phrase examined for its collocational and semantic preferences is far larger than is available here. But the focus on contexts of use is less full, or a more limited network of keywords and phrases is considered. I discuss fewer instances in fewer articles (a representative selection), but include much more explanation of the political background at the time of the articles' appearance – the political context. I am perhaps closer to Fowler (1991) in this respect. I offer a comparatively discursive treatment of these newspapers' discourses around wealth inequality, reading the texts as texts rather than attaching nearly all the importance to the nature of the immediate co-textual collocates of the keywords selected.

While this is clearly not a study of readers' responses to *Times* and *Mail* articles (that would be a separate project that could draw on the evidence in this study), I have tried to keep in mind an actual *Times* or *Mail* reader, often tailoring my interpretation to keep it congruent with how a reader might have noticed the language of a story – or not.

A crucial part of my method is an attempt to be conservative or minimalist in interpretation, in the sense of trying always to confine interpretations to strongly implicated meanings. On the one hand, in my view, there is simply no possibility of 'objective' analysis of the meaning let alone the effect of any discourse: the analysis is inescapably interpretive or subjective. On the other hand, it is desirable for critical discourse analytical interpretations to be open to falsifiability where at all possible, and that has been my intention with all the interpretations of linguistic patterns presented here.

1.11.1   Keywords

The study is bound together by its systematic attention to particular words and the phraseologies surrounding them, which are argued to be revealing of the newspapers' gradually changing stances toward wealth disparity and its consequences in Britain over the past forty-five years. Those 'keywords' include but are not limited to the following: *fair/unfair, class, Britain* and *British, afford(able), help, tax burden, Luddite/s, luck(y), lottery, Robin Hood, deserving*. The usual method is to follow these steps:

1. Identify all relevant instances of a particular item (e.g., *class*) in a suitable set of texts, especially where the term is disproportionately frequent or infrequent.
2. Examine KWIC (keyword in context) concordance lines for collocational patterns, trying to explain the marked frequency or infrequency.
3. Supplement the KWIC analysis by examining the word or phrase in its full sentential contexts of use.
4. Interpret the formulation – keeping as faithful to the source sentences as possible – of all significant assertions and inferences of the uses of the expression in their sentence frames.
5. Derivate, directly from the given corpus, a set of paraphrase-sourced propositions for the studied item, constituting a profile or description of what the item means in the corpus.
6. Attempt to integrate an item's propositions, so derived, into a local implicit narrative to which, by virtue of the use of the studied item in the sentences noted, the writer or newspaper seems committed. Each of these narratives should reveal something of the writer's or newspaper's attitude to wealth inequality in the UK.

When undertaking steps 4 to 6, we have to recognize that not all presupposition paraphrases are likely to be fully mutually consistent (author-internal ambivalences). Where possible, an attempt is made to express the presuppositions in a sentential format that renders the claim, report or evaluation unambiguous. This is to avoid the vagueness and unfalsifiability of observations such as 'In this discourse *class* is about/ relates to X'.

The study involves a variety of kinds of news story, although most attention is devoted to political news stories and reports of parliamentary debates, editorials, opinion pieces and letters to the editor. These are complexly intertextually related to each other; for example, some news event may trigger a political response, each of these being reported in the newspaper, and both these in turn may prompt an editorial, or letters, which may partly address each other as well as address the initiating event.

In this study of moderate length, I have had to be sharply selective as to the topics and the keywords explored, focussing on such topics as the economy, employment and industrial relations, housing and housing policies, welfare and pensions, wealth and lifestyle, while saying less about other relevant domains such as education and health care. There is some variation of format and methodology in the different chapters, to suit the different kinds of corpus or textual evidence being examined: looking at all the mentions of *Luddite* in political editorial items in *The Times* and *Daily Mail* across forty-five years, for example, calls for a different methodology than a comparative analysis between the 1971 budget speech and its news reception and their counterparts forty years later.

1.11.2   Subjective Interpretation

Like van Dijk, van Leeuwen, Fairclough, Teubert, Mulderrig and others, I believe the political and socioeconomic context of the texts I analyse is crucial to the interpretive process. But any statement of that context, whether making use of political histories or of theoretical explanations of social and economic change over the past half-century, is itself an interpretation. There is no such thing as an interpretation-free account of these matters. Like Mulderrig (2015), therefore, I see no embarrassment in the fact that CDA's methodology is, in her terms, 'reflexive and abductive' (p. 447). The latter of these terms, championed by C.S. Peirce, refers to a form of inferencing from evidence, where the conclusions reached are not guaranteed by the initial premises, as in deductive reasoning; rather explanations are proposed on the grounds of their likelihood in the given complex context, shaped by innumerable factors. Mulderrig describes how the analyst is continually moving back and forth between theory, method and data in order to achieve 'explanatory adequacy' in the research process. In this way the findings from the empirical analysis of text are set in dialogue with and interpreted in relation to (a theoretically informed understanding of) their social context. (Mulderrig 2015: 447)

My own approach intends to be similarly reflexive and abductive, moving between theory, method and data, with the proviso that mostly I have sought to keep uses of socio-political theory relatively simple and relatively close to the assumed viewpoints of the editors, journalists and readers directly involved in the production and consumption of these newspapers.

Also like many other CDA projects, in grammatical description and explanation the present one will draw from time to time both on traditional grammars and on the systemic functional grammar developed by Halliday and others (Halliday, 1994; Halliday & Matthiessen 2014). In particular it will use systemic linguistic categories when discussing transitivity (the kinds of processes and participants which represented states and events can be classified as, and what this may reveal about the habitual way of viewing social reality in one or a group of newspaper texts) and modality (the adding to a proposition of expressions of the author's qualified or subjective commitment to its validity or desirability, or their sense of its obligatoriness). But I will draw also on a wide range of other grammatical commentaries and pragmatics proposals (e.g., Grice's maxims) where useful. Many of these analytical models (transitivity, modality, Gricean cooperativeness maxims and the implicatures that exploitations of them or the presence of presuppositions may trigger) are widely used in stylistics and critical discourse analysis, their main elements summarized in many introductory guides, so that I will not describe them here.

1.11.3   Reformulatory Modifiers of Nouns

One interpretive procedure, however, merits fuller introduction here, since in the work that follows it is used extensively, it may seem contentious and counterintuitive and is not one I have seen discussed or explicitly adopted in extant CDA work. This concerns the semantic relations, specifically in op-ed evaluative journalism, between modifiers (e.g., adjectives) and the 'head' noun to which they are attached. I argue that they are very often in a paraphrase relation, with each modifier redescribing the referent of the head word, rather than contrastively specifying a subtype of the head.

Modifiers within noun phrases often have a contrastive, selective and sub-categorizing function: they distinguish the present entity from other entities that might be referred to if a different modifier were used. And they affirm that not all instances of the entity denoted by the head noun share the characteristic indicated by the present modifier. Ordering *black coffee* distinguishes the drink requested on this occasion from other types of coffee that are not black, such as *white coffee*. The use of *black* (or *white*) is selective and contrastive modification. But when someone proposes having *a nice restorative cup of tea*, the modifier *restorative* is not truly subcategorising and contrastive; rather it is a supplementary description, explicating what we are to understand is generally and significantly in the nature of nice cups of tea, namely that they are restorative. Similarly, in the cited example, it is implied that supplementary to the understood meaning of *a restorative cup of tea* is the fact that it is *nice*. There is little contrastive or delimiting meaning conveyed by the addition of *nice*: it simply adds to the characterisation, by cancellable presupposition, of all cups of tea or a typical cup of tea. I will argue that, in argumentative op-ed journalism, evaluative modifiers typically have such an explanatory, elaborative or supplemental function, which makes them a powerful basis for paraphrase-oriented analysis, and adds to their narrativising function in recurrent collocations.

If someone is described as a *rugged farmer*, why should we assume that the speaker is using the modifier as typifying, implying they think farmers generally are rugged, rather than as supplying a contrastive or distinguishing meaning? One constraint to note is that in nearly all the cases discussed here, the modifier is of the epithet or evaluative kind (usually gradable: *very rugged*, etc.) rather than of the non-gradable classifier type. Elaborative and 'typifying' interpretations seem to be confined to evaluative (non-classifier) types of modification. In *a Zimbabwean farmer*, or *a farmer in her sixties*, both of which have classifying modification of *farmer*, there is no justification for presupposing that typically or in most cases farmers are Zimbabwean, or in their sixties. In terms of the broad distinction between asserted and presupposed information carried by language, to assume a covert typifying function as more significant than the overt specifying function is to treat these modifiers as more presuppositional in nature than assertive (we already knew that cups of tea are nice and restorative; that information is virtually presupposed).

1.11.4   Selecting Textual Evidence

Establishing precisely what constitutes 'relevant evidence' in newspapers of representations of something as experientially diffuse as wealth inequality is challenging. When exploring homophobia or Islamophobia or ageism in discourse, a few key lexical items present themselves as likely to be especially salient, and this usefully constrains the task. Wealth inequality and newspapers' attitudes to this are mostly indirectly signalled so that they cannot be captured by a small, widely agreed set of key terms. Accordingly, while this study examines news items, leaders, commentaries and letters that thematise the gaps and differences between the rich and the poor, it also ventures beyond those stories in search of indirect articulations of the wealth gap, in discussions of employment, industrial relations, the economy, class and education, taxation and TV reviewing. In this it is grappling with methodological problems, and sometimes *ad hoc*-seeming solutions, faced by all forms of critical discourse analysis or critical linguistics.

Deciding just where to begin corpus searches is a matter of subjective judgement; one cannot simply take the phrase *inequality of wealth and income in the United Kingdom* and explore how this is represented and talked about in the newspapers, since that precise phrase is vanishingly rarely used. Nor can much progress be made, when looking at news discourses on 'UK wealth inequality', by looking at all mentions of *wealth* or *inequality* or *UK inequality*. On the one hand, most of the many uses of *wealth* will have little relevance to inequality and the United Kingdom, just as most of the mentions of *United Kingdom* will have no bearing on wealth or inequality; on the other hand, mentions of the phrase *UK inequality* (two occurrences found in *The Times Digital Archive*, from 1971 to 2012) or similar phrases are far too few to be a useful basis for study of such a deep and wide-ranging condition. Likewise a search in the same archive for *wealth* and *inequality* occurring within five words of each other yields only forty-seven hits, an average of just one per year, and many of these are irrelevant to the chosen topic. If such a large issue is to be explored by CDA at all – and surely it should be – then oblique or indirect methods of analysing the discursive evidence must be devised and applied.

1.11.5   Why from 1971 to 2016?

I have selected the particular span of four-and-a-half decades, from 1971 to 2016, for several reasons (although the December 2016 endpoint is based on practicality, the nearest I can reasonably get in a corpus study of this kind to genuine contemporaneity). Most crucial has been the fact that, as noted earlier, the early 1970s have been widely recognised as the high watermark of relatively reduced economic inequality, between the poor and the rich and all in between, in modern Britain; subsequent years have been marked by broadly continuous growth in the separation of the wealthy from the disadvantaged. Forty-five years is also, roughly, the extent of a typical working life in modern Britain: whether you were starting work aged sixteen or eighteen in 1971, coming straight from school, or did so a few years later after university, you might well be contemplating retirement in the early-to-mid 2010s.

The period studied is one that all British-born people now in their sixties or older will have lived and probably worked through, served by governments we have collectively voted for – people who, like me, are now approaching or in retirement so are in a position to look back on the period as one they have experienced personally. Nor is the early 1970s evidence, its traces and expressions of mainstream British ideology in those years, dismissible as utterly passé, as 'history', unconnected to 2011 or more recent years. It is perfectly possible, for example, that some of the same people who read the opinions and may have absorbed the attitudes of Peter Black in 1971 were reading Christopher Stevens's reviews in the *Mail* just over forty years later, or that those reading editorials and letters in *The Times* in 1971 about housing shortages, the Common Market, and low productivity were reading letters and leaders in the same paper on much the same topics, forty and more years later. Has the tenor of the articles changed, whether or not these readers have noticed the change?

1.11.6   Selectivity and Representativeness: Subjective but Not Arbitrary

Methodologically, then, this study derives paraphrastic descriptions of each selected key term, in the chosen corpus or sub-corpus, to pinpoint what *The Times* meant by referring to *Robin Hood economics* in the 1970s and later decades, or cumulatively to present a picture of what the *Mail* used *fair* to mean in the 1970s. The process is, I would argue, laborious of necessity: it is necessary to consider all the uses of *Robin Hood* that are relevant to economics, examining instances in their fuller context, to understand their use and underpin interpretive generalisations. On all occasions the aim is to be comprehensive, relative to the specific set of instances identified (thus all relevant uses of *Robin Hood* or *Luddite* or *fair* or *burden* in the specified corpus or sub-corpus, such as all *Daily Mail* comments and letters from 1971 to 2016, or all budget speeches, reported verbatim in *The Times* across the forty-five years, are considered).

This combination of selectivity and representativeness has been recognised as an analytical inevitability in discourse analysis and stylistics for decades. In the furtherance of a defensible strategic selectivity, I have adopted various 'workarounds', some of which I have not seen in extant studies. To give one example, consider the difficulties, short of working through the material over many days, of calculating the proportion of inclusive *we* relative to exclusive *we* in a half-million word corpus of forty-five budget speeches. (An inclusive use of *we* refers to and includes, beyond the speaker and his or her immediate circle, a large group of addressees – in the present case, the British people; exclusive *we* implies 'the government and I' or some similarly small set.) To assist in calculating trends of usage, factoring in the typical style of budget speeches, I proposed counting the proportion of *we have* and *we will* uses, as a proportion of total number of uses of *we* in budget speeches. On the assumption that *we* in those two forms will be exclusive, a reasonably accurate calculation of the proportion and extent of exclusive *we*, relative to inclusive *we*, can be made.

Another *ad hoc* but I believe justifiable strategy was adopted usefully to delimit and focus attention on all stories in *The Times* in the years 1971 and 2011 which used the adjective *fair* (a much more frequently used word than *equal* or *equitable*). Mindful of the importance of language-inscribed or inherent opposites, only those stories where both *fair* and *unfair* were used together were collected and analysed.

In the context of newspaper commentary on inequality and the evaluating of various acts of wealth redistribution, the name *Robin Hood* soon emerged as the most commonly and consistently invoked name and popular-cultural reference (e.g., both in the *fair* + *unfair* stories in *The Times* in 1971 and 2011, and in the forty-five years of budget speeches). In light of the varied uses of *Robin Hood* as a metaphorical encapsulation and evaluation of kinds of wealth redistribution, a chapter exploring the name's relevant uses across the period in the two newspapers seemed justified. Although heroic, the Robin Hood story is mostly invoked in the media to warn of naïve and impractical egalitarianism; its closest exclusively English cultural counterpart, often used in the newspapers to stir readers' memories of destructive and illegal attacks on factories and their owners and technological progress in general, is the story of Ned Ludd and the Luddites. Again, the words *Luddite* and *Luddites* were often found in stories across the decades of interest where major industrial disputes over pay and conditions were reported.

A different motivation again prompted scrutiny of TV reviews in the *Daily Mail* in the years 1971 and 2013 (two corpora of approximately 60,000 words of Peter Black's reviews and Christopher Stevens's reviews, respectively). The motivation was a conviction that in that newspaper's reviewer's extensive commentaries on a range of precisely the national TV programmes that a significant proportion of the British public were watching in those two years, a window onto the newspaper's values was opened. A number of surprising contrasts, in need of explanation, arise.

1.12   Brief Outline of the Chapters

Chapter 2 examines patterns of use of two terms at the core of discursive representation of the reasonableness and morality of wealth inequality: *fair* and *unfair*. It looks at how these are used in *The Times* in a wide range of contexts, in particular seeking to uncover whether some conditions judged not entirely fair in the 1970s – such as those concerning the dismissal of an employee, or the use of a lottery with its lure of millions for the lucky winner, to raise funds for good causes – had come to be regarded as not unfair in the 2010s.

Chapter 3 uses corpus linguistic resources to explore the discursive differences between the budget speeches (fully reported in *The Times*) of two new Conservative Chancellors (Barber and Osborne) in 1971 and 2011, respectively, before considering all ten budget speeches from these two chancellors. It looks at shifts in formality and tone, of audience and rhetoric, the different appeal to inclusive *we,* the different invoking of *Britain*, and the different assumptions about how much the government will *help*, and take steps that are *new.* Setting these two speeches in the context of all forty-six budgets across the period, the chapter also analyses the more creative metaphors in all the budget speeches, and traces the sharp decline in mentions of *taxation* as a process to which the electorate are subjected and of *burden* as an acceptable representation of what people – especially affluent people – should be expected to 'carry', for the common good and the national interest.

Chapter 4 briefly profiles two *Daily Mail* TV programme critics, Peter Black and Christopher Stevens, before analysing two custom-built corpora of nearly all their TV programme reviews from the years 1971 and 2013, respectively. Despite areas of shared interest, the discourses of the two critics are strikingly different in topics covered and evaluative stance. Black often offers aesthetic critique, but qualifies his verdicts, on programmes which, even when fictional, address serious socio-political topics. Stevens is only rarely critical and mostly enthusiastic and celebratory; his stories are nostalgic for the 'great' sitcoms of yesteryear and heavily oriented towards profiling celebrity performers and the public's 'interactive' involvement in talent shows such as *Strictly Come Dancing.* The word *class* is comparatively prominent in the Black corpus, evidently a contemporary concern, and recognised as indicative of inequality of opportunity. In Stevens's much longer stories, class has largely disappeared from the discursive agenda of contemporary Britain, and is only mentioned in relation to the past, or other countries. By 2013 it seems to have become natural not to discuss class or present-day wealth inequality in *Mail* TV reviews, while *sex* and *affair* are now frequent. The two critics' discourses also differ in their representation of *Britain* and *the British*, and these, too, seem to reflect changes as to what *Mail* readers assume and expect about 'we British' between 1971 and the near-present day.

Chapter 5 traces the rise and fall of *Luddite/s* in the newspapers, as used in the context of industrial relations between employers and employees. Used to denote individuals or groups who are resolutely opposed to a change in their terms of employment, *Luddite/s* has been strategically deployed over the years – chiefly by Conservative politicians and centre-right newspapers, mostly aimed at trade union leaders or their Labour party allies, and most noticeably in the crucial early years of the Thatcher governments, when the most abrupt revisions were made to the terms of engagement in industrial relations.

Chapter 6 examines how the name *Robin Hood* has been used across the forty-five years, with Robin Hood in some respects as a counterpart to Ned Ludd, committed to redressing inequalities of wealth by illegality and force.

In the 1970s there was honour as well as some criticism in a minister being described as practising *Robin Hood economics*. In more recent decades in *The Times* and the *Daily Mail*, however, the evidence suggests a hardening of attitudes towards any government interventions described as revealing a Robin Hood 'complex'. By the time the papers are probing every financial initiative from New Labour's Chancellor Gordon Brown for any 'Robin Hood tendencies', the background understanding is that all such ideas are extreme, unreasonable, indefensible or hugely damaging to the national interest.

Each of these chapters takes a very few distinct, inequality-relevant keywords as the basis of an exploration of the newspapers' discourse across nearly half a century. Each keyword's uses contribute to imagined narratives about reasonable expectations, responsibilities and entitlements in modern Britain. Sometimes, fortuitously, two or more keywords may feature jointly in a single narrative. The narratives are more often vague and variable than sharply defined, and only partially mutually congruent. But in underpinning the authoritative public discourse of newspapers (especially their comment or editorial material), the ideological influence of these keywords and narratives on faithful readers is likely to have been considerable.

1.13   Political Affiliations

Some critics of discourse analytic studies claim it is useful for analysts to 'state explicitly' their own political sympathies at the beginning of such a study, and then to consider how those sympathies may affect any claims of objectivity of the analysis. To my mind this is crude and simplistic. I cannot see that analysts declaring, at the outset, that they are passionately committed to international socialism or, for that matter, to neoliberal global capitalism, should make a difference to the nature or the merit of the discourse analyses that follow, which are of how a set of terms directly reflecting a newspaper's conception of wealth inequality, have been used over several decades.

Nor are the analyses and commentaries that follow easily subjected to a simple subjective/objective classification. On the one hand, interpretation of the evidence is constantly involved so that the commentary is as 'subjective' as many a scientific proposal or legal decision. On the other hand, I have continually striven to begin with extensive samples, explain the basis of calculations of frequencies, and ground all interpretations on the evidence of the newspapers' usage, read in context. At every step of the way, I hope, readers are given enough information to decide for themselves whether my analytic decisions are reasonable or arbitrary. I have aimed to 'show all my working' and to be objective in that sense. To take a very simple example: in the chapter where I look at whether and how the phrase *Robin Hood* is used by the newspapers as evaluative of various economic policies, I explain why I have disregarded the many newspaper mentions of *Robin Hood Airport, Robin Hood's Bay* in Yorkshire, and other toponymic uses. That is an interpretive decision on my part, and subjective, where an 'objective' treatment is hard to imagine. But my political sympathies – were I able succinctly to formulate them – are again irrelevant.

Humanistic sympathies may be a different thing, but these are rapidly summarisable and stand above political affiliations. The United Kingdom comparatively speaking is one of the richest countries in the world. Nevertheless a significant minority of people, including perhaps a quarter of all children, are living here in relative poverty, with well-documented life-long disadvantages accruing. These children, in particular, are living an unfairness that they have not earned. My interest is in whether right-of-centre newspaper discourse has used the language of 'natural and reasonable inequality' in ways that may have habituated and reconciled their readers to that unfairness.

2   What's *Fair* and *Unfair* in *The Times*

2.1   The Language of Fairness

In the newspapers, concern for equality sometimes manifests itself in talk of fairness. Fairness is an everyday way of invoking equality of treatment (or opportunity) or adequacy of reward for work done or other investment. The word *fair* is an approbatory term in many English idioms and phrases: *fair shares, a fair price, a fair wage for a fair day's work* and *none but the brave deserve the fair*. *To be fair* and *to be honest* are interchangeable conversational fillers. In rural Ireland, *a fair day* means two different things, and those meanings co-occur *a fair number* of times, when market day is mild and sunny, which is *fair enough*. To be fair is also sometimes to be white, with fair dealing as the opposite of the dark deeds of blackguards.

But even if everyone could be persuaded to be fair at all times, matters are complicated by the inequality of differences of endowment. People do not start out equal, given differences in ability, motivation and family resources and support, including private wealth under typical western conditions. At any given point in time, person A is so wealthy that he or she owns the enterprise and its profits, while person B manages the company for A in return for a comfortable salary, and person C is one of many who works to B's instruction for remuneration rather less than B's and considerably less than A's. Those inequalities predate the current moment (so in a sense are behind the historical curtain) and bear only indirectly on any present-time negotiation between the parties and any possible representation of it in the newspapers. Therefore 'fairness' in news reports is also invoked against a background of received and largely incontestable inequality, but it rarely alludes to that background. Rather, it is used in evaluating as equitable or not the immediate relations between the parties involved. And those parties do have to be 'in' the same domain – a single shared space, community or nation – often expressed by the 'container' conceptual metaphor, as in *we are all in this together*. If two groups are separated, made foreigners to each other, by an impregnable wall that puts them 'in' different polities, then intergroup fairness is of little concern. High walls are an effective way of countering egalitarian pressures.

The grammatical template by which we think of someone or something as *being fair (to someone/something)* means that all other unnamed affected parties may be overlooked. When CEOs received ten times the median company salary, that inequality was often called 'fair'; now that some CEOs are paid one hundred times the median wage, some still call this 'fair'. In lots of ways, fairness is different from equality, as company pay indicates. We shall see 'fair but unequal' pay – a discursive hotspot in a wealth-unequal society – discussed in several of the following sections.

In this chapter I look at how *The Times* reported matters related to personal wealth and income as *fair* or *unfair*. I focus on that newspaper's stories using these terms in the years 1971 and 2011 to explore whether its representations have shifted through that forty-year time span. Thus the study focuses on all the ways that the words *fair* and *unfair* were used together in the same text in just those two years. Attention is directed to *The Times* on this specific question because in those years there was limited co-occurrent use of *fair* and *unfair* in stories in the *Daily Mail* (the digital archive returns just 140 items in the 'Editorial and Commentary' category of stories in the *Mail* for the years 1971 to 2004 inclusive, and most are letters).

2.2   Why Concentrate on *Fair* and *Unfair*?

The rationale for examining how *fair* and *unfair* have been used, and especially how they have been used together, is simple: I hypothesised that if matters of wealth inequality are discussed in these opinion-shaping newspapers, *fair* (3,705 occurrences in *The Times* in 1971) and *unfair* (589 occurrences) are likely to be among the most basic evaluative terms to be incorporated into those discussions. They are the most basic evaluative vocabulary items associated with wealth (in)equality, both intuitively and as confirmed in listings of most frequent lexis, such as Leech et al. (2001) or the *Oxford English Dictionary* frequency bands for vocabulary. Thus *fair* and *unfair* are more frequently used separately and together than the following seemingly relevant words, listed here with their total frequencies of occurrence in *The Times* in 1971: *unequal* (57), *inequality* (63), *disparity* (168), *disadvantage* (299), *disadvantaged* (40), *privileged* (217) and *underprivileged* (40). Especially when *fair* and *unfair* are both used within the same story, they are among the most fundamental lexical touchstones in the discursive representation of equality as a socio-political concern.

At first glance some of the frequencies of other evaluative lexis – although still far below that for *unfair* let alone *fair* – look promisingly high, but a closer inspection reveals that many of the uses of these terms have no bearing on wealth inequality or on general conditions in the United Kingdom. *Disadvantage* appears on 299 occasions in *The Times* in 1971, but many of these occurrences are unrelated to the focus of this study. For example, the twenty-seven stories in the month of January that include the word *disadvantage* are about such disparate topics as the following: one-person-operated buses, a film review, the Russians and the cold war, doctor-patient relations, a ballet review, election of the House of Commons Speaker, a leader article about the Industrial Relations Bill, the Open University, Scottish rugby, etc. Only one story in this partial listing – a leader article about the Industrial Relations Bill – is in my estimation of potential relevance. Scaled up for the whole year, this would suggest that between twenty and thirty of the 299 stories (10% of the total) using *disadvantage* might be relevant to wealth inequality. This small yield is even smaller if only those stories using both *disadvantage* and *advantage* are identified: there are seventy of these, but only a handful are relevant to wealth and economics. By contrast, as noted earlier, the frequencies for *fair* and *unfair* are 3,705 and 589, respectively. Again, on the occasions of their separate use, the stories were rarely predicted to relate to wealth inequality, and extensive sampling confirmed this. Where the two terms were used concurrently, aspects of economic inequality were expected to feature significantly often, so these are the stories focused upon in this chapter.

2.3   The 1971 and 2011 Selections of *Fair + Unfair* Stories

Using *The Times Digital Archive* for 1971, I identified a total of 130 stories that used both *fair* and *unfair*. In terms of the archive's own classification of subgenre, the stories belonged to one of just six categories. The *fair + unfair* stories in some of these categories proved unrelated to my interest (e.g., advertising, people and features), so they were set aside, and just eighty-nine of the original 130 – all those classified as news or editorial commentary – were retained. In terms of a specific topic, the following were those most frequently addressed by the eighty-nine *fair + unfair* articles:

> more than twenty-five on the Industrial Relations Bill
> more than five on the Barber budget
> several on public sector pensions
> several on statutory pay controls
> several on fair rents and public housing reform
> several on disparate non-UK-related topics (Sweden, Laos, Nixon, Milan, etc.)
> single articles on subjects such as the jobless versus working families, benefit fraud, a 'Robin Hood' tax, the 'blade runner', taxing the rich, council cuts to charities, care for the elderly, employment tribunals, regional development, unfair economic competition

from Hong Kong, museum charges, interrogation of Ulster inter-
nees, the Immigration Bill, etc.
As the list suggests, a great many of *The Times* stories containing both *fair* and
unfair concerned industrial relations and government-employer-union relations. In fact more than half of the eighty-nine stories were on political issues
lying at the heart of the government's evolving policies regarding employment,
wages and pensions, rents and housing and taxes. In all these areas of government interest, where *The Times* of 1971 is using the *fair/unfair* pair, money is
intrinsically relevant: these are matters of possible (not obligatory) government
concern, where money is the essence of the activity. It is in the nature of wages,
pensions, housing rent and taxes (the most frequently recurring themes) that
they entail money or money-equivalent remuneration in ways that are *not*
directly entailed by health care, education, protection of the environment or
even defence. By contrast the *fair/unfair* terms do not seem to feature in many
of the 1971 *Times* stories concerning health care, education, foreign affairs,
sport or entertainment – areas of public and therefore newspaper interest, where
money is less obviously an intrinsic element for the parties involved.
The monetary connection is usually more oblique. In short, *fair/unfair* in
The Times of 1971 mostly relates directly and specifically to fairness in
money matters (e.g., in the form of fair pay or fair rent), and this emphasis
seems to be no accident.

More specifically how were *fair* and *unfair* used in these eighty-nine stories,
particularly in those that concerned government policies? Here is a preliminary
sampling from just four of those stories.

1. On the question of 'fairness' in government duties imposed, where dumping
   of goods is identified (P.H. Kinslow, Letter to Editor on 'Anti-dumping
   Duties', 8 January 1971: 16):
   *The United Kingdom might not be less fair than other countries. However it is
   difficult to understand how the word 'fair' is applied to the concept of dumping ...
   [T]he imposition of anti-dumping duties on some fertilizers in 1970 was considered
   by many as being positively unfair.*

2. Concerning categories of punishment in the armed services and 'dismissal
   with disgrace' from the army ('New Services Code of Punishments:
   Farewell to the Punjab Image'. Report of debate in Parliament,
   14 January 1971: 9):
   *It was unfair for a man to carry that with him for the rest of his life. It was fair just to
   be dismissed from the Army.*

3. With regard to protecting consumers from manufacturers or retailers who
   offer restrictive product guarantees ('Warning to Buyers on Guarantees
   Which Reduce Their Rights'. Report of debate in Parliament,
   16 January 1971: 4):

It was better to take action which was fair to all and which meant that everybody had to do the same thing, otherwise unfair competitive advantages might be given to one group of people rather than to another.

4. On a survey reported in a book studying the matrimonial (divorce) jurisdiction of magistrates' courts (John Clare, 'Divorce and Discontent', 28 January 1971: 12):

   [The survey] shows that 76 per cent of the spouses thought that the hearing was unfair, while 72 per cent felt that the atmosphere of the court was adverse to a fair hearing.

It is striking, first, that the two words of interest are so often used proximately – often in the same sentence – when it would be entirely possible, given the search conditions, to find them in the same story but widely separated. From just these four examples we can see that *fair* versus *unfair* treatment is invoked in a wide variety of situations where groups or individuals are subjected to the power and control of others. Implicit in all such news stories is the conviction that fairness is a good to be aimed at, over and above various other considerations (military morale and discipline, contractual relations between sellers and buyers, orderly procedures in divorce settlements or general economic or political principles). The implication is that the fair thing to do is the right thing to do, and there is little room in *The Times*'s use of *fair/unfair* for claiming that some way of proceeding could be economically or politically sensible, although unfair. For *The Times* of 1971, if something is unfair it cannot be entirely politically sensible.

Turning to *The Times* of 2011 (and again using the digital archive, updated to the end of 2011), a search for all articles containing both *fair* and *unfair* yields 147 stories – a slightly higher number than the initial capture of 130 for 1971, but actually a lower frequency per 1,000 words, since issues of *The Times* in 2011 were far longer than in 1971. Of the 147 stories, thirty-eight are editorial and commentary and thirty-four are news; all seventy-two of these were reviewed for relevance. A number of the news stories concerned sports and sports celebrities and so were disregarded, as were some about technical legal issues where, for example, a judge made a general reference to a defendant's right to a fair trial.

Rather than discussing each story separately in strict order of chronological progression, I have grouped the stories by major topic, comparing the 1971 articles and those forty years later, wherever this seemed illuminating (but sometimes concentrating on items in just one of the two years of interest when the topic did not noticeably recur in both one-year periods). The stories come from multiple sources: some are letters from readers, some are a verbatim reporting of an MP, some are unsigned editorials and some are from regular columnists. What unites them is that they are all in *The Times* and all may have been read by a loyal *Times* reader in 1971 or 2011 or indeed in both years.

2.4   A National Lottery

Wasteful, Illusory and Unfair is the uncompromising title of a leader article of 9 January 1971 that argues against the introduction of a national lottery or municipal lotteries (a national one had recently been mooted, and voters in Manchester had just approved a city lottery). Throughout the eighteenth century in Britain there had been national lotteries – long-term loans to the government that funded various projects and expenses (Raven 2016) – but they were abandoned in 1826 owing to maladministration or worse.

The 1971 *Times* editorial rejection of a new national lottery is read by us today in the awareness that a national lottery was in fact launched in 1993/4, something of a personal initiative of the then prime minister John Major. Approximately half of its ticket income is dispersed in prize money and a quarter is distributed to good causes. Contentiously, those who buy tickets and thus enable the lottery to function mostly come from lower socioeconomic groups. But in the 9 January 1971 *Times* editorial 'Wasteful, Illusory and Unfair', public lotteries are called *an equally illusory benefit to the public and to public finance*. As noted, *unfair* is prominent in the story headline, attracting what linguists call 'end-focus', while *fair* appears in the body-text: 'Perhaps it is fair to say that while not immoral in themselves, they [lotteries] have a tendency to demoralize'. The leader, though accepting of established opportunities for gambling, notes that '[i]t would be wrong for public authority to add to the opportunities and propaganda for gambling – if only because gambling implies a deliberate disjunction of effort and reward which must be prejudicial to society'. The implication of these generic sentences is clear: Britain should be a society where effort and talent (not 'luck') are rewarded; it should be a meritocracy of the deserving. *Merit* and *luck* are opposites here, and success should come through the former, not the latter [for a study which suggests that something far from this is the case today, see Frank (2016), who describes the role of luck in achieving success and how over time it unfairly magnifies initial advantage]. *The Times* of 1971 thus argues for a Britain in which rewards are earned and deserved rather than obtained by sheer luck.

This raises the question of whether there are any kinds of wealth and advancement, unearned by personal effort or merit, acceptable in *The Times*'s preferred Britain of 1971. What of the rewards that accrue to a child lucky enough to grow up affluent rather than poor, who as a result has far greater access than his or her impoverished contemporary to a full education, a good university and the more rewarding jobs and professions? Such a child's luck is of a different order from that of successful gamblers and presumably would not incur *The Times*'s censure. Interestingly, as evident in Polly Toynbee and David Walker's interviews with bankers (Toynbee & Walker 2008), highly successful people usually minimise the role of good luck in their success and emphasise their own merit and hard work, and this makes them less inclined to pay high taxes towards the common good, argues Frank (2016). However, in a society that regards luck as a legitimate basis of success (on a par with but different from bases such as talent or personal connection or market competitiveness), instruments such as a state lottery, which bypass a reward-for-effort contractual relation, would seem to be 'naturally' acceptable.

In the lottery-averse 1971 editorial just discussed, 'accelerating inflation' is also identified as tending to cause a loss of faith in saving, thrift and responsibility, as well as stimulating a lottery-friendly attitude of spending and *irresponsibility*. Targeted lottery fundraising is particularly criticised as 'a highly regressive principle of taxation'. Again the implicit reasoning can be spelled out: if something is worthy of state funding – e.g., a school, hospital or police service – then it should be paid for out of general taxation, to which all should contribute as a duty, rather than from a lottery, which individuals might choose to support or not, and, when doing so, might be motivated mostly by hope of financial reward. A lottery to finance the state's responsibilities turns a duty (one's tax contribution) into an option (charitable giving), and *The Times* of 1971 rejects such a turn.

Within two decades, centre-right thinking on these foundational principles has changed. The Conservative Party general election manifesto of 1992, having noted the recommendation of the 1978 Royal Commission on the subject, declares: 'We believe a well-run, carefully controlled form of national lottery would be popular, while raising money for many good causes.' Many stories in *The Times* of 1992 review different proposals for the precise terms and management of a national lottery; no leader questions the scheme's rewarding of the undeserving lucky. The tone is set instead by stories such as the feature by Anthony Everitt entitled *Have a Flutter to Stop the Rot* (16 December 1992), which identifies a variety of arts and cultural institutions in desperate need of financing for renovation, to which potential lottery grants would throw a lifeline. Buying lottery tickets is now characterized as good citizenship, affirmed by live draws on terrestrial TV and media coverage of the steady stream of big winners.

It is interesting to consider the lottery in relation to the much longer-established (1957), state-managed, finance-generating mechanism with a gambling element in it – namely National Savings (Premium) Bonds, also known by the acronym of the computer used to select the winning numbers each month, ERNIE. Premium bonds were (and are) a way for small savers to put money in an ultra-safe, interest-earning, government savings instrument, while enjoying the possibility of winning a cash prize if one of their numbered bonds was selected by the computer. Crucially, the bond was not a stake which, when ventured, was lost; a bond's winning a prize was a bonus. By contrast, there is no savings element in the National Lottery.

The words *merit* and *meritocracy* have more double-edged potential than is always recognised. There is little in the dominant narratives relayed by *The Times* and *Mail* in recent years, in particular, to disturb their readers' belief that Britain is in large degree a meritocracy, where those with ability and application can prosper and individuals and their families (rather than a large, bureaucratic, inefficient, interfering nanny state) are best placed to help them. This overlooks the fact that the term 'meritocracy', quite a new one coined in the 1950s by the sociologist Michael Young, carried in its original sense a warning about the dangers inherent in rewarding merit where this is done to the point of creating an entitled over-class, alongside relegation or neglect of all those who fail the merit test. Young described a dystopic possible future of unrestrained reward for the talented and subjection of the less able. As Young saw, the rewarding of the deserving, while reasonable when viewed in isolation, may easily contribute to acute and entrenched inequality. This has not discouraged the Conservative Party from using *meritocracy* twelve times in their June 2017 election manifesto (the term does not appear in the Labour manifesto), which talks repeatedly of aiming to make Britain the world's Great Meritocracy. But meritocracy is similar to social mobility: you can have a lot or a little of either, without it bringing any reduction in inequality.

2.5   Industrial Relations in 1971: Strikes and Unfair Dismissal

Fully one-third of the stories under review (twenty-seven of eighty-nine) are in the Politics and Parliament subcategory, and most report parliamentary debates on employer–employee relations, the role of the trade unions and the government's Industrial Relations Bill (IRB). In these articles, the *fair/unfair* paired terms are used in a variety of strategic ways.

The stated purpose of the IRB (it became law in September 1971) was to reset the balance of power between employers and workers. It defined and banned 'unfair industrial practices' on the part of workers or unions, largely by regulating and requiring the registration of the unions, by making unofficial and secondary (wildcat) strikes illegal and by imposing negotiation and arbitration procedures, including final reference (i.e., recourse and submission) to a newly devised National Industrial Relations Court. In return, forms of redress were created for sacked employees, where 'unfair dismissal' could be established. The bill and the subsequent act were bitterly opposed by the unions, and most historians judge that this political struggle weakened rather than strengthened the Heath (Conservative) government. The TUC voted for member unions not to comply with the act's provisions, including its requirement that unions be registered, and the Transport and General Workers' Union (TGWU) was fined for its noncompliance. The act was repealed when Labour returned to power in 1974. The legislation did not resolve matters, but it can be summarized as aiming to prevent two kinds of unfairness – on the part of workers and employers, respectively.

The first IRB story using *fair* + *unfair* comes on 29 January 1971 and reported a development summarised in the story headline: *Industrial Relations Bill: Mr Carr Undertakes to Consider Position of Trade Unions Like Equity.* The draft bill proposed to ban 'pre-entry closed shop agreements', which hitherto had prevented all but those who were members of the relevant union from obtaining work with a particular employer. So these clauses were aimed at protecting the right of workers not to join a union if they so wished. On the other hand, in the entertainment industry, for example, where there were always far more eager applicants than jobs, performers were vulnerable to exploitative pay and conditions unless there was a robust union counterweight to theatre management, such as the performers' union, Equity. It was a senior Tory MP (Sir Harmar Nichols) who argued against total abolition of the closed shop agreement as this could be 'unfair and damaging'. Yet another Tory MP (Mr Rees-Davies) spoke up, similarly, for the Writers' Guild, whose purpose was to maintain 'fair fees'; even if only a few writers withdrew from the guild, this 'would break the organization's bargaining power'. In using the latter phrase the MP may have intended an allusion to a classic concept in labour law and economics: the 'inequality of bargaining power', stemming from inequality of each party's resources, which generally obtains between employers and employees. Mr Carr agreed to reconsider such cases, while maintaining a major principle of the bill: the right not to belong to any union. This Conservative conceding that an all-unionised workforce might be fair for the protection of workers in the literary and theatre trades does beg the question why they might not be equally fair in all trades. But the voicing of these concerns, and Tory acknowledgement of the value of closed-shop protections in some professions, is strikingly different from the absolute rejection of closed shops in the 1980s and subsequently.

The next significant *fair/unfair* story in 1971 was on Tuesday, 2 February, concerning the management versus union stalemate over postal workers' pay. The story headline ran:

Post Office Dispute: Differences Simple but Difficult to Bridge: Minister on Problem of Assessing What Is a Just Wage

This article had Mr Carr (the Secretary for Employment) asserting that 'their [the Post Office employers'] offer was a fair one'. If the parliamentary debate on the IRB articulated the diversity of views on fair dealings in the workplace in theory, disputes like that of the postal workers (or those in car production, or the miners,) showed the clash of interests and different forms of power, in practice.

In both discourses, a proposal's being fair or unfair was a touchstone, used where the speaker hoped it would be accepted as the most compelling justificatory criterion for the mooted course of action.

Another parliamentary report, of Thursday, 11 February (*Unions Not the Untouchables* ...) had one Labour MP complaining that the government was forcing the unions to accept 'a biased [Industrial Relations] Bill', with contentious new 'definitions of what were unfair industrial practices'. The use of a registrar to decide whether a union was properly registered or not was *unacceptable* to the unions, she said. A leading Conservative replied in part that '[i]t was not unfair and unreasonable for society to lay down standards to which [trade union or professional] organizations must conform, and it was not unreasonable for registration to be the foundation of trade unions'.[1]

On 17 February, MPs were again occupied with the IRB; here, although he was a Conservative MP, Mr Nicholas Scott expressed the hope that the government would explain what it meant by 'induce' in the bill's clause that banned anyone from 'inducing' an unofficial strike. The government, he urged, 'must not allow the word "induce" to limit fair discussion in a meeting about the full range of possibilities of [industrial] action that might be open at any time'.

At this distance one could miss the fact that Scott's comment went to the heart of a contentious question, namely who, in what circumstances, was able to propose a strike without being open to prosecution for 'inducement of breach of commercial contract' (a protection known as 'tort immunity'). Again, these were not the kinds of employee-protective reservations that we will find *The Times* or Conservative MPs registering as little as a decade later.

Yet another record of parliamentary proceedings in relation to the IRB (17 February) reported Geoffrey Howe, the solicitor general, acknowledging that the bill's unfair industrial practices clause (clause 86, banning any unofficial call to workers to strike without union authority and due notice) could make any press dissemination of such a call open to prosecution. In the report on the following day, 18 February, Sir Geoffrey Howe complained that strikes were being too often used as a weapon of first resort, and that unofficial strikes were causing great damage. In the course of his defence of the clause, he used *fair* and *unfair* more than twenty times. Here, by way of example, was his explanation of how the bill continued to allow most secondary sympathetic ('borrowed strength') strikes, but outlawed one specific type of these: 'Once one accepted there were certain strikes the calling of which was unfair because

---

[1] A brief word is in order about the grammar of reports from Parliament in *The Times*. As the example just quoted demonstrates, these are in the past tense with the speaker either named or denoted by third-person pronouns. But this indirectness of form is a minor conversion of what is otherwise selective *verbatim* reporting of MPs and peers. In this example the reader is to understand that one of the sentences the Conservative MP actually said was 'It is not unfair and unreasonable for society ...' etc.

they were in pursuit of unfair objectives, a strike in support should be identified as unfair.' Thus for Howe and the government, some strikes were unfair and any secondary strike in sympathy would also be unfair. Certain questions were begged: What were 'unfair objectives' and on what grounds?

The general representation of the IRB in *The Times* of 1971 was that it aimed to make disputes more orderly, and that it balanced a new entitlement (redress in face of unfair dismissal) against new constraints (removal of 'closed shops', union registration, due notice, referral to an industrial relations court, etc.). The government hoped that the IRB's effect would be to reduce the number and length of strikes, which were deleterious to industrial output. Having formulated measures aimed at meeting that goal, employee-friendly 'unfair dismissal' clauses were added in a compensatory spirit (and to meet some of the Donovan report recommendations, discussed later in this section). But there was no genuine parity of governmental concern here, as between treatment of employers and of employees: unions' or workers' *unfair industrial practices* were the primary and driving consideration. And detailed research suggests that from its 1972 introduction up to the present day (incorporating subsequent changes to the legislation), 'unfair dismissal' protections for employees have proven insignificant, notwithstanding centre-right media portrayals to the contrary (Ewing & Hendy 2012).

On 24 February, the business journalist Innis Macbeath wrote an overview of the IRB, which in addition to two separate mentions of the concept of *unfair industrial practice*, also explained that in relation to their own union a dissenting worker had a right to *a full and fair hearing* and if sacked they may be entitled to a remedy if the dismissal could be shown to be *unfair*. It was only on 4 March that we find *fair/unfair* used together in a parliamentary report on something other than the IRB: it comes in a report on Labour MPs condemning the Immigration Bill as 'unnecessary' and 'sham'. Unlike the government, Labour *stand(s) for fair play for Commonwealth citizens* and rejects a Bill whose administration would be *complex and unfair*.

On 17 March review of the IRB was again the site of a *fair+ unfair* paired use, with Sir Geoffrey Howe reported as defending new clauses aimed at preventing the intimidation of employers (by unions, impliedly) so as to get workers sacked. Pressure on employers could be *unfair* and intimidatory, but employers had the primary liability for *unfair* treatment of an employee, so in the bill the government was providing *a fair and sensible system*. There should be a remedy, Howe declared, where cases arose of *wholly unfair and intolerable discrimination*; this would *secure fair play for the individual*. After all, all organizations, be they of employers or workers, *could be unfair*. The following paragraph from Howe in his account of the IRB reflects how *fair(ness)* clusters, with several near-synonyms (bolded) that were used to develop an implicit narrative of how the industrial workplace could be improved in the direction of a reasonable and balanced working-out of a civilized mutual accommodation:

They [the Government] could not believe it was impossible or **intolerable** to ask the trade union movement as well as the country to accept that this was a **sensible** alternative so that in the resolution of this kind of dispute, resort to industrial action became a weapon which was not one of first resort and was replaced by a **civilized** code for the resolution of these rights.

The unions and the country surely can **tolerate** being asked to accept that employees' disputes with their employers can be resolved in a different more **sensible** way: not with the weapon of industrial action but by a **civilized** code. [bold added]

Taken as a whole, this Howe speech argued that the IRB provisions were fair to both sides, and consequently a tolerable, sensible way of resolving (i.e., ending) disputes, by means of all parties complying with a 'civilized' code. The IRB code (or system, as Howe also called it) was said to be civilized, tolerant and sensible. The code was represented as an alternative to industrial action – in fact it was directly contrasted with it. The latter was twice described here, in adjacent sentences, as a weapon, and weapons connote war, violence, aggression and uncivilized loss of control. But if industrial action – such as striking – is a withdrawal of labour in protest at pay or conditions that were themselves seen as intolerable and unreasonable, then striking could be regarded as the employees' best shield (not a sword) with which to protect their rights and interests from the onslaught on them – another weapon – of an employer's imposing of those working conditions and pay. The word *strike* itself, verb and noun, can hardly escape the connotations of physical force in its other uses (*stoppage* is more neutral, but less used). The dominant representations of this clash of interests in *The Times* largely adopted the Conservative government's terms, so that a civilized 'code' was proposed in contrast to and in place of a 'weapon', sometimes wielded by 'wildcats' – terms that gave the discourse an evaluative colouring unambiguously hostile to organised labour.

A week after the budget, the next major item (6 April 1971) was a return to parliamentary discussion of the IRB, but this time in the House of Lords, where Lord Donovan was a speaker. Lord Donovan was the chair of a Royal Commission and chief author of its 1968 Report on Trade Unions and Employers' Associations, which informed the drafting of the IRB. It was the Donovan Report that proposed the idea of an employee being allowed to claim for 'unfair dismissal'. Now Donovan argued that for 'the best hope of cooperation' (from the unions, implicitly), the legislation 'must be made as fair as we can make it'. He went on to identify unfair industrial practice (by unions) and the penalties it attracted as 'the teeth of the Bill', but warned that if the latter turned out to be 'unjustly oppressive', then the legislation would fail. With the word *teeth*, Donovan used a different metaphor from Howe (for whom strikes were weapons), but an equally aggressive one, albeit attributing the aggression to the opposing side: management and government.

A 6 July House of Lords report about an amendment to the IRB provisions concerning 'unfair dismissal' used *unfair* a total of six times, always in the phrase *unfair dismissal* – in effect a term of art and a key concept in the bill. Accordingly there is some temptation for the discourse analyst to dismiss all such mentions of *unfair,* and by the same token all the uses of the word *fair* in the news items discussing debate on the Fair Rents Bill, as artificial inflations of the frequency of occurrence of *fair* and *unfair.* There are grounds for being more guarded, however, in the circumstances. It may reflect the greater centrality of ideas of fairness in the political and governmental discourse of those years, that *fair* and *unfair* should feature so prominently. It is implausible to suggest that governments and parties no longer care about fairness; rather, fairness is no longer invoked as the defining quality of a bill. It may not be without significance that there has been no bill or act since 1980 with *fair* in its title, except for the Fair Employment (Northern Ireland) Act of July 1989.

The general picture emerging as to the collocational semantic prosody, of and around *fair/unfair* and industrial relations in 1971, is one of ambivalence or even-handedness. *The Times* represented some industrial practices, and some strikes, as actually or potentially unfair; but discussion of possible action may be fair and therefore should not be 'limited'; then again, some workers' objectives are unfair, so a strike in pursuit of *them* is unfair. Some dismissals are unfair; but some hearings of protests against dismissal could also be unfair. An even more general 1971 trend may be emerging too, reflected in how often reports of major government initiatives on UK domestic affairs invoked fairness: a tendency for the government to justify policies wherever possible on grounds of fairness, rather than any more overtly political or ideological principles (such as competitiveness, or entrepreneurial innovation, or protection of the currency from inflation, or reduction of the deficit or national debt). Is there a similar ambivalence in the use of *fair* + *unfair* in industrial relations (with its implications for the balance of power between employers and employees, between the wealthy and those largely dependent on earned income) in *The Times* of 2011 and later, or has the tenor changed?

2.6   Industrial Relations in 2011: The Burdens of Employment Law and 'Abuse' of Tribunals

Forty years later, fairness in employer–employee relations continued to attract discussion and dissent, but some of the terms and expectations had changed. The intervening legislative history in brief summary was as follows: the Conservative government's Industrial Relations Act 1971 was repealed and replaced in 1974 by the Labour government's Trade Union and Labour

Relations Act (TULRA), subsequently replaced in 1992 by the Conservatives by a revised act with the same name. Labour also introduced the Employment Protection Act (1975), creating the employment tribunal system (in place of the earlier Industrial Relations Court) and the arbitration service (ACAS). But the legislation was ineffective in a number of key disputes in the 1970s (sometimes because an employer refused to recognise a union: see, e.g., the Grunwick case, in Chapter 5 on *Luddites*). Dysfunction culminated in the 'winter of discontent' of 1978–79, when public sector workers went on strike in disregard of their own union leaders' urging of restraint and cooperation. From 1980 onwards, the Thatcher and then Major Conservative governments introduced laws which gradually controlled trade union activity further: 'sympathy' (secondary) strikes were outlawed, picketing was restricted, balloting of members before taking industrial action was required from 1984; from 1993 the balloting had to be by post rather than more informally, and employers had to be given seven days' notice of an action. The closed shop had already been banned, and from 1982 union immunity from expensive damages suits in court was removed, although employers more often sought an injunction suspending a strike pending consideration of its legality. In all these ways, the campaigning freedom of employees and unions was restricted by a thicket of legal and procedural constraints.

The incoming Labour government of 1997 made few changes to the employment and trade union laws they inherited, advertising its New Labour stance towards the unions as a matter of 'fairness not favours' – thus, unsurprisingly, no abandoning of the 'fairness' criterion. The clear implication is that 1960s and 1970s fairness towards workers and unions (from Labour but also to a degree from the Conservatives) was protective to a fault, and in effect was unfair to employers, capital and other affected parties. The Labour white paper of 1998, *Fairness at Work*, promised there would be no return to 'strikes without ballots, mass picketing, closed shops and secondary action'; but certain 'basic canons of fairness' would be protected, such as those concerning unfair dismissal, joining a union or not, and unpaid parental leave. In the last twenty years, EU legislation has become an important contributor to industrial relations in the United Kingdom, notably in its Working Time Directive (implemented in 1998).

The first relevant 2011 story using *fair* + *unfair* came on 4 January from Helen Giles, an invited *Times* contributor, under this title:

Stop Legal Parasites Feeding on Small Business; Employment Tribunals Are Clogged Up with Claims of No Merit Encouraged by Opportunists

This uses *unfair* in the phrase that first came to prominence in the 1971 IRB: Giles approvingly reported that the Coalition government was contemplating extending the period of employment 'necessary [before an aggrieved dismissed employee could seek redress at an employment tribunal for what they believe was] . . . unfair dismissal from one to two years'. Describing herself as 'an HR adviser to small charities and businesses' (and using the *burden* metaphor that is examined further here in Chapter 3), she declared that small businesses and charities 'are groaning under the burden of complying with employment law that encourages employees to misrepresent themselves as victims of bullying and discrimination'. Besides, she complained, if the wrongdoing appeared to be an Equality Act breach, there was not even the constraint of a required qualifying period. 'It's easy and costs nothing for an employee to cook up a claim', Giles reported. 'Employment law needs a thorough shake-up to restore a fair balance between the interests of employers and employees.'

The Letters to the Editor on 6 January included several taking issue with Giles's call for reform of the employment tribunal system. One claimed that 'the law is loaded in favour of the employer. It allows an employer a very wide "range of reasonable actions" before [dismissal] is deemed to have been unfair', and reported the tribunals' own statistic that 'half of unfairly dismissed employees receive less than £4,300 compensation'. Some reform may be needed; the legal process was 'undoubtedly slow, complicated and expensive, but my experience is that it is at least fair'.

On 4 July appeared a profile (under the heading *It's Time to Put Tribunals in Firing Line*) of Charles Gallagher, the CEO of Abbey plc, who was described as 'on a crusade to alter Britain's "outdated" labour laws' (Gallagher is Irish). The profile contained an onslaught on the concept of 'unfair dismissal' as wishy-washy, costly to employers and stifling of dynamic management practices. It thus echoed exactly six months later the article on this topic by Giles, similarly invoking the terms *fair* and *unfair*. Gallagher's criticism contrasted with the *Times fair* + *unfair* stories in 1971 about the IRB, which approved the new 'unfair dismissal' protection as an important counterweight to the employer-friendly and union-constraining provisions of the bill, and also reported the advocacy of these provisions by Conservative ministers Robert Carr and Geoffrey Howe.

As a legal concept 'unfair dismissal' was first introduced in 1971–72, and in 2011 we saw extensive coverage of the beginnings of a campaign to weaken or even abolish it. Just such a weakening came in 2012, with an extension to the required qualifying period of employment before someone could submit an unfair dismissal claim. The 1971 time limit had been set at one year (changed to eighteen months for small businesses in the 1980 Employment Act) and reaffirmed by s.108 of the ERA of 1996; but in 2012 the qualifying period was extended to two years and has remained there since. Clearly, the longer the exemption period, the more employer-friendly the provision. More broadly Mr Gallagher, guardedly supported by *The Times*, declared the 'unfair dismissal' remedies as 'outdated' and made explicit his view that times have changed, and that within the new employment order, 'unfair dismissal' was inappropriate by being too employee-friendly relative to the balancing of the rights and interests of employers and employees. Over the forty years, the point at which dismissal potentially can be unfair in law shifted in the employers' favour, with a mooting of the idea that fairness/unfairness should not apply to dismissals at all, in legal terms. For *The Times* and the government some small but significant shift occurred over the forty years, as to what *fair* means, or what *dismissal* means, or both.

The Giles/Gallagher position reported in *The Times* was at variance with the facts, however, as noted in Hendy (2014), who reports Employment Tribunal statistics showing a drop of nearly 20% in the number of unfair dismissal claims between 2009–10 and 2011–12. Hendy also notes how 'contrary to the evidence, the media insist on promoting the myth of employers beset by rising numbers of claims' (2014: 3), citing an article by Louisa Peacock in the *Daily Telegraph* on 27 October 2011. In a subsequent paper Ewing and Hendy (2012: 121) conclude:

The truth is that unfair dismissal law does not impose undue burdens on business. Rather, it offers minimal protection for workers: too many are excluded from the legislation; it is too easy for an employer to justify a dismissal as not being 'unreasonable'; and the remedies for those who are dismissed remain wholly inadequate. This is the legal regime that needs reform.

In summary, while in 1971 *The Times* accepted 'unfair dismissal' protections, by 2011 it tacitly endorsed narratives which represented them as a drag on employment flexibility. Fitting this direction of travel, on 16 November 2011 came another op-ed piece titled *Red Tape Suffocates Job Creation* which argued, among other changes, that '[t]he concept of "fair dismissal" should be widened from neglectful incompetence and inherent inability to include inadequate performance' so that underperforming employees can be more easily dismissed. In such an atmosphere, it is perhaps less surprising that in July 2013 the government introduced compulsory fees (called exorbitant and immoral by some critics) to be paid by anyone taking their claim to tribunal, following which the number of cases (especially sex discrimination ones) pursued to tribunal dropped by 70%. In July 2017, however, the Supreme Court ruled that such fees were inconsistent with principles of equality and access to justice. What was deemed fair in 2013 was judged unfair only four years later.

There has been no 'cherry-picking' of industrial stories in the foregoing section. All the news/op-ed stories, using both *fair* and *unfair* in the two years that are four decades apart, have simply been gathered and compared to see better those values they share and those where with the passage of time a contrast has emerged. What has emerged in the use of these terms in

The Times is a change in their application, in favour of employers, managers, the controllers of capital or their agents and to the disadvantage of the employed and those with little wealth.

2.7   Mr Marples's Manifesto for the Control of Fair Incomes

On 22 March 1971 came the first of two fascinating 'blue skies' articles by Conservative MP Ernest Marples (the second appeared the next day) on what he saw as the most equitable basis on which an 'expansion policy' could be launched. By 'expansion' he meant a policy that would stimulate economic growth, growth in GNP – hence the article's title, *Legislating for Growth*. Using *fair* twelve times and its antonym once (when he denounced periodic past impositions of a *crude unfair wage freeze*), Marples argued that a strong growth economy needed a distribution of incomes and pensions that was affordable, relative to GDP; he added that it *must be fair, and seen and felt to be fair* (making this point at least twice). Income-distribution would be differential, he recognized, with the value of different kinds of work reflected in different levels of remuneration (lorry drivers versus airline pilots was one of his examples). He also recognized that values could change over time, so clerks might come to be valued and remunerated less than dustmen, for instance. But, citing the 1953 Priestley Commission on Civil Service Pay, he argued that an independent, unbiased, Parliament-approved 'Differential Incomes Board', assisted now by computers and more comparative data, should be able to devise a successful and enduring incomes policy. Marples concluded his first article by declaring that '[d]ifferentials compiled on such a basis would be acceptable to fair human beings', but he conceded that not all human beings were reasonable and that the 'naked power struggle' between employers and employees was at the root of the problem. Marples might be criticized for a naïve faith in the possibility of an 'unbiased' incomes board, functioning freely at arms' length from Parliament (doing so, one suspects, only until such time that it did anything that the government – not Parliament – disapproved of). It is not irrelevant, given the preceding information, to speculate as to what Marples's reaction might have been to the stratospheric remuneration packages of top executives in Britain in more recent years or indeed as to what Sir Raymond Priestley (recently retired from the Vice-Chancellorship at the University of Birmingham) would have thought of the CEO-style pay awards for heads of universities these days. And Marples, we must remember, was writing as a Conservative MP and a recent government minister: no Marxist radical.

In *Power for the Consumer*, his second and concluding article, published the next day, Marples warned that power had now shifted 'from the masters to the men', and 'workers can now damage or destroy a company at practically no cost to themselves' (he ignored the fact that striking – if that was what he meant by 'damage or destroy' – entailed total loss of wages, only partially mitigated if the union was wealthy enough to be able to provide strike pay for a period of time). Rather contradicting his own thesis of increased labour power, he noted that 'oddly enough ... wages and salaries are still the same percentage of national income' as they were decades earlier (the 'wage share' described in Section 1.2 of Chapter 1).

As a means of altering the present adversarial culture, Marples proposed the creation and funding by taxation of a totally neutral and independent 'Power Balancing Unit' (PBU) which would be 'like a neutral referee in a boxing match' and might prevent what happens at present, where both combatants 'end up clobbering the paying silent spectators'. As in the previous day's article, Marples decreed that the PBU, now allegedly holding the balance of power, 'must be fair and be seen to be fair'; 'fair procedures would emerge from the feasibility study', he confidently predicted.

The point of reviewing the *fair* + *unfair-* using Marples 'manifesto' is to show another example of 1971 *Times* discourse confronting wealth inequality, where what was deemed fair and what unfair, and what kinds of government progressive interventions might be contemplated as 'fair and reasonable', were far less inegalitarian, far less accepting of inequality, than the *Times* discourses of 2011 and surrounding years. The Marples plan assumed extensive government intervention to ensure fairness in pay levels and increases, in public and private sectors alike, alongside fair profits for employers. Long before 2011 such talk had been pushed to the margins in government and centre-right newspaper discourses. Fairness, as a principle, was undoubtedly still desirable (and invoked in Osborne's budgets, for example, in relation to tax rates), but it had long ceased to be regarded and discussed as a coherent basis on which the state might intervene to regulate profits or pay awards, felt to be best left to the free market.

2.8   The Squeezed Middle and Fair Pay in 2011

The Marples items are two of several 1971 *Times* op-ed articles on the economy that invoked *fair* + *unfair*. Others came from Brian Walden and Nicholas Scott (space limitations prevent discussion of them here) – both intensely political figures but outside government. In 2011 there were roughly comparable op-ed articles, using the *fair/unfair* terms, from Philip Collins, formerly a speechwriter for PM Tony Blair. Collins did not discuss central control of prices and incomes; such ideas had been swept off the agenda following the entrenchment of neoliberal free market principles and the privatising of many industries. But on 4 March 2011 he wrote a substantial column titled *Will the People in the Middle Ever Get Richer?*

Collins argued that the 'squeezed middle' in the country were those most affected by the stalling of wage increases over the last decade. And they were people, not 'the economy':

individuals and their families, 11 million of them, all earning more than £11,000 but less than £33,000 a year. These people have assumed, for most of their lives, that if the economy grew, their income would grow with it. All of a sudden, that is not happening. Wages stopped growing in 2003 and are not expected to start growing again before 2015.

Productivity had risen and the labour market had become more flexible, but wages had not kept pace. 'This isn't just unfair. It also has consequences for the rest of us', Collins said (e.g., in triggering the growth of personal or household debt to dangerous proportions). He continued, rhetorically: 'Does it matter that better work is not producing better pay? Is it fair that improving productivity from the workers should end up in the pockets of the man who owns the mill? And, if it is not fair, are we prepared to do anything about it?' Relevant to Collins's concern for the depressed pay progression of the 'squeezed middle' was the review chaired by Will Hutton, on Fair Pay in the Public Sector (nearly sixty years after Priestley's similar review). A commentary on the Hutton Review's proposals came from Duncan Exley on 18 March 2011, under the title *Fine Words on Unfair Pay Must Be Translated into Action.* The review was in part concerned with whether pay ratios in both the public and private sector should be publicly reported and justified, and whether top public sector managerial pay should be capped at twenty times the lowest-paid in their organisation. Hutton argued instead for reporting the top-to-median ratio, as 'less susceptible to manipulation' (e.g., by outsourcing of low-paid workers). Perhaps most significant is that there has not been the slightest hint of government action to implement a Hutton-style pay-cap – whereas regulation of pay and prices continued to be debated through the 1970s. The Exley commentary predicted as much; the *must be translated* in the headline is a journalist's contraction of *would need to be translated,* and the key phrase comes at the beginning: *fine words.* These, the idiom reminds us, butter no parsnips – that is, in themselves they have no practical effect; the implication is that the Hutton Review was fine words with no effect.

Later in 2011, on 26 August, came another op-ed piece from Philip Collins under the headline *Of Course the Rich Should Pay More Tax. But ... Ed Miliband Must Be Careful Not to Look Obsessed about It. That Will Only Turn the Voters Off Labour.* Written soon after Miliband was elected leader of the Labour Party, it predicted that, by contrast with the Blair period, with Mr Miliband 'we can expect an assault on inequality [of wealth and income] to be a conspicuous feature'. Collins rehearsed the facts about the comparatively low taxes imposed on the truly rich (e.g., the 86,000 people in the United Kingdom worth more than £5 million), and drew on Atkinson and Piketty's *Top Incomes: A Global Perspective* to rebut the standard objections that higher taxes would drive the rich overseas and yield little extra revenue. He also deplored the gibe that proposals to tax the rich more was the 'politics of envy':

When people on the Left criticise income distribution they are not motivated by a grudge; they are making a claim about justice. They are saying that it's not fair. And, indeed, many of the rewards in London's financial services are what economists would call 'super-normal'. Where labour markets are essentially rigged there is not even a crooked line between reward and desert.

Preserving a direct link from desert to reward, we noted, was part of *The Times*'s justification for rejecting lotteries in 1971. Now Collins was acknowledging a scandalous gulf between them, with London's banking elite as a 'rigged' labour market.

At the same time, however, Collins professed concern that Labour politicians were 'obsessed with income inequality, regardless of how people's wealth has been derived': 'But although inequality is part of fairness, it is not the same thing … An inequality is only unfair when it cannot be justified.' The latter general truth does not grapple with varying strength of justification and varying degrees of inequality, where all the difficulties lie. For all his arguments in favour of higher taxes on the rich, Collins ended by warning that 'taxes on the super-rich are a disguised trap for the Labour Party' and not a vote-winning policy. Thus in *The Times* in 2011 even a centre-left commentator drew back from any concrete proposal regarding what he recognized was markedly increased inequality of wealth and income.

On 3 November came an editorial titled *To Be Fair; A Robin Hood Tax Is an Impractical and Unworkable Idea, but the Government Must Take Steps to Show That Social Justice and Capitalism Run Best in Tandem*. It began with the maxim 'A fair exchange is no robbery' and proceeded to reflect on how 'the financial crisis has also produced a crisis of fairness'. The leader prescribed four pathways to meet 'the demand for fairness': economic growth, reform of public services to 'help ensure that taxpayers feel they are getting a fair deal' (value for their money), more 'responsible' rewards for chief executives ('when customers … and … shareholders … complain that remuneration for a few chief executives is unfair that is because such rewards are indeed unfair') and, finally, reform of property taxes. It also rejected imposing higher income taxes on high earners since 'such a broad measure is a disincentive to economic activity', even though precisely that argument had been rebutted in the August article by Philip Collins, who had declared 'there is no stable causal relationship between a nation's growth rate and the extent to which it taxes people at the top of the income scale'.

In Your Shout; Taxing Times (5 November) readers' online comments on the leader article of two days previously were reported. Some defended the big earners. One wrote:

'Anyone would think City workers don't presently pay tax. They do – huge amounts. And they go to work every day. Unlike the slobs hanging around St Paul's whining "It's not fair". Working people don't have time for protests, or scroungers.' The mention of slobs at St Paul's is a reference to the Occupy

London anti-capitalist protesters then camped and campaigning in front of St Paul's Cathedral – hardly the 'squeezed middle' Collins had in mind. Another reader agreed:

The pay of a chief executive of a private company is not the business of anyone but that company. It is ridiculous to say that it is unfair for a 'fat cat' to receive a percentage salary increase way above that of the lower-paid workers. That 'fat cat' may well be in charge of 200,000 people. Awarding all of those people the same percentage increase would dissolve a company . . . Some people obviously do not like this. Tough. Emigrate to a communist country if that's how you feel.

Another wrote: 'Before we go farther down the route of finding new ways to tax people in the name of fairness, we must look at the other side of the coin – spending [i.e., alleged government profligacy: MT].'

Four days later (9 November) another *Times* commentator, Daniel Finkelstein, was found arguing for what he found *fair* and what he judged *unfair*, in a discussion titled *We're as Angry with Welfare Cheats as Bankers; Labour Is Strong on the Greedy Rich but Will Have to Raise Its Game on Crime, Immigration and Benefit Fraud*. This 'we' that deplores both bankers and welfare cheats was surely another version of the 'squeezed' middle class. Finkelstein claimed to have detected in the speeches of the leaders of both main political parties a 'new' idea – that of people getting something in return for actually doing something, in place of a 'something for nothing' culture: 'But it isn't just about rich people. It is about anyone who gets something out without putting in *the same amount* . . . It is one part of the same populist anger that is commonly expressed about criminals, welfare fraudsters and bogus asylum seekers' [emphasis added]. Finkelstein's 'same amount' condition was unworkable or meaningless for any transaction more complex than A giving B a cup of sugar today and B giving A a cup of sugar tomorrow, except as a figure of speech invoking a principle of proportionality, of return or reward linked to contribution. It is even more opaque that Collins's invoking of 'justified inequality': the salary-for-work agreement by definition eludeed 'same amount' calculation. Finkelstein then cautioned that '[t]his demand for fairness is always there, but it becomes particularly strong when resources are scarce, as they are now'. Most resources are generally scarce and differentially available, to a greater or lesser degree, including good housing, good jobs, good food, good education; so one wonders if Finkelstein's 'when resources are scarce' phrase was simply an oblique way of alluding to the hardship of the announced austerity cuts. The mindset seemed to assume a world where resources were normally unpro-blematically available, a mindset placidly unaware of other people's poverty.

An op-ed piece on 2 December by Anushka Asthana also implied coali-tion government misspending and the resulting frustration of those in the 'squeezed middle'. It was titled *Clegg Is on the Wrong Side of the Fairness*

Divide; Favouring the Jobless at the Expense of Working Families Will Prove a Costly Political Error. Asthana profiled Natalie Cheshire, the mum in 'a typical British family' (two parents, two young children) who face losing their Stevenage home because of a sudden rent rise to £750 a month. The family wages were too low to save for a deposit to buy and too high to have priority on any social housing waiting list. Next door to Natalie, living in a similar house, a council tenant (evidently one such priority case) was being charged only £440 per month. Asthana wrote: 'Her [Natalie's] perception of unfairness – "we work hard but we've got nothing to show for it" – is widespread. And it goes to the heart of a battle raging in Westminster over the welfare state.' Asthana described some confusion in and between the political parties over welfare, with Iain Duncan Smith, the Work and Pensions Secretary, repeating a 'make work pay' mantra, but combining this with caring language about reducing poverty. Asthana added: 'Labour too is grappling with welfare, aware of just how important fairness is for voters.' But she singled out Nick Clegg's cabinet 'push' for out-of-work benefits to be increased by the relatively high figure of 5.2%, in line with one calculation of inflation, as in danger of back-firing with the 'squeezed middle' of families like the Cheshires because that increase was allegedly paid for by a Treasury freeze on any increase in the working tax credits for the two million lowest-paid earners. As for Labour: 'Mr Miliband is wrestling with the fairness issue: his talk of the squeezed middle and his attack on "something for nothing" reveal a change in language. But Labour will need to go further to tap into that anger felt by families such as the Cheshires.' She mentioned that some Tories, including Duncan Smith, advocate the idea of 'workfare' – doing community work to receive basic unemployment benefits – and suggested that for all its difficulties of implementation, 'it could instil a sense of fairness into the welfare system and provide a boost for the unemployed' (for CDA critique of government discourse on workfare, see Mulderrig 2015). Her final thought was that 'Labour too needs to challenge its beliefs on welfare. It is possible to be both radical and fair – and that will be the key to the next election.'

Taking Asthana, Collins and Finkelstein together, their combined message is that the 'middle' – those neither rich nor poor – are being treated less than fairly by the state (hence 'squeezed'); by contrast both the rich and the poor are being treated more than fairly by the tax system and the welfare system, respectively. A possible solution with regard to relations between the middle and the poor, aired rather than emphatically endorsed, would be a 'change' to welfare, in a 'radical but fair' way, in both the language about it and its actual provisions. Hence the mention of 'workfare' – unemployment benefits made conditional upon so-called community work – which some critics have seen as a regression in the direction of nineteenth-century workhouse principles.

2.9   Fair Rents, Fair Housing

In the light of the 2011 housing rent grievance of Natalie Cheshire reported in the precious section, a long news item that appeared forty years earlier (11 November 1971) by Ronald Butt, entitled *Labour's Emotional Ambiguity over Housing,* is of considerable interest. Butt's article came six months after a brief report on the government's emerging ideas concerning 'fair rents' for state-owned housing ('council housing'), a policy aimed at raising such rents to be in line with those charged for private rented accommodation. This is presumably not the solution, with regard to affordability, that Natalie Cheshire would have wanted; nevertheless it promised to equalise private and council rents and, crucially, regulation of private rentals, as per Labour's 1965 Rent Act, would have stayed in place. Butt's article was one of several items about the Fair Rents Bill (renamed a Housing Finance Bill) that appeared in November of 1971 and contained the *fair + unfair* combination.

Butt argued that the bill 'more lucidly and logically perhaps than any other of the Government's social measures, embodies essential Tory philosophy and, in consequence, embraces ideas of which the Labour Party is deeply and instinctively afraid'. He acknowledged that the old system of 'blanket' housing subsidy of council housing tenants overcame the postwar housing shortage, but 'it has been unfair as between council and non-council tenants and as between both tenants and landlords in different areas'.

Five days later, on 16 November 1971, an entire parliamentary report was given over to the Environment Minister Peter Walker's moving of the second reading of the Housing Finance Bill (titled *No Family in Future Would Be Crippled by Rent*). This reported Walker's statement in detail, beginning with the claim that the legislation promised to be the most important reform in housing to take place that century. The Bill's principal aims were said to be two: to provide local authorities with 'far greater' funds (*via* council rent rises, to more closely match the fair market rate) that will address 'a serious housing problem'; and to ensure 'much greater equality' among different council-housing tenants and local authorities. Mr Walker chastised the Labour opposition for objecting to his initiative in 'practical socialism'. As for uses of *fair* and *unfair*, there were three of these: Walker explained that '[i]f the fair rent was lower than the existing rent, a rebate would be given to the tenant'. He went on to call Labour's system of historic cost rent assessment 'an unfair way of fixing rents for local authority housing', and later argued that the bill would extend the new *fair rent system* to voluntary housing movements (housing associations).

In the forty years between Mr Walker's act and the 2011 crisis in housing affordability, major milestones included Labour's 1975 Housing Rent and Subsidies Act, which reversed the policy of 'fair' rents and empowered local authorities to set rent levels. But the dual system of housing provision (market-rate private purchase or rental for the better-off; rental of subsidised council-owned properties for the less well-off) persisted until the 1980 Housing Act of the Thatcher government, which gave council tenants the right to buy their home, at a heavily discounted price (depending on length of residency). Subsequent acts of 1984 and 1986 removed restrictions and raised discounts (e.g., up to 70% on flat-purchase). At the same time, the Thatcher governments applied 'spending controls' sharply to curtail central government housing grants to local authorities, and this forced councils to reduce their building programmes as well as increase their rents. There is no question that these policies were part of a wider project of 'shrinking the state' (here, local government particularly), privatisation, and the transferring of responsibility to the individual.

Alongside this massive handover of housing stock ownership from councils to private individuals, new build of council housing since the mid-1980s had dwindled to a negligible number: compare 151,000 council house completions in 1971 with 3,000 in 2011. As for total new house completions (private and public), 2013 government statistics (DCLG) report 364,000 house completions in 1971 and 141,000 in 2011. In the Conservative government period 1979–97, the proportion of UK housing stock that was council housing fell from nearly a third of the whole to 17%. Social housing came to be increasingly occupied exclusively by low income, socially disadvantaged families.

What is remarkable about a great many of the housing-related 1971 *fair/ unfair* instances noted here is that this *equality-* and *fairness*-worded approach, protecting the power of local authorities to provide new council housing, was being promoted by a Conservative Party government. The contrast with *The Times*'s reporting of the post-2010 Conservative-led Coalition government's attitude to local authorities and any responsibility they might be judged to have for taking a leading role in housing provision within their boroughs is very clear.

The Anushka Asthana December opinion article described earlier, which complained of unfairness in private sector and public sector housing rent, triggered a letter on 5 December from Rev Paul Nicolson, Chair of the Zacchaeus 2000 Trust:

Sir, It is unfair, says Anushka Asthana, that the rent of a council house is £440 a week and the rent charged by a private landlord is £750 a week for a similar house next door.

It certainly is but the private tenants' indignation should be aimed at landlords, who have been the beneficiaries of billions of pounds of their taxes in housing benefit every year since lending was deregulated in the 1980s, rising to £21 billion last year.

It is not the welfare system which is to blame but the governments who allowed that flood of lending to push up prices and rents, and housing benefit, in a housing market in short supply. There has been, and there remains, no coherent housing policy to keep rents and prices under control to provide all tenures with affordable housing.

It is depressing to read this letter's sober assessment in 2011 ('no coherent housing policy', etc.) against the background of the 1971 articles regarding Peter Walker's Housing Finance Act, noted earlier. It is as if the intervening forty years have seen a decline rather than progress in ensuring there is affordable housing for all. Rev Nicolson mentioned the deregulation of mortgage lending in the 1980s, which was part of a wider deregulation movement. The Housing Act of 1988 began the deregulation of private sector rents, also reducing protection for tenants and removing the right to independent assessment of 'fair rent'. Eligibility for housing benefit (rent rebate/allowance) of students under twenty-five was restricted (and further restricted in 1996 for all single people under twenty-five). But the steep decline in the funding and building of new council or social housing plus the steady rent rises allowed by deregulation led to a tripling in housing benefit expenditure in the ten years to 1997–98, when it amounted to £12 billion, before nearly doubling again by 2010, as Rev. Nicolson noted. A study could be made of how deregulation (the freedom of the market) ousted fairness as a priority of government policy. Critics of the neoliberal capitalism that has taken hold in Britain as in other OECD countries in the past thirty years argue that the increasing reliance of the economy on such state supplements to counteract low incomes (via working tax credits) and high rents (via housing benefit) point to the failure of that neoliberal system. These two provisions have been seen as implicit recognition of and resigned acceptance of the unfairness of neoliberal market capitalism. The latter has failed to deliver, for many in work or otherwise, affordable housing or decent wages; neither state intervention nor these press commentaries on what is fair housing have counteracted neoliberalism's tendency to increase wealth inequality.

2.10   Pensions 'Reform' in 2011

Pensions, whether from the state following a person's National Insurance contributions or earned through an occupation-based scheme, were of some concern in 1971 but much more so, and more often invoking the *fair/unfair* paired terms, in 2011. The one striking instance in the earlier year, on 29 October 1971, came in a six-page special report on pensions and retirement, prompted by the government's recent white paper, *Strategy for Pensions,* and assessing the government's proposed changes from every angle. The *fair/unfair* terms occurred in the first article in the report, from Paul Dean, then a junior minister, introducing the government's proposals, which were in essence to provide people with two pensions – a basic state one and an earnings-related one. 'Earnings-related contributions [also] relieve the unfair burden on the lower-paid', Dean explained. For those not covered by an earnings-related occupational scheme, there was a state reserve scheme: 'The scheme will operate on a strict money-purchase basis as the only fair way of catering for those who may be in and out of it at different periods of their working lives.'

While the discussion around pensions in 1971 was in terms of fair and practical provision, in 2011 it was in terms of reform of long-established arrangements, especially in the public sector, now argued by some to have become unaffordable. *Summer of Strikes Feared as Pensions Lose 'Gold Plating'* (11 March) was a lengthy item surveying the kinds of adverse consequences that the government's proposed pension reforms would have on particular categories of employee. Jill Sherman reported that '[p]ublic sector employers could face industrial tribunals over changes to previously agreed contracts, although the reforms could bring the end of the Fair Deal, which forces companies to guarantee public sector pensions when staff transfer'. A dinner lady says, 'I think it is unfair to make people work longer', and a policeman suggests that the only fair way to change pensions is to introduce new rules for new entrants, rather than for those on a previously-agreed package.

In the letters to the editor on 17 June, several contributions were about the proposed changes to public sector pensions, and their fairness or otherwise. One person wrote that those who 'complain that the changes to their pensions are unfair . . . should remember that it is the same for everyone'. Another wrote:

Leaders of the teachers' unions ask if it is fair that they should be asked to pay more, work longer and get less. Is it fair that the children they teach – and their children – should through taxation pay their teachers' (and their parents' teachers') index-linked final salary pensions, when those children and their children will be able to acquire equivalent pensions for themselves only by contributing 12–15 per cent of their earnings over their working lives?

Concerning threatened union strike action over the pension reforms, columnist Matthew Parris (18 June) wrote that he suspected the strikers would win little general sympathy: 'An immense and sometimes rather unfair national scepticism about the public sector runs deep and is of very long standing in Britain.' With this stance Parris can neatly rise above two clashing publics: hard-pressed state employees and the 'general' public.

The Truth about Public Sector Pensions (25 June) was a *Times* Money article which announced that with the strikes imminent, it would assess the claims made by both sides of the dispute 'to help you to make up your mind about who is in the right – the strikers or the Government'. One local authority worker, attracted by the promise of a good pension, complained that 'the way the Government keeps changing the goalposts for public sector workers is unfair ... I am resigned to working until I am 66, but that doesn't seem fair as when I started in the public sector I was told I could retire at 60. We are being asked to pay while bankers get massive payoffs.'

The same topic was resumed in *Playing Fair with People's Pensions* (30 June), where Ian King reported TUC General Secretary Brendan Barber's criticism of the government proposals as setting a 'gold standard for unfairness' (a rejoinder to the talk of public sector pensions being 'gold-plated'). King conceded that most public sector pensions (averaging £7,800 *per annum*) were modest, but that each would need a pension pot of more than £200k to finance them. By contrast the average private sector worker currently retires with a pension pot of just £30k. 'What is genuinely unfair is that these people [one in eight private sector workers, working beyond retirement] have to do this and then, through their taxes, pay for the pensions of better-off public sector retirees.'

An opinion-editorial on 25 November returned to the question of public sector pensions reform, now the subject of a strike by affected workers: *Why the Strike Is Wrong; It Is Hard on Public Sector Workers to Be Asked to Contribute More to Their Pensions and Work Longer but It Is Fair to Taxpayers and an Essential Reform.* The leader noted that '[t]he case being advanced for the proposed action is that the reform of public sector pensions is not fair on the recipients'; it agreed that the reforms would be hard and unwelcome, but observed: 'Being hard and unwelcome is not, however, the same as being unfair.' The government has made generous concessions to ensure these public pensions are still valuable, but '[t]o go any farther [in the way of conceding to union demands] would be very unfair to taxpayers'. Again we see here that what counts as unfair is never fixed, but open to continual adjustment in response to changed conditions.

Throughout the discussion of pension 'reform' (sc. reduction), there is a sense that those affected by the reform are powerless to shape what is decided; this is in some contrast to one public reaction to proposed reform of another large financial sector, the banks, where access to ministers and power to influence them seems to be different. Thus a 28 January item from the Davos global affairs conference reported that Jamie Dimon, chief executive of JP Morgan Chase, had denounced all the public criticism of bankers following the global banking crisis: the 'constant refrain of "bankers, bankers, bankers" is an unfair and unproductive way of treating people', he said; also, the expectation that banks would not question proposed reform measures but simply 'bend down [sic] and accept them just because we are banks – that is not fair'. Mr Dimon's pay package in 2011 was $23 million; in June 2015 his net worth was calculated to be $1.1 billion.

2.11   *Fair* and *Unfair* in Other Contexts

As in 1971, a variety of other *fair* + *unfair* stories on government-related topics appeared in 2011, but with less prominence. One of these concerned fairness in the state support for care of the elderly. A 5 July 2011 item warned that government reform of funding for care of the elderly, previously criticised by a government-appointed review commission (the Commission for the Funding of Care and Support) as a 'confusing, unfair and unsustainable' system, might be derailed by the general spending cuts. That commission's key recommendation was that an individual's contribution to his or her care should be capped at something between £25,000 and £50,000, with Mr Andrew Dilnot, the economist chair of the commission, recommending £35,000 as 'an appropriate and fair figure'. Further costs would be paid for by the state.

The letters to the editor on 8 July returned to this topic under the headline *How to Pay for the Care of the Elderly*. The first letter stated:

In fact what is proposed is very fair; in that all citizens contribute towards global provision from their taxes and those who need help can be confident it will be provided when needed; just as would be the case with any other form of healthcare or public service. If we construct a benefits and welfare system such that the burden of contribution falls only on the well-off but the benefits accrue only to the poor, then the former group will soon be unwilling to maintain the funding upon which all rely.

The next correspondent suggested that the well-off may exploit the rules:

My advice to wealthy clients will be to place Mum in the very best care home, incur the maximum £35,000 cost after about six months and then get the State to pick up the tab for the rest of her life. Very good for Mum and her beneficiaries but very unfair on the taxpayer.

Then there is the matter of university tuition fees. An item on 16 July argued that university tuition fees were a bargain:

The tuition fees policy can be criticised on the ground that it is inter-generationally unfair because previous generations did not have to pay as much, if anything, for their education. But if you consider only the current generation of 18-year-olds, then it is fair that those who go to university pay for it and those who don't do not.

But setting aside the 'inter-generational' or historical comparison, if in 2011 it was fair for those who go to university to pay for it, would it not have been fair also in 1971 (when nearly all did not)? On the 'unfairness' of university funding in 1971 *The Times* now, as then, is silent.

Six weeks later (27 August) an op-ed article criticized the Scottish government for charging 'rest of the UK' (RUK) students at the £9,000 p/a level as a solution to their own funding gap: 'It has always seemed unfair that, while EU students can come to Scottish universities on the same terms as the Scots, those in the RUK can be charged extra. Unfair, and mean-spirited ... it is a diminution of the reputation for fairness and equality for which Scottish education has long been celebrated.' Here, in direct contradiction of what had been argued six weeks previously, it was the paying of fees by the individual rather than the not-paying that was deemed unfair.

Many other topics were discussed in a story using both *fair* + *unfair* on just one occasion. The topics just discussed were those where *fair* + *unfair* was recurrently used, and therefore those best reflecting what *The Times* represented the place of fairness and unfairness to be in contemporary politics and economics.

2.12   Conclusions

The core of the chapter has reviewed uses of *fair* + *unfair* in a range of topics, from industrial relations to pay restraint to pensions to housing, using qualitative, critical and interpretive methods. My interest is not in the narrow question of what the immediate collocates of *fair/unfair* in *The Times* were, in 1971 and forty years later (the evidence of clear trends is anyway slight), but in the way *fair* and *unfair* were jointly used in the earlier year and then in the more unequal world of the United Kingdom in 2011, and in what those uses tell us about the social world in and between those two years. The aim of this chapter as for future ones is to draw out, from interpretations of all relevant joint uses of these keywords, a number of core propositions that encapsulate the central meanings of these words for these newspapers, in relation to wealth distribution and then to try to produce (in a sense, reproduce) a narrative, where those propositions are plausibly combined. For some keywords or phrases, a synthesis of the main detectable propositions into one or more narratives is far from automatic and may be difficult to make transparent. Nevertheless, the foregoing examination of uses of the *fair/unfair* paired evaluative terms in inequality-related contexts in *The Times* in 1971 and forty years later has revealed a number of patterns and developments.

• In assessing policies and government-managed conditions, fairness and the minimizing of unfairness is only slightly less prominent in 2011 than it was in 1971. The words and concepts are still important, but what they are applied to has sometimes changed. My preliminary thesis that governments and newspapers will always advocate fairness as an unqualified good seems to prevail in all the 1971 stories, but a few in 2011 suggest that *it's not fair* can be the whine of the slob, and reflective of something negative or regressive. Some 2011 stories say or imply 'Life is not fair, toughen up!' and certainly caution against costly 'nanny-state' intervention aimed at redressing every conceivable form of unfairness, misfortune or disadvantage. Those are implied to be 'fair but unaffordable'.

- *Fair/unfair* co-occur in *The Times* in relation to those government policies where monetary gain or loss is directly concerned. Thus they repeatedly figure in discussions of taxes and pay awards and pensions, but rarely in discussions of health, crime, education, defence – although in principle fairness is just as relevant to these.
- A national lottery which *The Times* rejected in 1971 as unfair and rewarding luck and gambling rather than merit is thoroughly entrenched by 2011, and characterised as both fair and a social good (with an enthusiasm absent when taxes are discussed). The entrenchment of an acceptance of 'lottery culture', of the power of fate and good or bad luck seems reflected in the recurrent descriptions of inequality in schools and health care as subject to a 'postcode lottery', of certain kinds of happy outcome as 'like winning the lottery', and of genetically inherited characteristics as 'a lottery'.
- *Fairness* is a key criterion in 1971 in the evaluation of proposed changes to employment law and the regulation of strike actions and dismissals. But there are limits to its application. *Fair* or *unfair* are key descriptors of strike objectives, dismissals and hearings, but are rarely found collocating in *The Times* of 1971 with *pay* or *remuneration* or *conditions*. By 2011 *The Times* was reporting how employment law is too employee-friendly, giving rise to costly cases brought to tribunal.
- Towards the close of 1971, but first adumbrated in a *fair/unfair* story on 12 May, the government is repeatedly reported, with implicit *Times* approval, striving to create a fair rent system for all housing. There is no comparable discussion in *The Times* in 2011 (e.g., no reports of government interest in intervening to attempt to control housing rentals).
- Alongside continued appeal to what is fair, just where the scales are set so as to achieve fairness seems to have shifted by 2011 in ways that might surprise the 1971 reader: completing two years of employment (not one year) before a claim for unfair dismissal can be lodged is now deemed fair, but only grudgingly, as further reform of the rules regarding 'unfair dismissal' and recourse to a tribunal are advocated. Very different university tuition fee regimes in Scotland and England are now fair (but non-EU rules with regard to English students in Scotland are unfair). A shift to less generous terms for public sector pensions is now fair; large salaries for CEOs and relatively low top rates of tax are now fair, and any higher rate in 2011 would be unfair. Pensions are one of the topics where the idea of fairness is especially valued, perhaps reflecting the special place of the pension in the idealised life 'script', of diligent educational training, productive employment, the raising of pro-social children, and final release into healthy and financially secure retirement. If that is the implicit social contract, one of the unfair variants of that script is one where you cannot afford to retire at the expected age, or where the pension amount bears little relation to the quantum previously promised.

Thus there are many signs of change here, in what is represented as fair (or unfair), from the first extended example, the ethics of state lotteries, onwards. Being a centre-right 'small c' conservative newspaper throughout the period, *The Times* can be expected to have maintained a broadly Conservative ('large C') set of values in terms of what its stories judged to be *fair* and *unfair*, and this was by and large confirmed. But the shifts of position are equally striking. Arguably the very broadest shift from 1971 to 2011 in *The Times's* *weltanschauung* is away from a concern with state responsibility for fairness (for many things, including ensuring fairness – if not in 'life' altogether, at least in health care, education, employment and housing) and towards the assumption that fairness is mostly the individual's responsibility. That broad shift is not the present study's focus of interest, but rather the growth in inequality. After all, a state could move from a more collectivist to more individualist politics without any such growth – indeed, with further reduction of wealth inequality.

In 1971, admittedly not always enthusiastically, *The Times's* stories recognised that pay or pensions or education or employment terms or dismissal may be comparatively and historically unfair for a whole group of people, by virtue of their being involuntary members of that group (being working-class or a grammar-school reject or badly housed was not the individuals' *choice*); relatedly, where society as a whole could afford to intervene and ameliorate a groups' disadvantages, it was only fair to do so. By 2011 *The Times's* stories had mostly shifted to a worldview in which individuals are responsible for their own fate, and if they choose to exert effort and show enterprise, then they will prosper (and if not, they will decline); certainly, the state cannot afford to intervene at every turn, nor would it be fair (on 'society', on those contributing to the economy) for it to do so. It is best – fairest – for the state simply to secure the basic conditions (efficient infrastructure, competition, a market within which citizen consumers can choose for themselves) and to allow individuals to flourish or flounder using their own talents.

The logical difficulty with the 2011 *Times* worldview is that it makes claims about acting fairly towards people who are superficially equal (in, for example, each of us having one vote in elections) but who in reality live in deeply unequal conditions with access to acutely contrasting wealth resources.

One of the few situations where the poor person is on an equal footing with the barrister or the banker is when playing the National Lottery; but the wins or losses on the lottery have no realistic political chance of becoming a model for random distribution in other matters (imagine allocating all school places, state or private, or all political offices, by localised lottery; or all university places or teaching jobs also by lottery, by discipline applied for: why not, exactly?). Besides, we can be confident that infinitesimally few barristers or bankers play the lottery, knowing the odds and, more importantly, knowing that they have far more reliable ways of adding to their wealth. Meanwhile the less well-off are the lottery's mainstay, indeed are assured that this is a form of public service, funding such good causes as the National Cycle Network, thousands of after-school clubs, or the new wing of London's Victoria and Albert Museum – a small voluntary tax, in effect. Lottery conditions are entrenched as part of British identity and British values (just as, some might note, fixed odds betting terminals are: legal and fair, despite causing catastrophe for the addicted). In the summer of 2016, around the time of the Rio Olympics at which UK athletes did so well, advertising posters appeared in countless public spaces such as bus shelters proclaiming in very large font: BY PLAYING THE NATIONAL LOTTERY YOU'RE PART OF TEAM GB. THANK YOU. *The Times* of 1971 knew all the pro-lottery arguments, but concluded that even within the extant Conservative framework it endorsed – individual responsibility and personal freedom and enterprise for personal gain – a lottery was unfair and unethical. By 2011 it had decided it was quite fair and indeed to be welcomed. It concurred with the idea that the kind of fairness that the National Lottery entails is the kind of fairness that Team GB as a whole (or the United Kingdom) should now play by.

When *The Times* changed from viewing a state lottery as 'prejudicial to society' to something like a public good, this accompanied a wider and deeper change in how it viewed wealth inequality and what it regarded as fair dealing with the different economic strata of society. In part, the broader change came because by 2011 *The Times* had accepted and articulated – as fair and normal – a smaller state than the kind of state presupposed, as common sense background, in its 1971 representations. In the smaller state, the government is supposed to enable rather than provide (that is the new *fair*). It is assumed to enable more of the people to take personal responsibility for their own employment, health care and pension provisions, and even their education (at least at tertiary level following the sharp reduction of state tuition and maintenance grants, if not at post-16 level, too). But over the past decade and more, as many of the 2011 news reports of what had become *unfair* intimate, that enabling task is not being achieved. To the young, especially those from less affluent backgrounds and worried about oppressive debts, the scarcity of quality jobs, and the exorbitant costs of housing, the government's promise to *enable*, by providing the right background conditions, must ring hollow.

3   Budgets and *Burdens*, from Barber to Osborne

3.1   Introduction

The budget speech, which until 2017 was delivered in the House of Commons in late March each year (it is now delivered in the autumn), is the UK government's key statement of its financial plans for the coming fiscal year. The speech is a high point of the political year – an attempted financial implementation of the government's political agenda – and is extensively discussed before and after its delivery. The budget is an ancient institution, emerging in the premiership of Walpole in the 1720s; one happy milestone came in William Pitt's of 1798, when income tax was introduced. The budget is delivered by the Chancellor of the Exchequer (the finance minister), the second-most powerful person in the government (after the Prime Minister). This annual statement, which invariably includes some comment on the country's past and persisting economic difficulties, powerfully reflects a government's guiding attitudes concerning private wealth and inequality, and the desirability or feasibility of redistributive actions.

The budget speeches that are the first interest of this chapter were delivered forty years apart by the Chancellor of the day, namely Anthony Barber in 1971 (on 30 March), and George Osborne in 2011 (on 23 March). Both were Conservative MPs, serving in a Conservative government in 1971 and a Conservative-dominated coalition government, respectively – both of which administrations were relatively new. In each case this was their first spring (March) budget.

The print newspapers have always paid a great deal of attention to the budget speech and its sometimes foreseen, sometimes surprise announcements of adjustments to taxes and spending. Throughout the twentieth century, *The Times* faithfully reproduced the text of the Chancellor's speech in its entirety (often a speech of 10,000 words or more, covering two pages of the next morning's newspaper). In that respect, then, *The Times* provided a platform for the government to express very much on its own terms what it saw as the 'economic contract' between citizens and the state, the private sector and the public sector. At least, the representation was governmental until readers turned their attention to the newspaper's leader article assessment and other influential commentaries from the paper's political, economic and financial journalists. The print edition of *The Times* continued to reproduce the speech in full until the first years of the present century, at which point readers were directed to the *timesonline.co.uk* website to read the speech verbatim, while the print newspaper devoted an increasing number of pages to explanation, graphic visualisations and commentary and reaction from many sources. As for the *Daily Mail*, while it never reproduced the budget speech in full, it has throughout the period of interest reported it quite fully, with extensive commentary.

Together with the specific verbal content of the speech, the numerous discursive commentaries on the budget in *The Times* and *Mail* have collectively shaped readers' conceptions of the state of the economy and what the budget proposes, and of the newspaper's own views on the economy. But the budget is a 'state of the citizen' assessment as well as a 'state of the nation' one – a commentary on whether the 'putting in' that citizens are doing (e.g., in terms of work done and taxes paid) and the 'taking out' that they are benefitting from (in pensions, health care, education, etc.) are both about right and roughly in balance.

It may be argued that the Barber and Osborne speeches were political discourse, and therefore tangential to a study that purports to be on newspaper discourse. But budget speeches are so fully embedded into the news media that they become newspaper discourse. On budget day, they are often the chief reason why readers purchase that day's paper. The fact that these speeches have been reported so fully in both papers is an extreme form of what regularly happens, in the media, to authoritative and privileged 'real world' discourse (as noted by many analysts, e.g., Bell 1991 and van Dijk 1988). Such discourses may be contextualised and critiqued by the newspaper, in adjacent articles, but they are also granted full direct discourse rights, being reproduced extensively within the newspaper itself and prominently placed on the page and in the edition.

The Barber speech in 1971 took one and three-quarter hours and is approximately 15,000 words long; Osborne's speech in 2011 took one hour and is just 8,670 words long. The former was not broadcast live in any form (Mr Healey's 1978 budget was the first to be broadcast, but in sound only), and no audio recording, let alone a video one, is widely available, even if the Hansard officers made one. Thus, at the point of its delivery in its spoken form, the 1971 speech was addressed solely to fellow MPs in the House of Commons. Summaries of the speech's main provisions would have been broadcast by the press agencies and on radio and TV later the same day. In terms of extensive and inspectable availability, only the printed version (and especially the one printed in the next day's *Times*) was addressed to the wider public. We cannot 'revisit' the Barber speech audiovisually by clicking on a URL, as we can now so easily do for the budget speeches of the last few years. In 2011 Osborne's speech was broadcast live on various television and internet channels as well as on radio, so even at the point of original delivery in the House, with periodic interruptions of cheering, laughter or protest, Mr Osborne was in a sense speaking directly to the nation (the world, even). This co-temporally variegated audience (including friendly MPs and hostile ones, the press, voters, the financial industries and markets and other countries, including EU partners) will have influenced his wordings and his delivery. Despite these textual and contextual differences, a deep comparability remains. It is hard to think of major texts that address matters of wealth and fairness in either a British newspaper of 1971 or its descendant forty or more years later, which would be more comparable than the national budget speech transcripts and their journalistic reception.

3.2   Style and Genre Differences between Barber 1971 and Osborne 2011

In this section I begin by briefly reviewing some of the differences of style and tenor between the Barber and Osborne speeches and then suggest ways in which these might be relevant to changing assumptions about inequality. That the speeches are stylistically different is intuitively apparent simply by juxtaposing a typical passage from each. Here, for example, are a couple of paragraphs from the middle of Barber's text:

The Finance Bill will contain provisions to implement two particular undertakings in the Government's election manifesto. The first relates to the case where both husband and wife are earning. It is, as we said, a nonsense, and a substantial disincentive, that above a certain level of earnings a married couple can pay more tax than two single people with the same earnings.

I propose therefore that husband and wife should be able to elect to have their earnings charged to tax as if they belonged to separate individuals, but on condition that the husband receives the single personal allowance instead of the married allowance. For administrative reasons this new provision cannot come into effect until the tax year 1972–73. The full year cost is estimated to be about £12 million.

And here is a typical paragraph from the middle of the Osborne speech forty years later:

But if Britain is really to become a home of innovation then we want research and development to take place not just in our great universities, but in our smaller businesses too. One of our greatest high tech innovators, James Dyson, has urged me to increase the support they get. I have listened to him, and gone even further than he recommends. From April this year the small companies Research and Development Tax Credit will rise to 200% – and from next year it will rise again to 225%. We also want to encourage manufacturers to invest in the latest machinery and technology. So I propose to double the limit on the capital allowances for short life assets from four years to eight years.

The Barber speech is far more formal than the one by Osborne, and this is reflected in the wider range of lexis in the Barber speech (2,410 types versus only 1,973 types in the admittedly shorter Osborne speech), with greater use of impersonal constructions. Even Barber's use of the formal phrase *husband and wife* without a preceding indefinite article has an impersonality that Osborne and other recent Chancellors would not adopt. Also notable is the complexity of Barber's construction when he goes on to say that couples *should be able to elect to have their earnings charged to tax as if they belonged to separate individuals*; today we might just say *partners can be taxed independently of each other* (the *as if... separate* wording may reflect the tendency in those years to regard those making up a 'married couple' as having a more attenuated individuality than we would today). Another small index of formality is the *I turn now to* construction, a long-established device for signalling a topic shift in a speech or lecture; this is used fifteen times in Barber's three budgets (1971–73), but only six times in Osborne's seven budgets (2010–16).

Evidently aiming for a style that would be more accessible to the ordinary voter, Osborne comes close to narrating how the inventor and entrepreneur James Dyson urged something upon him and of how he, Osborne, listened and responded. There are more names and more numbers in this speech. Osborne's sentences begin with cohesive conjunctions (*But, So*) far more frequently and interactively than Barber's. There are thirty-one sentence-initial *But*s and only two instances of sentence-initial *So* in the Barber speech, totalling 0.24% of the text; in the much shorter Osborne text, there are twenty-four sentence-initial *But*s and twenty-four instances of sentence-initial *So*, amounting to 0.58% of his text. His far more conversational style is also apparent in the extract in his use of *really* (redundant, strictly speaking, but rhetorically implying a contrast between imagining something desirable and actually effecting it); in the booster terms *great* (universities) and *greatest* (innovators) and in the volitive modality of *we want* (used twice), of what Dyson *urged* and of Osborne having *gone even further*. There is personalization too, beyond that of the plural first person *we/us/our* (discussed later in this chapter) in the orientation to Osborne himself, as an *I/me*. Accordingly it is not a matter of Dyson asking the government for greater support for research and development and 'we' (or 'the Government') responding; rather *Dyson has urged me ... and I have listened ... and gone even further... So I propose.*

3.3   Lexical Contrasts

In the remainder of this chapter and several subsequent ones, the online corpus processing tool called Wmatrix (see, e.g., Rayson 2009) is used in the identification of various lexical patterns and the calculation of their significance. Wmatrix is a sophisticated suite of programs that enables the user rapidly to obtain frequency and alphabetised lists of all the words in a given text, and a concordance showing the immediate co-text surrounding each use of each of those words. It can also report, for example, all the four-word sequences that occur more than five times in a text – a particular kind of prominence. For any word of interest, it can identify those words with which it markedly often co-occurs; that is, its collocates (other computational tools that offer similar manipulations of texts include WordSmith Tools and Antconc). And because the tool is linked to the USAS and CLAWS annotation tools, all words in a text can be assigned to a part of speech category and a semantic category, respectively. Drawing on these as background resources, comparisons can be made of the frequency, in a given text or corpus, of specific words, parts of speech or semantic domains with their frequency in a large reference corpus. As a result a text's keywords, key parts of speech and key semantic domains, statistically speaking, can be identified. Selecting a suitable reference corpus often requires judgement as to suitability, but for many of the calculations in the present chapter, the sample of general Written British English which is preloaded in Wmatrix was judged sufficient. That sample is part of the British National Corpus, a 100-million-word corpus, mostly of written English, collected from a range of sources and designed to represent the diversity of British English from the late twentieth century, both spoken and written in the 1990s (see www .natcorp.ox.ac.uk).

Consider this invented example: a specific *Times* editorial, 300 words in length, uses the word *deserving* six times (a 2% frequency), while a corpus of all *Times* editorials in that year, 130,000 words, uses *deserving* sixty-five times only (a 0.05% frequency); the frequency in the single text is so disproportionately high that *deserving* will be one of the keywords of that text, and a useful indicator of what the text is chiefly about. Statistical comparative calculation, known as log-likelihood, similarly enables the analyst to identify significant differences – here, a text's disproportionately frequent or infrequent parts of speech or semantic domains (known as positively or negatively key, respectively). It is not appropriate or necessary to explain log-likelihood (but see, e.g., Baker 2006); the crucial point is that such statistical procedures can underpin claimed significant difference between two frequencies, relative to all the other differences of frequency of words, parts of speech or semantic domains between a targeted text and a reference corpus.

Table 3.1 *Top Keywords in the Barber and Osborne Budgets of 1971 and 2011*

Barber	Osborne
tax	Tax
will	We
taxation	Will
propose	Our
rate	Budget
income	Today
earned	that's
year	Enterprise
investment	Duty
surtax	Businesses
S.E.T.	
income	
this	

I now return to the two budget speeches: the simplest initial corpus linguistic calculation for the two texts is to identify in each of them those words which are markedly more frequently used than in a sample of reasonably comparable text, with a statistical calculation, measured in terms of log-likelihood (sometimes abbreviated as LL), to confirm the significance of a strikingly high (or low) frequency. In using the BNC written sample as reference corpus for both budget speeches, what emerge as the most key keywords in the two speeches are listed in Table 3.1. All of them except *businesses,* in the Osborne speech, have a LL above 100.

The precise order and LL scores for these words is less important than their unambiguous keyness, which is confirmed even if a rather different reference corpus is used. But the keyness of many of these items is neither surprising nor, since they occur in both speeches, a pointer to an interesting contrast. Of all the differences between the listed top keywords (lexical or grammatical) in the Barber and the Osborne, the most striking is the presence of *we* and *our* in the Osborne list, and their absence from the Barber list; this is explored further in Section 3.4. At variance with this section's title, *we* is not a lexical item but a grammatical one, and grammatical items do not normally emerge as disproportionately frequent in comparison to an appropriate reference corpus, so they are all the more interesting when they do.

Far more than half a dozen lexical items, however, have a high keyness score in the Barber or the Osborne texts or both, so a consideration of not just the top ten but the top fifty items is advisable, thereby considering all of the items in descending order of keyness down to a LL rating of 50 or so (still quite significant, by corpus linguistic standards). When this is undertaken, two words from among the top fifty keywords in the Osborne speech stand out by virtue of their not being an obvious reflection of the speech's predictable content: *fair* (13 occurrences, 0.16% textual frequency and a keyness LL of 48) and *help* (25 instances, 0.3% of text and keyness LL of 54). All the other top lexical keywords are more directly a reflex of subject matter: *tax, Budget, duty, today, that's, forecast, taxes, growth, rate, rise, price* and so on. Accordingly, in Section 3.5 I examine why *fair* and *help*, neither of which is remotely key in the Barber speech, are so prominently used in the Osborne budget of 2011. Here are two items that stand out even in relation to the other keywords for being both unpredictably present (given the genre and subject matter) but also 'common core', everyday vocabulary, with nothing of the esoteric about them. Their very high frequency suggests they may be prominent in Osborne's intended underlying narrative.

When a similar search is made in the Barber speech, to identify any non-technical but general and evaluative lexical items among the fifty most keywords with a LL above 50, the list contains almost nothing unexpected: *tax, will, taxation, propose, rate, year, income* and so on. With one borderline exception, there are no top keywords in the Barber that are not intrinsically related to finance and the national economy, thus confirming the impression that the Barber text is more sober, less rhetorical, less aimed at projecting an interpersonal persuasive intent upon the addressee, than the Osborne. The solitary exception is the word *burden*: this is the first residually 'expressive' lexical keyword I can find in the Barber text, ranked a lowly forty-ninth among the top fifty. The presence of *burden* prompted a broader study of the frequency and specific discursive contexts of *burden* across the forty-five years of budget speeches from 1971 to 2016. Discussion of *burden* is accordingly presented in Section 3.7, somewhat separately from the specific Barber versus Osborne comparison.

3.4   *We* in Osborne

With 163 occurrences comprising 1.86% of the text, *we* is almost three times as frequent in the Osborne as in the much longer Barber (97 instances, 0.67% of the text). A dispersion plot shows that *we* is most heavily used in the opening ten minutes or 600 words of Osborne's speech (21 uses), with further prominence at the close. Therefore I will focus on the opening and closing passages of both Chancellors' speeches, reproducing them, with all instances of *we* bolded. It will transpire that these extracts are also the most relevant to Section 3.8's analysis of metaphor in these budgets; accordingly the chief metaphorical phrasings are underlined. Here are Osborne's first eleven instances of *we*:

Mr Deputy Speaker, Last year's emergency Budget was about rescuing the nation's finances, and paying for the mistakes of the past. Today's Budget is about reforming the nation's economy, so that **we** have enduring growth and jobs in the future. And it's about doing what **we** can to help families with the cost of living and the high oil price. **We** understand how difficult it is for so many people across our country right now. That **we** are able now to set off on the route from rescue to reform, and reform to recovery, is because of difficult decisions **we**'ve already taken. Those decisions have brought economic stability. And without stability there can be no sustainable growth or jobs. Without stability governments have to keep coming back to their citizens for more – more taxes and more spending cuts. In Britain, **we** do not have to do that today. **We** inherited a record Budget deficit. But **we** have set out a credible, comprehensive plan to deal with it. **We** have had to undertake difficult measures. But **we** have already asked the British people for what is needed, and today **we** do not need to ask for more.

Another flurry of especially frequent use of *we* comes at the end of Osborne's speech:

I know that by itself this [fuel price freeze] will not end the pressure on family Budgets. But **we've** done what **we** can to help. Help for families. Help for businesses. A Government that listens and helps. Mr Deputy Speaker, There were some who said that this year my job was to help families with the cost of living. There were others who said 'no', my task was to back enterprise, support business and undertake far-reaching reform to help the economy grow. It is the central understanding of this Government – and core to our strategy – that these are not two separate tasks. They are one and the same thing. **We** are only going to raise the living standards of families if **we** have an economy that can compete in the modern age. So this is our plan for growth. **We** want the words:
> 'Made in Britain'
> 'Created in Britain'
> 'Designed in Britain'
> 'Invented in Britain'

To drive our nation forward. A Britain carried aloft by the march of the makers. That is how **we** will create jobs and support families. **We** have put fuel into the tank of the British economy. And I commend this Budget to the House.

Here by contrast is an extract from the opening of the Barber speech forty years earlier, showing how much rarer is his use of *we* (in the first 1,100 words, as noted earlier, one-third as frequent). All of these are interpretable as inclusive *we*, where Barber intends to speak for all of us.

Over these years **we** have become accustomed to unfavourable comparisons with other industrial countries – slow growth, recurring balance of payments weakness, faster-than-average inflation, a low rate of investment, a falling share in world exports, and increasingly bad industrial relations. These are problems not for government alone but for the whole nation. What is needed is a new realism and a new determination: a new awareness of where the ruts **we** have been following will lead us and a new national effort to change the direction.

If **we** are realistic **we** should recognise that, unless there is a change in the trend – a change not only compared with the last five or six years, but with the trend over the last two decades and more – the prospect is that by 1980 our standard of living in this country will have fallen considerably behind that of most of the countries of Western Europe. Before too long, I hope that **we** shall know the outcome of our application to join the E.E.C. I have never doubted that, given fair terms, this historic venture would bring us great economic benefits in the longer term. But, whether **we** go in or whether **we** stay out, it remains essential to improve Britain's economic performance.

And here are the five instances occurring at the end of Barber's speech (with some intervening paragraphs ellipted):

In this year's Finance Bill, **we** shall legislate to replace the existing income tax and surtax with a new and simpler system of personal taxation. The Bill will provide also for the reduction of corporation tax.

During the coming months, **we** shall be consulting representatives of industry, commerce and the professions about the reform of corporation tax and about the value-added tax.

Next Session, **we** shall legislate for the introduction of the value-added tax.

In April, 1972, **we** expect to be ready to announce our decisions for the reform of corporation tax, and to implement them in next year's Finance Bill . . .

It is right that I should end with this warning. All our hopes for the future will be but dust in our mouths if **we** do not repel the assault upon the value of our money. This must remain our first priority.

By contrast with those in his opening paragraphs, Barber's few instances of *we* here at the close are mostly exclusive, reporting what the government intends to do. But the final example, part of a striking metaphor-deploying construction which also refers to *our mouths* and *our money* is unambiguously inclusive (everybody's mouth, everybody's money, are what he has in mind). Among other things this has the useful effect of encouraging all MPs and indeed all citizens to understand the 'first priority' in the next sentence as belonging to them (or us) all.

The examples of *we* reproduced from the Osborne speech are representative of how the word is used throughout his speech: after an initial inclusive use (*so that we have enduring growth*), it is used overwhelmingly exclusively, to denote 'we, the Government', understood as distinct from the British people. While *we* in the Barber speech is also mostly exclusive in reference, there is a large and significant minority of inclusive uses, where Barber is speaking about 'we in Britain', as noted in the opening passage quoted earlier, for example.

This Osborne versus Barber contrast with regard to *we* should not be under-estimated. Whenever *we* occurs in standard English, it is inevitably the clause

Subject; and the Subject is more likely to carry the agentive role than any other grammatical element (such as Object or Complement). So a government-originated text that makes extensive use of exclusive *we* is likely to be one in which the speaker is repeatedly asserting what they (and their colleagues) have done and are doing, as active parties (here, responsible authorities), while the larger 'we' (i.e., the British people) is implicitly consigned to a more passive and reactive role. Politicians periodically declare that they are the servants of the people, but a speech from one of them that makes heavy use of 'exclusive' *we* may be telling us a different story, of the empowered politician and the populace cast as distanced participants. A couple of ambiguities in the opening passage of the Osborne speech further hint at this asymmetry. The fourth sentence mentions the current difficulties facing *so many people across our country*: in light of the reference here to *many people*, it is hard to see how the *our* can be interpreted as anything other than exclusive of those people, as if the country belonged to Osborne and the government (or, at most, to him and his parliamentary audience). And in the eighth sentence, a generic one about what all governments must do when there is no economic stability, there is the awkward usage of *their citizens* (rather than, e.g., *the people* or *the citizenry*), when governments do not 'have' citizens, only countries do.

It is true that inclusive *we* can be patronising, or a hard-to-resist co-opting or fake inclusivity. But the distancing function of exclusive *we* is inherent rather than just a possibility; the implication is that the addressees are distinct from the addresser experientially and agentially. The spokesperson for the 'we' affirms that their experience and powers are different in kind from those of the addressed 'you', who are not part of the 'us'. And that implicit separateness is prominent in the Osborne speech (with its high frequency of exclusive *we*) but not in the Barber.

It is possible that dominance of exclusive *we* and diminishing use of inclusive *we* has spread far wider than Osborne's budget speeches; it may be a broad trend that has taken hold in government discourse over the past twenty years or so. For example, Mulderrig's CDA study of the language of education policy documents (white papers, etc.) in the period when New Labour was in power finds that unambiguously inclusive *we* amounted to just 3% of instances (83% were judged to be exclusive, and another 13% were ambiguous as to inclusive or exclusive reference). But Mulderrig is looking at the very different genre of written policy document. What of other budget speeches in the modern period: do these have a sizeable minority of inclusive *we* uses, like Barber, or plenty of exclusive *we* and very little inclusive *we*, like Osborne of forty years later?

When the texts of all seven of Osborne's budget speeches are combined (from June 2010 to March 2016), *we* emerges as the topmost keyword (referenced against BE 2006, a sample of British English from 2006, preloaded in Wmatrix), with a text frequency of 2.24%. Thus on average every fortieth word in Osborne's budgets is *we*. That contrasts with the comparatively low frequency of *we* in the three Barber budgets of 1971–73 combined: a text frequency of 0.58%. It also contrasts with the 0.76% text frequency across all five of Geoffrey Howe's Conservative budgets from 1979 to 1983, and even the 1.10% frequency for *we* in Gordon Brown's eleven Labour budgets (1997 to 2007). Thus while there seems to be a gradual rise in use of *we* in budget speeches as we move from 1971 towards the present day, still Osborne is far and away the most frequent *we* user of modern Chancellors (more than twice Brown's frequency of use).

But can we be confident that the Osborne uses of *we* are as rarely inclusive as in 2011, across all six of his recent budgets, and that Barber's larger minority of inclusive *we* uses is maintained in all three of his 1970s budgets? Ideally that requires close examination of collocational and contextual patterns, case by case. Without going to that immense trouble, however, I propose using, as an indirect indicator of prominent exclusive *we*, a budget speech's high frequency of use of *we have* or *we will*, which can be identified and counted automatically. Treating high frequency of those particular strings as symptomatic assumes the following: *we have* will mostly be used in budgets followed by a past participle verb in a construction reporting what *we* (exclusive of the people) have already achieved; similarly *we will* followed by an infinitive verb will often report actions we (the government, Cabinet or Treasury, exclusively) intend to undertake, and the frequency of such exclusive *we have* or *we will* will be higher in a text which has a smaller proportion of inclusive *we*.

In the Osborne 2011 budget, there are 19 occurrences of *we have* and 52 of *we will*; in all seven Osborne budgets combined, *we have* occurs 152 times, *we will* 308 times, thus amounting to 460 instances (920 words) of a 59,540 word text, or 0.015%. In the Barber 1971 budget the *we have* frequency is 21, that of *we will* is just 1 (which amounts to just 0.003% of the text, one-fifth of the Osborne 2011 frequency). For comparison, in the five Howe budgets of 1979–83 *we have* occurs 105 times, *we will* a mere 7 times – a total of 112 instances, or 224 words of a 68,400 word text, or 0.003%, thus exactly the frequency found in the Barber 1971 speech.

By comparison with these earlier Tory Chancellors, then, there is much more *we will* than *we have* in Osborne, and the *we* involved has a strong tendency to be exclusive. All modern Chancellors' budget speeches have protested a concern for national unity and have striven to project a collective national agenda to which everyone despite their different interests can subscribe. It was Osborne, in that vein, who repeatedly proclaimed *We are all in this together* (first in his June 2010 emergency budget). His exceptional and frequent recourse to exclusive *we* not only in the 2011 budget but in all his budgets paints a different picture, of we the duly-empowered government and you the people, whose compliance is (given the election result) assumed. This division, like all divisions, lends itself to a hierarchy or inequality of status, of managers and managed; and this inequality by division projects a worldview in which hierarchy and inequality are acceptable in many other respects too.

3.5   *Fair* and *Help* in Osborne More Than Barber

Why do *fair* and *help* have a prominence in Osborne's 2011 speech that is absent from their use in Barber 1971? The prominence is not just relative to Barber 1971; it is in comparison to all modern budgets. Table 3.2 presents the comparative frequencies of these words in the Barber 1971 and Osborne 2011 budgets, in two small corpora of all their budgets (the 45,000 words of Barber's three budgets and the 56,000 words of Osborne's seven), in a corpus of all forty-six modern budgets and in Wmatrix's BNC written sample. For comparison, frequencies of a third evaluative word with a slightly elevated keyness rating in Osborne 2011 are given: *new*. While both Barber and Osborne have slightly elevated frequencies of *new* relative to all modern budgets, that frequency in turn is considerably higher than in the BNC sample, so *new* is confirmed as non-contrastive here and simply characteristic of budget language. But Osborne's high frequency for *fair* in all his budgets and especially in 2011 is confirmed, as is his high frequency of *help*, again in 2011 especially, while Barber's *help* frequency is consistently low against all modern budgets, but not as low as the BNC sample frequency. In short, Osborne's *fair* and *help*, in all his budgets, stand out.

Let us begin with *fair*, in the process considering whether there are any connections to the discussion, in Chapter 2, of inequality-related stories using *fair* and *unfair* together in *The Times* in 1971 and 2011. There are just three instances of *fair* and one of *unfair* in the Barber speech:

Table 3.2 *Relative Frequencies for* Fair, Help *and* New *in Various Budget Texts and BNC Written Sample*

	Barber 1971	All Barber, 1971–73	Osborne 2011	All Osborne, 2010–16	All Modern Budgets	BNC Written Sample
fair	0.02%	0.02%	0.16% (13 items)	0.06% (36 items)	0.02%	0.01%
help	0.08%	0.08%	0.30% (25 items)	0.25% (147 items)	0.18%	0.04%
new	0.39%	0.35%	0.44%	0.44%	0.33%	0.13%

1. I have never doubted that, given **fair** terms, this historic venture [joining the EEC]
2. Britain has many good points. It is **fair** as between one taxpayer and another
3. eas income which I believe would be **fair** and reasonable. This is not, however
4. S.E.T. to be a thoroughly bad tax. It is un**fair** and it is arbitrary. It discrimina

In Osborne's markedly shorter text, however, there are thirteen instances of *fair*, and none of *unfair*:

1. with. And our tax system should be **fair**, reward work, support aspiration a
2. g in. Of course, taxation must be **fair**. Its right that the wealthiest shou
3. the wealthiest are not paying their **fair** share. So as well as reviewing reve
4. property can not avoid paying their **fair** share. Help for small businesses.
5. of many many families. This is not **fair**. So I can announce that – from the
6. ructure. To ensure customers get a **fair** deal, we will closely follow develo
7. ur public service pensions are both **fair** to those who give their working live
8. working lives to help others, and **fair** to the taxpayers who have to fund th
9. iety who seek to avoid paying their **fair** share of taxes. Tax avoidance and e
10. working families. And that is not **fair**. Unfortunately, not enough has bee
11. on families, we think it would be **fair** to delay this Aprils Air Passenger D
12. something else. We can introduce a **Fair** Fuel Stabiliser. From tomorrow
13. l price falls and stays low. Its a **Fair** Fuel Stabiliser. And the result is

What distinguishes Osborne's fairness from Barber's? First, the paucity of mentions of *fair* in Barber means that what is *fair,* or fairness, is far less thematised: it is not a focus of discussion. This could be because fairness simply was not of concern in 1971, but this seems unlikely. Of just three mentions, one relates to entry into the EEC, another treats *fair* as paraphrased by *reasonable,* and the third comes in a sentence (#2) which rather implies a general agreement that matters are already 'fair', and goes on to make a claim that I doubt any recent Chancellor would concur with in today's climate of tax evasion and avoidance: '[Our system of taxation in Britain] is fair as between one taxpayer and another; it is held in good repute and as a result is relatively little abused.' By contrast what is *fair* is a theme repeatedly returned to by Osborne, and it is possible that he does so partly because there is not, as there was in Barber's time, any general confidence that the fiscal system (or individuals' and companies' compliance with it) is already fair: *the tax system should be fair . . . must be fair,* Osborne insists, also mentioning those *not paying their fair share*. It is noticeable that in the Osborne instances just shown, to the left of the node *fair* there is nearly always explicit or implicit negation (*not, avoid*) or a modal comparator (*should, must,* etc.) or other means (*to ensure . . . a fair deal . . .*) that amount to tacit admissions that the present system is not already fair. Several instances of *fair* occur in sentences about the wealthy *paying their fair share* of taxes, again a tacit admission that there is no present certainty that they are (see items 3, 4 and 9). Two things are declared *not fair* in the Osborne lines: one is the way high costs are putting home ownership beyond the reach of many families; the other is the way tax avoidance adds to the tax burden on working families.

Here now are the KWIC lines for the twenty-five uses of *help* in Osborne's 2011 budget, his other most key nonfinancial word:

1. and its about doing what we can to **help** families with the cost of living and
2. people – and this is one way we can **help**. It is still too early to say what
3. s most successful firms, that will **help** people start and grow businesses. T
4. sinesses. Today we can add to that **help**. From 6th April this year I am doub
5. not avoid paying their fair share. **Help** for small businesses. A boost for e
6. ut specific measures we can take to **help** a wide range of businesses. In life
7. 2012. We will also take action to **help** the construction industry. Stamp Du
8. fford the high deposits. This will **help** 10,000 families get on to the housin
9. he sector in the last 3 months. To **help** this continue, the Government annou
10. al and create new export credits to **help** smaller businesses; Launch Britains
11. we can find another 100 million to **help** councils repair the winter potholes
12. sury will publish a paper on how we **help** their private sector to grow. To de
13. l come forward with public money to **help** bring their bills down. Mr Deputy
14. to 80% from April 2013. This will **help** our most energy intensive industries
15. s is another major reform that will **help** Britain live within her means. We a
16. ose who give their working lives to **help** others, and fair to the taxpayers w
17. the right thing by you. It's a big **help** for the Big Society. But our charit
18. , in a fiscally neutral Budget, to **help** those families who do pay their taxe
19. ng. We have already taken steps to **help** from this April. I am glad to repor
20. ze rates for Heavy Good Vehicles to **help** our hauliers. I am also propos- ing t
21. gets. But we've done what we can to **help**. Help for families. Help for busin
22. But we've done what we can to help. **Help** for families. Help for businesses
23. e can to help. Help for families. **Help** for businesses. A Government that l
24. o said that this year my job was to **help** families with the cost of living. T
25. nd undertake far-reaching reform to **help** the economy grow. It is the central

Help is far more common here as a verb than as a noun. The dominant pattern is shown in Figure 3.1.

But surprisingly rarely is there a *to* + Infinitive clause directly following the naming of the group who have been helped. It is simply asserted that such and such a policy helps businesses, or families, as if *help* were

| we (the Government) our provisions | have helped are helping will help | people families businesses the economy our most energy intensive industries |

Figure 3.1 The dominant pattern of *help* in Osborne's 2011 budget

a simple, transitive, two-argument verb that required just a Subject and an Object or, in semantic terms, an Agent that *helps* an Affected (the Patient or Theme in some grammars). But it isn't.

The first definition and explanation of *help* as a verb in the *Collins Cobuild English Dictionary for Advanced Learners* (2001, 3rd edn.) reads as follows: 'If you help someone, you make it easier **for them to do something**, for example by doing part of the work for them or by giving them advice or money' (bold added).

The underlying grammar of the verb *help* reflects the Cobuild explanation. With regard to the process of helping, there is always the implication that someone is trying to do something, and another person or thing assists that person. In simplified format the structure in Active voice sentences is

NP_1 *help* NP_2 S (where S is a non-finite clause like *to decorate the table, decorate the table, decorating the table*)

With verbs such as *advise, coax, urge, persuade, enable* – and *help* – there is always implicitly an intermediate entity (usually a person or group) quite distinct from the party identified as doing the helping (or advising, coaxing, etc). And the 'intermediate' entity in principle could perform the process specified in the non-finite clause, without the helper. One discursive complication is that in the case of *help,* Active voice, there can be optional omission of either the NP_2 or the S, with the addresser relying on context to help the addressee 'recover' this ellipted information.

But perhaps deletion of the clausal complement after *help* + Object NP is a common pattern, and overt realization of the complement clause (the S) is rare, so that Osborne's way of using *help* is unexceptional. To get some sense of which patterns were most common, a search was made for instances of the sequence *help them* in the written, non-ephemeral subcorpora of the Bank of English (622 million words), yielding 7,070 instances, of which a random sample of 100 KWIC lines were examined. Just over half these lines (55) were of the explicit '*help them* + (*to*) + Infinitive' type (the *to* may be ellipted); thus in that Bank of English sample, presence of the following S complement, which makes explicit just what 'second Agent' goal the helping contributes to, is mostly explicitly stated. Here are a few indicative instances (interestingly, none is a V + -*ing* non-finite S):

1. Information that would **help them find the girl** who had shot both his parents.
2. d casting fertility spells to **help them conceive their dream baby**.
3. How that would **help them avoid machine-gun bullets**
4. s which will **help them gain confidence in themselves**.

In the nearly half-million words of the forty-six budget speeches from 1971 to 2016, *help them* occurs twenty-eight times (thus five times as frequently as in the Bank of English), and sixteen of these are of the *help them* (*to*) S construction – thus, similarly, a majority of cases. This confirms that the Osborne speech is noticeably different in its 'we can/will help families/businesses' constructions which omit mention of what it is the group being helped wishes to do.

The tendency in Osborne 2011 to declare that the government has helped, is helping or will help some group without specifying what the group needs help with, appears to parallel a trend noticed by Jeffries and Evans (2013) in the use of *choice* in the recent election manifestos of the political parties. In earlier manifestos, the named choice tended to be explicated in the noun phrase within which *choice* occurred: *a choice between Europe and the Commonwealth, a school of parents' own choice,* etc. In later years, particularly the 'peak' years of use, *choice* often occurred as an unmodified noun phrase (the way *freedom, democracy* were used) and 'the reader is given comparatively little indication as to what options the choice in question might present' (18). A final observation worth noting about *help* concerns its semantics: when you help someone with a problem, there is some hope but no guarantee that the problem will be solved. It is therefore semantically weaker than the more formal *enable* (only 82 uses in the all-budgets corpus), *provide* (262 instances) or *ensure* (286 occurrences), although much more frequent (813 uses).

What does *help* do in the Osborne budget speeches? It is widely agreed that a Conservative neoliberal market view of government is that it should 'free' people to thrive and earn rewards individually, while confining state aid and intervention to those clearly unable to help themselves. By contrast a Labour social democratic approach often aims to provide or enable, rather than merely 'help', perhaps on the basis of their perception that in an unequal society a large sector of the less advantaged are unable (or even prevented) from succeeding without some initial assistance. It is possible that these differences are reflected in how *help* is used by Osborne.

I have shown how Osborne tends to omit the clausal complement that could clarify the nature of the process that some agentive party is being helped with; and he does so even where there is insufficient co-textual disambiguation elsewhere. Just the NP_2 or direct Object Agent is named: *we have helped working families, we will help small businesses*, etc. This proclaims that the government is doing something to some affected party, but downplays that affected party's own agency – they appear more a beneficiary than an agent. The helping asserted by other, earlier chancellors more often specifies the process for which help is being extended, thereby drawing more attention to the shared goal that the two agents are in partnership to achieve. Here, for example are some random examples of the contexts of use of *help* in the first and last of Gordon Brown's budgets:

1. My changes in monetary policy were designed to **help** companies make long-term investment decisions with confidence.
2. Lone parents will be … offered **help** in finding work that suits their circumstances.
3. [T]he best way to **help** the income of families with children is to raise child benefits.
4. … more **help** for parents to do the best by their children.

A purposive progression is enacted, with the state helping a named group to reach their goal, in which the state also has an interest. By contrast in Osborne's pattern with the complement process absent, the implication is that some participant is the beneficiary (families, businesses, etc.), and they will then be agentive in some activity for which the state is not responsible.

In the Barber 1971 budget, not only are there fewer *help* instances, they are also more scattered, with a vaguely defined scope, such as *some of those who are worst hit by [inflation]* rather than an identified group of beneficiaries; more impersonally, he says that reducing Selective Employment Tax by half *will help in the fight against inflation* and another measure *[will] help with the financing of working capital and investment*. The final *help* is in Barber's closing sentence, one that is far from the ringing peroration attempted in the Osborne but indicative of the restrained 'parliamentary' spirit that Barber evidently sought to observe:

This Budget alone will not solve all our economic problems; but it does herald a new approach, an approach based on the belief that lower taxation and simpler taxation will, over the years ahead, **help** to create a new spirit – a new spirit of personal endeavour and achievement which alone can provide our nation with growing prosperity.

Stripped of the embeddings and hedgings which make it so unlike Osborne in style, Barber's claim at its core is that the right taxation will help to create personal endeavour, and this alone can provide prosperity. His Conservative credentials, prioritizing individual effort and reward, are clear. The verb *provide* is used, but Barber is unambiguous in his conviction that only personal enterprise, and not the state, has the potential to provide prosperity. In short, the kind of helping Osborne promises is masterfully vague and general, protesting it will do more than it can be measured delivering; the Barber makes almost no such promises to help.

Drawing the foregoing threads of evidence together, we can conclude that the fairness leitmotif is frequently used to bolster Osborne's self-description as doing all he and the government can, within inherited constraints, to *help* and to be *fair* to families, taxpayers and businesses, quite often by doing *new* things. If businesses and families are helped, then logically they will be better off than they otherwise would have been. But the goals or purposes of the helping are not specified, as if to say those are for the families and businesses to decide upon, freely.

3.6   Taxation

Earlier, *tax* and *taxation* were noted as among the top keywords in the Barber budget in 1971, while *tax* was among the counterpart top keywords in the 2011 Osborne budget. At first glance the absence of *taxation,* alongside *tax,* from among the Osborne keywords seemed inconsequential – a minor usage shift. But an interesting trend emerges, when the frequency of *taxation* is calculated alongside that of *tax* in the corpus of all modern budgets: Barber and Osborne both talk about *tax* with a frequency only slightly above the all-modern-budgets mean of 0.64%. But the frequencies with regard to *taxation* diverge markedly, with forty-four mentions of the word in Barber 1971 (0.33% of the speech), but only seven in Osborne 2011 (0.09%), compared with a frequency in all modern budgets (nearly half a million words of text, and 505 instances) of 0.11%. The contrast is even clearer in the frequency across all three Barber budgets and across all seven from Osborne: 0.27% and 0.04%, respectively. Thus Barber mentions *taxation* disproportionately often, while Osborne, most particularly, mentions *taxation* extremely infrequently; could it be that talk about taxation is avoided, by the time we get to the Osborne years? And what meaningful difference is there between talking about *tax* and talking about *taxation*?

Examining Barber's 1971 speech in context, it is clear that he talks about *taxation* as a process affecting the many and perhaps inescapably so. In an early section of the speech, about 200 words in length, he uses *taxation* eight times – doing so in the course of promising a comprehensive reform of the system, which he three times describes as a *burden*. In 2011, Osborne mostly prefers to talk about the product, *tax* (like chancellors generally: the mean frequency suggests *tax* appears on average once every 150 words), with minimal mention of the process, *taxation*. A clue may lie in remarks in Osborne's 2015 budget, where he promises that the annual self-assessment tax return will be replaced by an online account, 'a revolutionary simplification of tax collection' because 'we believe that people should be working for themselves, and not for the tax man. **Tax really does not have to be taxing**' (bold added).

The collocates of the many instances of *taxation* in the Barber 1971 speech include *system, direct, indirect* and *personal*, all immediately to its left; in Osborne 2011's scant seven instances, we cannot speak of trends at all, but the contexts of Osborne's use of *taxation* are that taxation must be fair, that the United Kingdom needs a much simpler and shorter tax code (and this will better resemble *good taxation*), that air passenger duty should widen to include those who enjoy private jets and that it should apply to very high value property and 'non-domiciled' residents (three of his seven uses). Thus 'taxation' is here something to be spoken of very sparingly, and mostly as something concerning the very rich; it is not associated in Osborne's speeches with the state's relations with ordinary citizens. In a sense this might be regarded as something to be expected, in a party committed to having the coercions of taxation and the state institutions that depend on it occupy a much smaller place in life in Britain than in a Scandinavian-style social-democratic state. On the other hand, the Barber speeches with their comparatively frequent allusions to taxation show that the discourse – and perhaps the thinking behind that discourse – were not always thus. Even Conservative chancellors committed in principle to a smaller state did not always, in the past, eschew mentions of taxation and redirect addressees' attention elsewhere.

3.7   The Disappearing Burden of Taxation . . .

It was noted earlier that, reflecting the sober restraint of Barber's 1971 speech, it is difficult to identify among the top fifty lexical keywords of Barber's 1971 speech any that are unrelated to the genre and topic – any that are instead of a 'general evaluative' nature (to set alongside the positive evaluative top keywords, *help* and *fair*, in the Osborne 2011 speech). The one partial exception in the Barber – if this item is judged to carry some evaluative charge – was *burden*. Even *burden*, however, occurs only eleven times in the Barber speech, with a keyness LL of 57 (relative to the BNC 2006 corpus) or 41 (against the BNC Written sample as reference corpus). This frequency seemed prominent enough to warrant a closer look at how *burden* is used in the 1971, 2011 and other budget speeches. In Barber 1971, *burden* is mostly used in phrases such as *the burden of taxation, the burden of estate duty* and *the tax burden on distributed profits*. By contrast there are only two occurrences of *burden* in the Osborne 2011 speech, and one of these concerns a burden on HMRC rather than on the taxpayer, the other being about the price of petrol as *a huge burden* on families; thus neither of these is actually a *tax* burden. How frequent and how key is *burden* in other budget speeches of the forty-five-year period? Figure 3.2 is a block chart listing, by Chancellor and year, the number of uses of the word *burden* in each budget since 1971. A broad trend of decline is clear: *burden* is used on average between twelve and thirteen times per budget speech in the

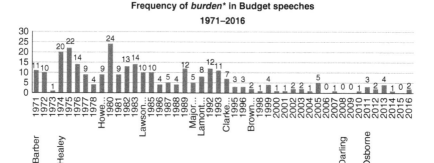

Figure 3.2 Frequency of *burden** in budget speeches, 1971–2016

first decade surveyed, reducing to just one per speech since 2001. Chancellors Healey and Howe (Labour and Conservative chancellors in the mid-1970s and in Mrs Thatcher's first government, respectively) average fourteen uses of *burden* in their five speeches each. One clear contrast then is between *burden*'s prominence in the early budgets and its comparative absence in the recent ones, regardless of whether the budget deliverer is Labour or Conservative, of the left or the right. But later in the chapter I suggest that the tapering use of *burden* reflects a second broad but diminishing difference between Labour and Conservative conceptions of the kind of burden that taxation is – indeed, as to whether taxation is some kind of social good or not. For the Labour chancellor Healey in the 1970s it was, implicitly, but it was not for Conservative ones or even Labour ones, nearer the present day.

But is it correct to describe an average, in the 1971–80 budgets, of twelve to thirteen uses of *burden* per speech as 'prominent' or 'extensive'? Although a keyword in Barber's 1971 speech, perhaps *burden* is not a budget keyword across the whole decade? Compiling a small corpus of all ten budget speeches from 1971 to 1980 and conducting a keyword analysis on this (with BNC Written Inform as reference corpus) confirms that with just two other 'evaluative' items as doubtful rivals (*full*, ranked 43 but mostly used in the phrase *a/the full year*, and *right*, ranked 48 but mostly used in the phrase *my right hon. Friend*), *burden* is the most highly ranked evaluative lexical keyword, ranked 49 and with a LL of 245.

The once extensively used word *burden* (twenty-two in Healey's 1975 speech, twenty-four in Howe's 1980 speech) has since about 1995 fallen completely out of use, for budget purposes. Is this mere chance, or indicative of a larger shift? My tentative suggestion is that *burden*, which in these speeches often collocates with *taxation,* is another of the discursive 'tell-tales' that are important to this study. When *burden* is examined in its collocational environments, it is revealing of a broad change in government attitude, from one in which taxes (and other government-managed assets) are mostly assumed to be a social good, notwithstanding local wastage or inefficiency and unsuccessful investments – that is, a burden worth carrying. In the changed viewpoint, taxes are presumed to be a nuisance at best, and often implied to be an ethically dubious removal from deserving individuals of the wealth they have earned, and are entitled to save or spend as they see fit.

It might be speculated that *burden* has sharply declined in use simply because it has been displaced by some near-synonym in the budget speech genre. But despite searching for collocationally appropriate alternatives, guided by the Macmillan online dictionary and the Wmatrix semantic tagging system, I found no evidence that the attrition in the use of *burden* is because some more suitable term has emerged and supplanted it.

In fact these whole phrases, *the burden of taxation* and *the tax burden,* have virtually disappeared from the budget speech discourse since 1990 – as if what they denoted had ceased to exist too. There is no instance of either in Osborne's budget speeches of 2013–16 inclusive. A search among all seven of Osborne's budgets for the phrase *of taxation* uncovers just one instance (among just twenty uses of *taxation*), in the phrase *the scope of taxation*; the *of tax* phrase – forty-seven instances – occurs just once preceded by a word which is at least similar in sense to 'burden': *the gross cost of tax relief.* What is noticeable in these recent budgets, and possibly in contrast with Brown or earlier Labour chancellors, are copious references to *tax cuts, tax credits* and *tax simplification.* These are now central to the new discourse of wealth diversity, while the old-style collectivity-minded mentions of tax as burden (and especially the wealthier person's burden) dwindle to near invisibility.

Let us look at how *burden* is actually used in two 'high-*burden*' budget speeches in the earlier period – Healey's of 1974 and Howe's of 1980 – and in two almost '*burden*-free' recent budgets – Brown's of 1999 and Osborne's of 2013 (thus, four speeches with a rather higher frequency of *burden* than the average for their respective ten-year spans). Here are the KWIC data for *burden* in the Healey 1974 budget:

1. t rates, I know, imposes a heavy **burden** on some businesses and individuals
2. convincing the whole nation that the **burden** of our sacrifices and the rewards o
3. , we have to ensure that the extra **burden** falls on those best able to bear it
4. not bear a proportionately larger **burden** in supporting the alliance than her
5. mentioned will help to reduce the **burden** imposed by our proposed increases

6. better-off are best able to carry the **burden** and are likely to reduce their cons
7. all if the whole of the additional **burden** could be imposed on people so rich
8. rich bear a higher share of the tax **burden** than they have under the last Gover
9. necessary to ensure that the total tax **burden** through duty and VAT was not, on a
10. only limited scope for putting the **burden** on those best able to bear it. But
11. th two children will find that the **burden** of their income tax and national in
12. nal unity we need. Yet though the **burden** is now more fairly shared, burden
13. burden is now more fairly shared, **burden** it is. In one way or another my Bu
14. s would increase the total tax **burden**–including the consequential VAT effect by
15. so propose to increase the tax **burden**–including VAT–on all wines, including Bri
16. re propose to increase the tax **burden**–including VAT–on beer by the equivalent of
17. as will increase the total tax **burden**–including VAT–on cigarettes by an average
18. considered redistribution of fiscal **burden**s so as to help those less able to be
19. concerned to carry the additional **burden**s I must now describe. Corporation t
20. her hand, will place the heaviest **burden**s on the broadest backs. First, the

In this, Labour Chancellor Denis Healey's notoriously long first budget speech, *burden* occurs twenty times, used subtly differently from what we will find in the Howe budgets. The phrase *burden of taxation* does not appear; there are six uses of *tax burden*, three of which talk of *increase(ing) the total tax burden* and many of the twenty uses talk of *sharing the burden* more fairly, by asking *that the rich bear a higher share of the tax burden* than under the previous government. There is frequent mention of *bearing* the burden.

While with indirect taxation there is only limited scope for 'putting the burden on those best able to bear it', with his direct taxation changes, Healey says, he will give some relief to the poorest but 'will place the heaviest burdens on the broadest backs'. (Interestingly, a similar wording returns at the twilight of New Labour in the party's general election manifesto for 2010, to describe its policies: *We have made our choice in ways that put the greatest burden on those with the broadest shoulders.*) Towards the end of his speech, Healey says: 'Yet though the burden is now more fairly shared, burden it is. In one way or another my Budget calls on the majority of the British people to make some sacrifice for the survival of their way of life.' This noticeably emphasises the sharing of the burden, with the suggestion that it cannot be avoided, and that somebody has to bear it. In the text to either side of the quoted sentences, Healey says his redistributive actions will set Britain on course towards 'that just and fair society' required 'to build the national unity we need'; the budget is 'a further step along the road to realism and a united nation'. This emphasis on national unity has an echo in Osborne's 2011 insistence that 'we are all in this together'. But for Healey, its preconditions are redistribution and burden-reallocation, an egalitarian making society fairer; in Osborne's 2011 speech there is no mention of burden-reallocation, which might have added to the demands on the very rich.

How does the equally copious use of *burden* in Howe's (Conservative) budget of 1980 compare with that in Healey 1974? Here are the KWIC data for *burden* in Howe's budget:

1. . My first Budget switched the tax **burden** from earnings to spending and great
2. et without putting too much of the **burden** on interest rates, a public sector
3. get, a very large increase in the **burden** of taxation would have been unavoid
4. p or down. This places the entire **burden** of adjustment on the working popula
5. itably, a substantial part of the **burden** of adjustment then falls on profits
6. find room for lightening the tax **burden** and so to provide scope and encoura
7. ete. This country carries a heavy **burden** of Government payments overseas:
8. form for business is to reduce the **burden** of financing the public sector and
9. ad users to face a constant fiscal **burden**, it would not be fair to disregard
10. g like its present rate. As the **burden** of income tax is reduced, I would
11. t start on reducing the oppressive **burden** of direct taxation. At every incom
12. bles and reduce the administrative **burden** on employers and on the Inland Reve
13. result in an increase in the real **burden** of income tax for the higher rate t
14. tions from many quarters about the **burden** of stamp duty on house purchasers.
15. transfer tax. This is a particular **burden** on the small business, when it pas
16. ernment can help by reducing the tax **burden**. I propose, therefore, to cut th
17. ch will lighten the administrative **burden** of the scheme and change certain fe
18. in order to ease the administrative **burden**. I propose that from midnight, th

19. and greatly reduced oppressive tax **burden**s on enterprise. But during the year
20. fect will be a marked shift in the **burden**s imposed by the Government and in th
21. stronger case for reducing the real **burden**s on companies and small businesses t
22. changes to ease the administrative **burden**s borne by small businesses about whi
23. it would impose particularly heavy **burden**s on those with the smallest incomes
24. experience sharply increasing tax **burden**s in times of inflation. In the ord

This speech is as *burden*-heavy as the Healey one, but the collocational patterns are different. Notice the recurrent phraseology that precedes mention of the burden. The burden has a *tax* or *administrative* basis (one of these two terms often precedes and modifies *burden(s)*) and is often **on** *companies* or *businesses* (which follow the node word), and seldom on the ordinary working taxpayer. The phrasing is mostly about reducing or lightening the burden or shifting it or acting to avoid causing the imposition of a heavy or oppressive one. There is no talk here of a necessary or worthwhile taxation burden that is linked to redistribution and inclusion. For Howe, the burden of taxation needs reducing, and this requires commensurate reductions in 'dangerously oversize public spending plans'. Naming the same desideratum that Healey had invoked in his 1974 budget (*national unity*) but in the course of arguing for rather different policies, Howe declares, 'Nothing, in the long run, could contribute more to the disintegration of society and the destruction of any sense of national unity than continuing inflation.' In Healey 1974, the budget's burdens of taxation foster national unity; in Howe 1980, national unity is preserved by those measures that combat inflation (*inflation* is mentioned in his speech – when Consumer Price Index (CPI) inflation stood at 18% – sixty-six times; in the earlier 1974 Healey budget, when CPI inflation was a very similar 16%, it is mentioned just twenty times). Howe specifies 'restraint of the growth of money and credit', or monetarism, as essential to defeating inflation. That in return required reductions in taxes and government borrowing, and in public expenditure. The latter had grown as a proportion of GDP in the last twenty years but must now be curbed 'if we are to find room for lightening the tax burden'. As the KWIC evidence shows, for Howe the tax burden can be *heavy, oppressive* (twice) and *real*; it is repeatedly characterised as something needing to be lightened, reduced or shifted, and never as an onerous means to a worthy end.

Here, now, are the many fewer KWIC instances of *burden* in the Brown budget of 1999:

1. , with no overall increase in the **burden** of taxation on business. Because w
2. sers in the tax system. Their tax **burden** has risen by nearly 20 per cent und

3. en. So under my proposals the tax **burden** on the typical family will fall to
4. will fall next year. And the tax **burden** on the typical family with children
and in Osborne's budget of 2013:
1. se in interest rates and leave the **burden** of debts to our children and grandc
2. times the largest reduction in the **burden** of corporation tax in our nations h
3. employers will have to absorb the **burden**, as is always the case with tax ch
4. The cost of employing people is a **burden** on small firms. And it is a real b
All mentions of *burden* in the Brown budget are in relation to *the tax burden*
and occur in the course of assurances that the burden will be reduced for
families with children (and at least not increased for businesses). Example 2
is not an exception: Brown is criticizing recent previous governments for
causing a 20% increase in the tax burden on families with children, before
proposing correctives. In Osborne there is equally scant mention of *burden*, and
where it does appear, it denotes the tax burden on companies not individuals
(examples 2–4), or on individuals but only counterfactually (example 1:
Osborne will not approve an increase in public borrowing that would bequeath
a debt to later generations). The general point is that taxation in recent years has
ceased to be talked about by chancellors as a 'good' burden or a 'bad' one on
individuals, or any kind of burden, except very occasionally on businesses; it is
as if that language and conceptualisation have become largely obsolete, part of
a *passé* language of mutual obligation in which the strong help the weak.

3.8   Chancellors' Metaphors: *Ruts* and *Dust* versus *the March of the Makers*

Metaphors, especially 'fresh' or creative metaphors, can be as persuasive in
political discourse and media commentary as anywhere else – more compelling
than literal or conventional language. If words are birds, metaphors are birds in
flight. An effective use of figurative language can be powerful advocacy for
a speaker's representation of matters, making his or her argument strike the
addressee as especially insightful and coherent. As much because of as despite
their unfalsifiable 'looseness', metaphors can nudge a budget's narrative in
ways that contribute to its seeming coherence, doing some of the political work
of explanation and reassurance, in hard-to-challenge ways. And as Musolff
(2016) argues, metaphors used in political discourse can have the effect of
reconceptualising a given situation, powerfully simplifying a complex problem
and encouraging the recipient to view it from the speaker's preferred perspective. It is therefore worth looking at metaphors in the budget speeches, to
consider just what they contribute and whether those of Barber in 1971 and
of Osborne in 2011 are significantly different from each other, in ways that
might bear indirectly on the naturalisation of economic inequality. Might the
metaphors (if any) of the Barber and Osborne budgets have articulated shifting

political assumptions about the relations between the state and the taxpaying citizen? Were their striking metaphors sufficiently 'resonant' to be taken up by the commentaries on their budgets in *The Times* and *Mail*?

Many words can be said to have some residual metaphoricity, but as indicated in Chapter 1, I believe it is important, not least for psychological realism, to focus attention on those metaphors that are comparatively unexpected, and therefore more attention-attracting and memorable. My simple criterion is to treat only those words or phrases as creatively metaphorical that are used in senses that are not recorded in the Collins Cobuild Advanced English Learner's Dictionary or the Macmillan online dictionary, or are not broadly synonymous with those recorded senses.

A first observation concerns the distribution of metaphors through a typical modern budget speech. Here there is a very clear trend. The more metaphorical uses of language in the 1971 and 2011 budgets are overwhelmingly concentrated in their opening and closing few minutes or paragraphs, and this distribution is apparent also in all the budget speeches over the past forty-five years. Those are the points at which a preliminary general overview is offered (the opening), and a reiteration of the main objectives is provided, usually in quite positive terms, as the concluding 'take-away' message (the closing). Once the chancellor turns to the technicalities of the financial outlook and the government's proposals in response, topics occupying the body of the speech, there is little evidence of anything but the most conventional or bleached kinds of metaphor. Guided by this textual pattern, the following observations focus on whatever creative metaphoricity is to be found in the speeches' openings and closings. The metaphors, and how the newspapers report them, help tell each chancellor's story.

3.8.1   Barber

path   In light of previous analyses of the Barber 1971 speech here, it is not surprising to find that it is also far less noticeably metaphorical than the Osborne of 2011. Very near the opening of Barber's 1971 speech, after he has briefly summarized the nation's financial problems and poor economic performance in recent years, comes one of the few metaphorical formulations (shown in bold) in the entire speech:

These are problems not for government alone but for the whole nation. What is needed is a new realism and a new determination: a new awareness of **where the ruts we have been following will lead us** and a new national effort to change the direction.

This metaphor of the nation's economy as people unthinkingly travelling along a well-worn but no longer suitable route, is not particularly attention-attracting. It makes the following mention of 'changing direction' more palpable, but the latter uses a quite basic, dictionary-recorded meaning. Barber's main purpose here seems to be to announce major change and difference of approach (he uses the word *new* four times in this short extract, urging *a new national effort*).

No other modern chancellor mentions *ruts*, but a great many have used versions of the *path* metaphor to which it is metonymically related. *Path* occurs fifty-two times in my post-1970 corpus of budget speeches, more metaphorically on some occasions than others: sometimes it is synonymous with *rate* or *level*, as in *the path of unemployment* and *the forecast path of public expenditure*; these 'rate/level' examples I set aside to concentrate on the 'route' uses. Even these are so familiar that their impact and power to encapsulate is weaker than it might once have been. When the Labour Chancellor Denis Healey gave his first budget speech in 1974, he chided Barber and the Conservatives for running *substantial risks on the balance of payments and inflation for the sake of forcing Britain on to the path of higher growth* – a gamble that failed, he noted. *The important thing is not to allow the difficulties to prevent us setting our feet on the right long-run path*, said Geoffrey Howe in 1980; and in the difficult year of 2009, after the world banking and finance crisis, Alastair Darling advocated at different points in his speech *a clear path to recovery*, a *sensible pathway*, and (twice) a *sustainable path* for public finances. When George Osborne gave his first emergency budget speech fifteen months later, he quoted the new Office of Budget Responsibility to support his view that *to actually follow the fiscal path set out by the previous Government* would raise interest rates and depress economic activity. In his 2013 speech Osborne assured us that *with this Budget we can stick to the path of deficit reduction*. The phrase *downward path* is quite popular, as the thoroughfare which chancellors promise they are keeping government borrowing on; and Gordon Brown was fond of *path-breaking* initiatives. One probable attraction of the *path* metaphor to the chancellors who used it is its implication that the minister is in control of the economy, at least to the extent of having identified a best path through whatever difficult terrain they expect us collectively to encounter. If we are now or soon to be on the right path, the chancellor is impliedly an accomplished guide and leader, rather than lost and without insight as to which direction to proceed in, and by implication powerless to control the economy.

In addition, where the *path* metaphor is invoked, not journeying is not an option: 'we' cannot 'put down roots' or stay put, in some notional already-settled homestead within some ideal country. The background is a world of uncertainty, difficulty and perhaps danger, analogous to an uncharted land or sea which must be traversed. The metaphor chimes with ideas of ambition, growth, change, improvement, innovation, of acting to make (or keep) one's life safe, free, different and better.

Also crucial to the 'on the right path' metaphor is the assumption that as a nation we are 'travelling' to some preferred destination. The stated or implied path destination(s) in the Osborne budgets are deficit reduction, and reduction of public spending, with a view to balancing revenue with spending. In Barber's three budgets, the stated destinations of the three fully metaphorical uses of *path* are *expansion and growing prosperity* and *higher growth* (twice). Howe 1982 is nuanced enough to say *We must, however, tread a very careful path between safeguarding the interests of the taxpaying community on the one hand and avoiding economic damage on the other.* In his first budget in 1984 Nigel Lawson prefaced his reforms by saying *I am well aware that the tax reformer's path is a stony one.* Lawson was also exceptional when the next year he admitted that the economy had diverged from the path he had set for it: *it is now necessary to return to the path I outlined last year.* And it was Lawson who invoked the *path of prudence and caution* (1988) long before Brown was associated with being prudent. None of these *path* metaphors, then, with the partial exception of Barber in the early 1970s, specifies any more uplifting destination for the journey than fiscal responsibility in which state spending and state taxes are balanced and both are 'kept within bounds'. While the *path* metaphor is perhaps the most frequently used, its application in the budgets is strictly to fiscal matters, rather than such profounder goals as peace, freedom, justice or equality of opportunity. If the budgets allude to the latter at all, it is by less prominent means.

dust in our mouths   Near the close, Barber produced what is the only striking metaphor in his entire speech. It comes in the course of his warning that inflation threatens all other economic plans: 'It is right that I should end with this warning. All our hopes for the future will be but dust in our mouths if we do not repel the assault upon the value of our money. This must remain our first priority.' Whether this powerful image of hopes turning to dust in our mouths is original to Barber or an adaptation from a religious or literary source is unclear. While the language sounds biblical, the nearest phrasing seems to be verse 9 of the Lamentation Psalm 102, which in the King James version reads: *For I have eaten ashes like bread, and mingled my drink with weeping.* The Barber metaphor implicitly contrasts the vital sustenance of food and water with their opposite, dust. We speak of various good things, including human beings – golden lads and girls in Shakespeare's *Cymbeline*, Alexander the Great in *Hamlet*, and the everyman addressed by the words of the Christian Ash Wednesday liturgy – eventually coming or turning to *dust.* So the theme of cruel reversal, from collective prosperity to financial disarray, is exceptionally vividly condensed here in the idea of hopes turning to 'dust in our mouths'. Macbeth's 'all our yesterdays have lighted fools the way to dusty death' (*Macbeth* V: 5) may also have been in Barber's mind. The metaphor is intimately physicalist, alluding to the senses of human touch and taste, and to hunger and barren desiccation. The sense of potential crisis, of emergency, is physicalised too in how Barber continues, characterizing inflation as an assault that the nation must *repel*. In the event, the rate of inflation, 9% in 1971, was already on a steep rise that peaked at 24% in 1975 and stayed well above 10% in every year but one until 1982. Since inflation has never risen above 5% in the years since 1991, it may be hard for younger Britons to appreciate the impact of high inflation on a society, particularly where an immediate compensatory rise in income does not occur.

The phrase *dust in our mouths* appears on just three other occasions in *The Times Digital Archive,* all in 1971. The first is *The Times*'s first leader article of 31 March evaluating Barber's budget (*A Radical Tory Budget*), and published the morning after he had delivered his speech (this commentary is analysed later in this chapter). Tellingly, in this long editorial (1,010 words), the 'All our hopes … dust in our mouths … value of our money' sentence reproduced earlier is the only extract from Mr Barber's speech that it reproduced *verbatim*, in direct speech.

The second occurrence of *dust in our mouths*, just two weeks later, comes from the then-journalist Nigel Lawson (himself the Tory Chancellor in the 1980s), writing in the Business/Finance section (14 April): a long assessment of Barber's policies, and how Lawson might best control inflation and unemployment, while stimulating growth. It begins:

'All our hopes for the future', declared the Chancellor in the one burst of imagery he permitted himself during his Budget speech, 'will be but dust in our mouths if we do not repel the assault upon the value of our money'. As Ford roar off into the middle distance with their two-year 16 percent-a-year wage agreement, closely followed along the primrose motorway by Vauxhall and British Leyland, the dust from their wheels seems to be making a beeline for the mouth of Mr Anthony Barber.

Acknowledging in passing the exceptionality of the *dust in our mouths* metaphor ('the one burst of imagery'), Lawson deftly exploits Barber's figure (together, indeed, with a 'path' metaphor), literalising it in his own metaphor of the car workers' inflation-stimulating wage settlements as akin to cars roaring away and scattering dust, to be savoured by hapless bystanders, such as Mr Barber. There is an echo here of the 'eating dust' idiom, the fate of those in any race left behind by more successful competitors, and for me also a fainter cultural one of Mr Toad (of *Wind in the Willows*) selfishly roaring past in his expensive motor vehicle. The one jarring note is that of *making a beeline*. Bees, beelines, and nectar sources certainly fit with the *primrose* mentioned in the previous line; but *primrose motorway* is sarcastic, and an image of pastoral productive harmony is no part of Lawson's intended depiction. This awkward mixing of metaphors scarcely matters, however: a certain amount of metaphor mixing, an avoiding of excessive care in one's formulations, seems almost to be welcomed in caustic political commentary.

The third mention is in a letter of 19 June to the editor from a J.A. Ballard in Cambridge about French nuclear tests; noting that the United Kingdom is likely soon to sign the (Common Market) Treaty of Rome, Ballard warns *The nuclear test ban treaties [will] turn to dust in our mouths if we celebrate a new entente and deliberately ignore the other side's flagrant disregard for every principle of scientific responsibility.* Although his topic is nuclear contamination rather than inflation, it seems likely that Ballard has taken and adapted this phrase from Barber and Lawson, using it to similar vivid effect, describing a defeated hope.

The *Daily Mail's* archival evidence with regard to *dust in our mouths* is similar to that in *The Times*: just two mentions, both from 31 March 1971. One is in the page one comment/editorial, entitled 'This Daring Gamble', where again the sentence of interest is one of just two passages from Mr Barber's speech that are quoted verbatim. The second comes in an 840-word assessment of the budget by Eric Sewell, *Masterly Barber Is Hailed by Joyful Tories: Budget Special.* This surveys the budget in its entirety, but finds room to say: 'He wasn't overselling his cure for the nation's ills. Already he had warned: *All our hopes for the future will be but dust in our mouths if we do not repel the assault upon the value of our money.*' All this evidence confirms that novel metaphors in chancellors' budget speeches are noticed and have a potential to be the focus of discursive comment and reader reflection far in excess of most of the surrounding nonmetaphorical discourse. Like all metaphors, they are also risky: if judged inapposite, contextually incongruous (a wider notion than 'mixed metaphor') or self-indulgent they may provoke mockery from journalists and readers.

Other than the 'dust in our mouths' warning of 1971, there is little use of metaphor in Barber's two subsequent budgets. In his 1972 budget I detect no novel metaphors whatsoever. That budget's core message is that the government aims to stimulate growth by applying a cut of about £1 a week to the standard rate income tax. This prompted the *Daily Mail* to use the headline *It's a Pound in Every Pocket!*, which uses conventional metaphors and probably mockingly echoes a famous assurance expressed by the previous prime minister, Harold Wilson. The title of the *Mail's* comment judges this budget: 'It's Fair, Adventurous . . . and It Sets Us on the Road to Europe', and reports that Barber is reforming our constricting tax system: *Our taxes must be simpler. They must be lower. They must promote progress, not put a brake on it.* (Here the *Mail* uses an 'economy as vehicle' metaphor that is not present in Barber's speech, but is evoked at the close of Osborne's 2011 speech, where he talks about 'putting fuel in the tank' of the economy.) The *Mail* comment concludes by saying *[Barber] has given us [the British people] a rich meal to chew over which, we believe, will leave a lasting and pleasant taste behind.* The phrase *a rich meal* is not used again in the *Mail* until 1992 and later, and then only in conventional uses related to food and diet. In short, and perhaps unsurprisingly, the *Mail* introduces one or two metaphors where none is apparent in the Barber speech on which it is commenting – as if the *Mail* had to metaphorise and try to add shape or story to a speech that lacked these.

Barber's 1973 speech has similar low metaphoricity, mostly close to the opening and related to his concern with inflation:

Not only does inflation create injustice as between one individual and another. It also blinds us, as a nation, to our real achievement. Instead of satisfaction it breeds resentment. There is only one way of removing the causes of this attitude, and that is by attacking inflation itself . . . we must conquer inflation. The battle against rising prices is crucial not only in its own right because inflation is bad, unfair and socially disruptive.

Blinds is not literal, but it is not a creative metaphor either (sense 2 for the verb *blind* in the Macmillan online dictionary is 'to prevent someone from realizing'); similarly conventional is the metaphor of inflation 'breeding' resentment; and the mentions here and later of attacking and conquering inflation are all conventional 'war' metaphors. In short, in all of Barber's budgets, with the one *dust in our mouths* exception, creative metaphor is absent.

3.8.2   Osborne

What of George Osborne, forty years later? His 2011 budget opens with two relatively conventional metaphors, bolded in the quotation already reproduced here in Section 3.4. The second of these, the 'change of route' reminder, is as predictable as Barber's about getting the economy out of the ruts. More striking are the closing sentences of Osborne's speech (also reproduced in Section 3.4). The last of these metaphors, the 'fuel in the tank' figure, is a familiar one – but on this occasion it is cleverly made literal again, since Osborne has just announced a consumer-friendly freeze on fuel duties, thus enabling people to afford to put more fuel in their vehicles. The most arresting and complex metaphor comes when Osborne envisages his budget leading to *[a] Britain carried aloft by the march of the makers.* It is hard to see how any kind of march could carry anything aloft, so metonymies and implications must be invoked to yield a plausible sense here: if more people in Britain worked in innovative manufacture (ten thousand James Dysons, perhaps, hoovering up foreign sales), they would be 'the makers', and their dynamic progress would be a 'march', like that of an army or mass movement. Their efforts would cause the British economy to prosper, with profits and standard of living 'rising'. But this 'carrying aloft' cannot easily be interpreted as becoming airborne, despite the appropriateness of applying such a metaphor to a 'slow' economy, in view of the asserted agency (*by*) of the march of the makers. Instead an awkwardly different image is suggested, where the marching makers are carrying Britain aloft rather as mourners might shoulder the coffin of a deceased loved one. Or Britain could be being raised high like a sports hero on the shoulders of their team-mates – except this would be to narrow the conception of Britain to a single champion, whereas the context suggests Britain is a group, and the many are holding up the many. Overall this is an example of a less successful mixed metaphor because it does not project a clear and persuasive picture.

Prior to his March 2011 budget, Osborne had delivered an emergency budget in June of 2010, and this contained several conventional and therefore low-impact metaphors. To respond to difficult economic conditions, Osborne said that *we have set a brisk pace since taking office*'; he commended the new Office for Budget Responsibility as a body *immune to the temptations of the political cycle* and described the government's policy as intended *to raise from the ruins of an economy built on debt a new, balanced economy*. The closing was equally unremarkable in its conventionality of metaphors: Osborne repeated that his measures were tough but fair, and said both that *we have provided the foundations for economic recovery* and, ten lines later, that we have *laid the foundations for a more prosperous future* – a presumably inclusive *we* have *had to pay the bills of past irresponsibility* and have *had to relearn the virtue of financial prudence*.

In 2012 Osborne opened with a declaration that his budget rewards work and earning one's way in the world, since *[t]here is no other road to recovery.* He seeks to support a range of industries where Britain is strong, rather than focussing too much on financial services, since they *are not the only string to our bow.* At the close he declared this is far from being *'a do-nothing Budget':* *We have not ducked the difficult choices; we have taken them head on.* In 2013 the opening announced that this is *a Budget for people who aspire to work hard . . .* [and] *who realise there are no easy answers to problems built up over many years. Just the painstaking work of putting right what went so badly wrong.* Osborne says *Today, I'm going to level with people* about persisting problems. But *we must hold to the right track,* he says, and we are *in a global race.* In time, those who aspire, the *aspiration Nation,* will be rewarded. In 2014 Osborne opened by again reminding everyone that *with the British people, we* [the Government] *held our nerve* and *stuck to our plan,* although *the job is far from done.* He closed by declaring *we're turning our country around* and that *[t]his is a Budget for the makers, the doers, and the savers.* The 2015 budget opening is more buoyant, asserting that *[w]e made difficult decisions in the teeth of opposition, and it worked: Britain is walking tall again . . . We set out a plan, that plan is working, and Britain is walking tall again.* In following the deficit- and debt-reducing plan (what critics called austerity cuts), Osborne twice says that *we choose the future,* emphasising 'choice' a good deal: *we choose the whole nation . . . we choose aspiration . . . we choose families.* In all these declarations, *we* is intended in its exclusive sense (Osborne is declaring what the government is choosing), but the pronoun may encourage the addressed public to think of themselves as actually included, as co-participants in these acts of choosing. The closing of the 2015 speech is equally rhetorical in its use of anaphora concerning several good things *returning*; confidence, growth, optimism and Britain itself are all said to be returning 'from the depths' metaphorically: *The share of national income taken up by debt – falling; the deficit – down; growth – up; jobs – up; living standards – on the rise. Britain: on the rise.* In Osborne's final budget speech, of spring 2016, the most noticeable use of moderately metaphorical language is, as in other budgets, in relatively short passages at the opening and the closing. And as in past Osborne budgets, there is considerable echoing of the opening's language in the closing sentences. This is most evident if the metaphor-using introductory and concluding passages are viewed together, with the intervening 9,300 words (forty-five minutes in the spoken delivery) set aside. Consider, for example, the first sentence of the most metaphor-heavy passage of the closing:

'**Five years ago**, we set out a **long-term** plan because we wanted to make sure that Britain never again was **powerless** in the face of **global storms**' (bold added).

Almost every lexical item in it can be linked back to one or more phrases, literal or metaphorical, in the few sentences of the speech's opening. Four phrases in particular – *five years ago, long-term, powerless* and *global storms* – carry multiple lexico-semantic links to the wording of the opening. To give just one example, the closing mentions *facing global storms*, while the opening talks of *strong headwinds, facing a challenge, turbulent markets* and actively choosing *stability.* One important feature of storms is that they are 'acts of God' and therefore not attributable to human or government action (at least, until the Anthropocene era). But the level of repetition of themes, phrasing and metaphors in the opening and the closing has a clear reinforcing effect as to the story of Britain that Osborne wishes to tell. The final paragraph of the closing is notable, particularly in light of earlier observations in this chapter about the absence of 'higher' goals for the frequent *path* metaphors. Here Osborne identifies several nobler purposes for his budget:

This is our Conservative Budget. One that reaches a surplus so the next generation does not have to pay our debts. One that reforms our tax system so the next generation inherits a strong economy. One that takes the imaginative steps so the next generation is better educated. One that takes bold decisions so that our children grow up fit and healthy.

The opening ends with talk of the government's efforts to *make Britain fit for the future* (where the fitness is metaphorical). Now the closing concludes with literal fitness, when asserting that the budget's bold decisions are *so that our children grow up fit and healthy* (*our children* links cohesively with *the next generation,* named in each of the previous three sentences, as the intended beneficiary of the budget actions).

3.8.3   Osborne's Story

What can we learn from Osborne's seven budget speeches' creative and semi-creative metaphors? The nature of the narrative that a reader can derive from his spring 2016 budget speech is affected by the metaphors prominent at its opening and closing, which make the narrative positive and uplifting, a story of success and recovery, with a happy ending, while understandably silent about particular consequences. The repeated and metaphorised parts of Osborne's opening and closing tell something like this story:

Five years ago we in Britain found ourselves *'powerless in the face of global storms'* and, vowing never to be powerless again, we the Government have fastidiously followed a difficult path since, which has enabled Britain to emerge as one of the strongest economies; now we will continue (if not more so: redoubling our efforts) on the same path for the years ahead, to ensure we are fit to cope with emerging conditions.

A narrative must have a situation and then report a change in that situation (Toolan 2015): the initial situation here is very clear (powerlessness) and the change is equally clear: Britain as fit, strong, stronger than others, bequeathing to the next generation health, strength and wealth. The 2016 narrative is not significantly different from the 2011 budget one, which (again, as most clearly pointed up in the opening and closing sections and their metaphors) told a story of *past mistakes,* the need to *rescue the nation's finances* and acts of present-day economic *reform* as 'we' travel the route away from rescue to reform to recovery, a route travelled by *the march of the makers* (widened in 2014 to include *the doers and the savers* too) who will carry Britain aloft. The 'high or up is good or positive' metaphor implicit in carrying aloft was present also in the emergency budget of June 2010, where a new balanced economy was promised, which the government would **raise** *from the ruins of an economy built on debt.* The old economy was a shoddy structure that impliedly could not withstand any of the shocks and *global storms* (2015) it met with; hence the idea, in 'raising', of total rebuilding, from the newly *laid foundations* (2010) up. This route-march, or thorough rebuild, we are reminded in most Osborne budgets, is a job, hard work, for government and people alike (the 2013 budget is for *people who aspire to work hard*); it requires that all hold to the plan and thereby *walk tall* (2015), eventually to emerge *healthy, strong* and future-proof. The planned changed fortunes of the economy, as distinct from the people or society, are the focus of this story.

3.8.3   Barber's Story

What story, by contrast, do Barber's three budgets at the opening of the 1970s tell, taking their openings and closings and any metaphorising there as chief guides? The story tells of how the government is addressing 'problems' by newness and change, especially change of direction to get out of the ruts, but always keeping the 'fight' against inflation as a priority to save the 'fruits' of prosperity from turning to dust in our mouths. But notice that the latter, Barber's most powerful and memorable metaphor, vividly represents the outcome to be avoided, rather than a desired destination.

In fact it is hard to see a clear narrative extractable from Barber's three budgets. The 1972 speech's opening and closing announce that the budget aims to help modernise and *revitalise* British industry and to help the economy to grow significantly faster, partly doing this by reforming (i.e., reducing) taxation, while battling the 'twin evils' of high unemployment and, especially, high inflation. The 1973 speech reports some progress, in that growth has risen 5% and unemployment is down, but the goal of reducing inflation has not been achieved, and the language about having to *conquer* inflation is more urgent than ever. Barber's talk of lifting the economy *on to a path of higher growth* cannot conceal the fact that the growth is not in real terms where it is outpaced by inflation. The 1973 budget also describes a patchy plan for curbing inflation by means of pay settlement restraint, and the disjointedness of the Barber narrative is reflected in the scattered press responses: that year, the *Daily Mail* chose mainly to bask in the victory of its campaign to have the new Value Added Tax removed from purchases of children's clothes and shoes. Its editorial, under the title *More Daring Than It Looks,* criticizes Barber for not cutting government spending more, and doubts that enough has been done to secure the co-operation of the unions in the holding down of wage demands. As for *The Times*'s editorial, *Mr Barber's Big Gamble*, it is unequivocal in its criticism regarding the high rate of growth fuelled by a large balance of payments deficit financed by reserves and borrowing as a high-risk strategy, notwithstanding the government's laudable wish finally to bring inflation under control. The leader ends: *The Chancellor's plunge is neither necessarily nor obviously disastrous. But it is certainly incautious; and we fear that it is ill-judged.*

There *is* a story that could be derived from this cumulative description of the initial situation and the promised tellable change; the main features of the promised narrative outcome are a Britain with modernised industries competitive in Europe and the world, with low unemployment, low and controlled inflation and reformed taxation. But there is very little in any of Barber's three budgets that can be seen as him confidently telling his audiences – for example, in vivid metaphors – that 'this is what will soon happen'. This failing to narrate a story of economic prosperity may have been for entirely honourable reasons: the government may have believed that such a story could not be reasonably maintained, and that later exposure of its fictionality could do more harm than not telling it at all. But the lack of a strong narrative here in the early 1970s budget statements makes for a clear contrast with the confident narrative carried in the Osborne budgets forty years later.

3.9   The Editorial Reception of the Barber and Osborne Budgets in *The Times* and the *Daily Mail*

How were the 1971 and 2011 budgets discursively reported, interpreted and critiqued in *The Times* and *Mail*, in terms that were relevant to readers while also reflective of the journals' own views? These are the questions addressed in this section; since newspapers' editorial commentaries often carry the greatest authority, attention here is mostly directed at these.

The Times's 31 March 1971 leader mentioned earlier, *A Radical Tory Budget*, carries that newspaper's overall assessment of Mr Barber's budget of the previous afternoon, and worries whether the chancellor's policies are 'reflationary enough' to halt rising unemployment and inflation. It declares this to be the first 'clearly Conservative' budget for many years, adding, 'It is absolutely right that Conservative Governments should produce Conservative Budgets and Labour Governments Socialist ones; democracy is served by choice as well as by compromise.' The leader then observes that most Conservative government budgets of the past two decades have followed 'the fiscal consensus' of the war years and the ensuing Labour government of 1945–51:

'They generally accepted the high priority given to equalizing society as against making it dynamic. They assumed that an underlying hostility to private wealth was normal, quite apart from the needs of the revenue; they were ashamed of private capital.'

Although it believes 'Mr Barber did not produce a socially unfair Budget', nevertheless his various tax reforms and reliefs are judged capitalism-friendly, of a kind that less radical Conservative chancellors might have regarded as a 'a major political gamble, or even as an offence to the spirit of the age'. Implicit in this assessment is that Barber's tax and spending cuts are more friendly to the wealthy, and less concerned with what it calls 'equalizing' than has been the normal, mainstream approach. *The Times* approves but recognizes that the approach is 'radical', and may need justifying to those of its readers who wish to see budgets that are positively 'socially fair'. Even this early in the leader, a number of abstract ideas have been cast in opposition to each other, in two camps: on the one side choice, dynamism, private wealth, radical action; on the other side, compromise, consensus, equalising, prioritising society as a whole.

Barber is described as committed to the logic of the capitalist system, including 'the earning and retention of high incomes' and 'the profit motive as a normal part of economic and social life'. *The Times* suggests this chimes with 'creating a society with strong rewards for success', and is a 'reasonable course' on economic grounds. The leader then reminds *Times* readers of the guiding Conservative commitment to private wealth, in a formulation that merits detailed analysis:

Conservatives are Conservative because they believe that a system of private ownership and private opportunity is in the end both more efficient and more fair than the alternative system of public ownership and public responsibility.

The strong implication is that *The Times* endorses this belief in private owner-ship as fairer and more efficient than public, as expressed here in sweeping or unqualified terms. This absence of qualification of the abstract claims is an inevitable consequence of the pervasive use of oppositions in this commentary. Unlike a spectrum, an opposition treats the phenomenon it describes as redu-cing to two radically different conditions.

In the leader article, some of the oppositions are of the 'constructed' kind studied by Jeffries (2010a) and Davies (2012): paired phrases which, outside their use in this text, would not be recognised as opposites. In the extract just quoted, *public* is contrasted with *private*: an established opposition. But there is also a contrasting of *opportunity* with *responsibility*, a text-constructed opposition asserting that these are not merely different from each other but diametrically opposed. The underlying message is that if readers really want *private opportunity* they must reject *public responsibility* (itself a euphemism for public control). The phrasing asserts (plau-sibly) that ownership cannot be public and private at the same time, so a choice must be made; and with that choice, it is less logically asserted, comes one of two very different kinds of good: opportunity or responsibility. It is implied that individual opportunity opens up only if private ownership obtains, but then there is the risk of 'irresponsibility' in public affairs arising; by contrast collective responsibility or duty is taken on where things are in public ownership, but at the risk of being less efficient and fair and of denying individual enterprise and reward.

There are many questionable assumptions in this narrative, which is directly derived from the text, but the most noteworthy and dangerous assumption concerns the validity of binarist oppositional and equative discourse itself, the idea that something cannot be anything but X, if it is not Y, or conversely that X and Y amount to the same thing (e.g., where *The Times* is found contentiously equating fairness and meritocracy). When public ownership is called here 'the alternative system' to private ownership, the implication is that it is the *only* alternative. This is softened, but not cancelled, by the paragraph's doublings (ownership + opportunity versus ownership + responsibility; more efficient + more fair versus less efficient + less fair). The central doubling means that the reader is being told that in opting for Conservative rather than

Labour policies, they are selecting the more efficient and more fair, as if these two were a unitary good. It treats efficiency and fairness as ('in the end', to use the editorial's language) a natural combination, joint contributors to some unified desideratum.

Some readers may accept this promptly; others, more effortfully, may measure the claim against real-world experience, which suggests that efficiency and fairness are sometimes, perhaps often, at odds. For example, the reasonable adjustments a society may make to treat all people fairly, regardless of their physical or cultural differences, involves more time, work and cost than if only some privileged 'mainstream' group is catered for: less 'efficient', but much fairer. Where what is fair and what is efficient diverge sharply, a practice can only be more efficient if it is less fair, and vice versa. So at this discursive moment especially, where efficiency and fairness are rhetorically equated or assimilated, the 'naturalization' and normalization process is most visible. Even if a reader is suspicious of the vagueness of nominalizations such as *fairness* and *efficiency* and generalisations invoking them, the fact remains that just such broad and ill-defined terms are central to *The Times*'s response to and almost unqualified endorsement of Mr Barber's budget provisions.

A further pair of textual opposites occurs at the end of the first quoted sentence from the 31 March 1971 leader *A Radical Tory Budget: choice* versus *compromise*. A script in which Conservative, capitalist, free market conditions are said to give people 'choice' became very familiar in the late twentieth century, so this is an early instance; what is more discursively awkward is the notionally opposed script in which Labour Socialism entails compromise. Beyond threats to national security, newspaper editorials are usually welcoming of compromise, as implying anti-doctrinaire pragmatism and a commitment to unity and inclusivity. The use here also diverges from another mainstream assumption in UK media and public discourse, that socialism is *un*compromising, extreme and dogmatic. So there is a script or story 'tension' here, perhaps caused in part by the leader writer's sense that it is Barber's Conservatism which is the more extreme (hence the word *radical* in the headline) and uncompromising.

The editorial concludes by saying that, although wage inflation remains 'unmastered', *this does look like a Budget which opens a new political prospect*, and *it could be the starting point for a revival of confidence in British industry*. The invoking again of *confidence* (it is mentioned at least twice earlier in the editorial, including a lament about *British lack of self-confidence*) is noteworthy since it seems often to be incorporated into the narrative of a normal and necessary inequality in a 'well-functioning' western economy: without enterprise rewarded (the story states), the economy stagnates, no new wealth is generated, potential stays unfulfilled and – theoretically – everybody suffers. Central to the conditions necessary for market-driven enterprise, it is always argued, is confidence. The standard market-oriented narrative is that a heavily regulated, high-tax economy is one in which investors and entrepreneurs 'lose confidence' and choose to invest elsewhere. Presumably what they lose confidence in is the strong likelihood of generating an acceptable and secure (long-term) rate of return on their invested time and money. The term *confidence* is applied to businesses and investors; it is also routinely ascribed to those educated at private fee-charging schools.

The *Daily Mail* reception of the 1971 budget is far less extensive and thorough than *The Times*'s, but no less distinctive. Two weeks before budget day, a *Mail* comment (*Let's Make a Start*) urges Barber to 'make a start on reducing the monstrous burden of taxes which is suffocating this country', by reducing Selective Employment Tax, Corporation Tax, Surtax, with a small increase in Family Income Supplement. The *Mail* predicts that '[t]he Socialists will shout "rich man's Budget"' in response to these proposals, but insists that seeing the 'Tory bulldozers get going on this great rubbish heap of taxes' is the way to release a 'go-ahead nation'.

A Comment on the day before the speech urges Barber to *[g]o for the open road* – to reduce personal taxes and business ones to stimulate growth while also curbing inflation. Two days after the budget, a further Comment (*The Budget Row Begins*) reports Labour's shadow chancellor complaining that the budget is 'socially divisive' and does little to restrain prices. While the budget is judged in the comment to be 'fair enough', the real question (which 'even the experts' cannot answer) is said to be 'whether these tax cuts will create new prosperity [i.e., growth, reflation] or whether they will be swamped by inflation', but Barber's 'dash for freedom' is 'well worth a try'.

The *Mail's* front page report on Barber's budget celebrates it through verbal and visual metaphors of the economy being freed to rise and grow rapidly – to 'take off': accompanying the text is a large cartoon in which Mr Barber's bald head and prominent nose are superimposed on the cockpit of a Concorde-shaped aeroplane, pictured cheerfully surging into the air. The headline is *Take off with Tony!*, and a subhead above this runs *Flying High for Expansion*:

His Budget gives Britain a chance to break out of the tightening mesh of taxes that has bedevilled enterprise and effort for years.

A revolution in the way we pay our taxes, fewer of them, and bigger prizes for those who work and save – this is the formula he offers for putting the nation back on its feet.

The comment editorial, in a narrow sidebar to the left of the main story, is headed *This Daring Gamble* and calls Barber courageous for cutting taxes and taking steps to revive confidence and employment. In view of the contemporaneous debate over a possible national lottery, it is interesting to find the *Mail* approving the following initiative, explicitly aimed at encouraging people to save: 'We particularly like the cheeky offer of a £50,000 first prize on the

Premium Bonds.' Eric Sewell's report on the same day describes Mr Barber's provisions and their reception by his own party and the Labour opposition, calling the Tories jubilant and the Opposition 'glumly dumbstruck' by Mr Barber's 'tax revolution' (*Masterly Barber Is Hailed by Joyful Tories*).

Forty years later, *The Times* comments on Mr Osborne's in its 24 March editorial under this title and subheading: *Bad Hand, Well Played; The Budget offers a well-constructed plan for recovery without endangering the public finances. But low growth rates and high oil prices present long-term risks.* From the evaluation *well-constructed plan* in the headline onwards, the article is peppered with guardedly approving evaluations of the chancellor's budget. The following phrases appear: *plausible, an achievement, deft, accurate analysis, seriousness in cutting public spending, credible, plausible forecast* and so on; the newspaper declares: *Mr Osborne is right not to toy with a Plan B. That is the correct strategy package* [for recovery]. The Labour Opposition's criticisms are *an intellectually weak line* and postponing cuts is *no answer* to sluggish growth. Osborne, it states, *rightly set himself the task of promoting growth in ways that would not reduce the revenues coming into the Exchequer* (as tax cuts would). *Overall, the Chancellor did well*; while he is now *one of the big beasts in the Government*, he will need all his strength in future years.

In 2011, a week before budget day, the *Daily Mail* published a comment which takes a similar line to that of forty years earlier: it begins by reminding the chancellor of 'a remarkable fact of economics: governments often raise more money by cutting taxes than increasing them' and ends by asserting that 'high taxes are the enemy of growth, and only growth can rescue us, rich and poor alike, from our calamitous debt crisis'. On the morning of the budget speech, in *Focus on the War That Matters Most*, the *Mail* declares its support for Mr Osborne's rumoured plans to merge income tax and National Insurance contributions. This would be 'a major step towards restoring clarity and honesty to the system. Indeed, by revealing the true picture of the enormous amount the state takes from hard-working families, it could change the way Britain thinks about tax'.

On the morning after the speech's delivery, the *Mail*'s headline judges it to be an *astute Budget for these terrible times* whose best feature is that it shows *no weakening of* [Osborne's] *resolve to shrink Britain's grotesquely inflated public spending and boost the private sector.* Echoing some of Osborne's language of steadfast sticking to a path but additionally using the rather esoteric idiom of 'shroud-waving', it writes *despite months of shroud-waving by the public sector unions and the BBC, he refuses to be deflected from his course.* And the *Mail* particularly welcomes the provisions also applauded by *The Times*: the fuel duty price-freeze, the raising of the tax threshold for the low-paid and the cut in corporation tax. Like *The Times*, it is hostile to the 50p income tax rate for high earners, so welcomes the promised review of this, reminding the reader that *this paper has long argued, high personal taxes crush incentives and often cost the Treasury more than they raise* (in Chapter 2, Philip Collins was noted as telling *Times* readers in August that this claim is documentedly false). The *Mail* ends by arguing that *at times like these* (it particularly blames *global conditions and Labour's grim legacy*) there is only so much a chancellor can do, but Osborne *did what he could.* In the same newspaper Hugo Duncan writes an evaluation (*Chancellor Sticks to the Plan*) largely echoic of the comment, that similarly argues that Osborne had limited room to manoeuvre, having *inherited a basket case from Gordon Brown,* but – here echoing the *Times* leader's subhead – *he played a poor hand well.* At the same time the *Mail* does more than grudgingly accept Osborne's proposals. In the same issue of the paper it prints, from its 'new star columnist' Iain Martin, a 1,335-word article titled *The Speech Mr Osborne Should Have Made.* Amid some column-filling knockabout, Martin articulates the essence of the *Mail's* political creed: a reliance on *low taxes and those who work hard* as the way to economic recovery and *national renewal.* As was done in *The Times,* Martin rejects the 50p tax band, although his reasoning verges on the self-contradictory when he implies that the 'immoral' 50% rate is in practice 'avoided' by the rich: 'It is immoral for the state to take 50p in the pound of anyone's income. It raises no extra money because the rich find ways of avoiding it, and discourages risk-taking.' Martin relatedly rejects what he calls 'employee rights', which he says get in the way of enterprise: 'We simply cannot afford the expansion of maternity and paternity rights that was planned. They are luxuries from an age of irresponsibility.' The semi-fixed expression Martin uses here – *(simply) cannot afford* – has a long and informative history of use in news discourse addressing political and economic provisions throughout the forty-five-year period (see, e.g., Gomez-Jimenez, forthcoming).

   In this chapter I have probed the differences in language between the Barber and the Osborne budgets of 1971 and 2011, and then all the Barber budgets and all the Osborne ones, and then more selectively among all the budgets of the past forty-five years, to see whether those language differences might reflect changing attitudes to inequality. I have suggested that, by dint of their inclusive and exclusive *we* pronouns, the different prosodic or complementation patterns around their use (or avoidance) of the words *help, fair, burden* and *taxation,* and their different uses of metaphors, Barber and Osborne, and several of the intervening chancellors too, have told a gradually revised story about Britain, its economic strengths and weaknesses, and its best way forward fiscally (in the early 1970s and the 2010s, respectively). We have seen a contrast between Barber's (and Healey's) discursive orientation towards society as a whole, to people, and Osborne's orientation specifically towards the economy.

   The story that *The Times* or *Mail* reader absorbs through the discourse of and around those budgets is also informed by everything else within those speeches and, particularly, by the newspapers' own reactions, which I have shown is in many respects similar to the chancellors' own, in the cases of Barber and Osborne. Where these chancellors saw the need for tax and spending cuts, *The Times* and *Mail* agreed; where they oriented everything to the curbing of inflation and stimulating of growth (Barber) or to austerity measures, deficit-reduction and economic growth (Osborne), these newspapers largely concurred. These newspapers can be seen very largely sharing Osborne's view of the economy and of the need to prioritise, as if this were the only sure route to general prosperity, enterprise and growth facilitated by the normalisation of wealth inequality rather than the 'burdens' and 'unfairness' of redistribution. If this involves accepting a 'we/you' division, in which the government and powerful institutions are a 'we' that is set apart from the general citizenry, then that is a necessary accommodation to modern conditions, they argue. The government, it is insisted, is committed to being 'fair' and to 'helping' its favoured clients, businesses and families, although the specific goals of these kinds of help and the clients' own agency is left vague. In these ways Britain will not only be on the march and fit for the future, it will also nurture and reward its strivers and winners, rightfully carried aloft. If the price of this is some protection of the privileges of the talented, gifted or wealthy so that they can ultimately make the nation as a whole more successful, and if part of that price entails continued protection of stark wealth inequalities, then this must continue, these voices contend: there is no commonsensical alternative.

4   Peter Black, Christopher Stevens, *Class*, *Britain*, and Last Night's TV

4.1   The TV Reviewer as Spokesperson of Everyday Ideology: Peter Black and Christopher Stevens

It was while reading extensively in the *Daily Mail* of 1971 that I began to notice that alongside its diversity of content – the hard news stories about the postal workers' strike and the Industrial Relations Bill, the feature articles and sports pages and readers' letters and so on – there was a particular person recurrently and prominently present in the paper, speaking in his own voice about specific recent experiences that many in the readership had surely shared. This was Peter Black (henceforth often PB), the *Mail's* TV critic, who two or three times a week throughout the year was to be found occupying roughly half a page of the newspaper, reviewing one or more of the previous night's television programmes.

Black began reviewing television for the *Daily Mail* in 1952 and continued up to 1973, and is often mentioned as one of the pioneers in the critical reception of BBC television (later, ITV also). He came to the emerging new medium from theatre criticism, and according to Rixon (2011: 6), together with Philip Purser (in the *Sunday Telegraph*) and Mary Crozier (in *The Guardian*) 'borrowed from theatre and literary reviewing to create what they saw as a serious way of writing about television'; he treated TV plays and documentaries as 'a serious form of culture' (Rixon 2011: 32), to be assessed seriously. Black was well aware of the power of TV programmes to inform and influence viewers. He saw how, with greater ease and potential danger than older media, TV productions could disturbingly blend fictional drama with factual documentary, raising doubts about political neutrality or bias. Of Peter Watkins's TV film *Culloden*, depicting the notorious ethnic-cleansing wreaked upon Scottish highlanders in 1715, Black commented (in *The Biggest Aspidistra in the World*, 1982), '[It] told the audience more about Scottish nationalism in an hour than most of them would have picked up from a hundred books'.

Once or twice a week, every week, the faithful *Daily Mail* reader of 1971 would open the newspaper to find (often on page 3 – thus after the first page turn) a 500-word piece under the familiar name and face of Peter Black, looking out at them and their world (see Figure 4.1 for one of the four photographs the *Mail* seems to have used, in rotation). The graphic invariably comprised three elements – photo, name and some mention of TV, such as *on last night's TV* – often set within a landscape-orientated, curved-cornered, thick-lined rectangle, perhaps intentionally echoic of a television screen. Black's columns addressed the reader in precise but straightforward language about the themes and effectiveness of one or two programmes from the previous night's television.

This was at a time when a third, noncommercial, station had only recently been launched (so that the UK public's choice of viewing encompassed BBC1, BBC2 and ITV), and at a time when far more people watched television. Thus there was every possibility that Black's commentary would be about a programme that readers had also watched, and on which they might have their own opinions. This accessibility to all made television and the TV review far more 'ordinary' than, for example, theatre or operatic productions, which

Figure 4.1 Graphic accompanying Peter Black TV reviews in 1971

few could attend, and their review; it conferred 'ordinariness' on the reader, too. Some sense of participation as addressee in a conversation was arguably involved, such that the viewer-reader's unstated assessment of a documentary, contemporary play, soap opera or historical dramatisation was 'answered' by Black's considered and entertaining commentary. Unlike later reviewers, Black enjoyed no special experience of the programmes he wrote about; without benefit of preview or videotape recording, he watched them under much the same conditions as his readers. All these factors fostered, I suggest, a kind of trust between Black as named and visually presented writer and the individual reader, making Black more influential with readers than most of his fellow journalists.

Figure 4.2 shows a representative Peter Black column, with the body-text set out alongside it, for legibility. As in many of Black's pieces, the column is mostly devoted to reviewing one programme, but a short assessment of an entirely separate one appears towards the end (under the heading PROBLEM), without prominent formatting indication of this change of subject matter.

The non-permissive society was the best thing on in Smethwick

AS a title *Black Girls in Search of God* was too good for *Man Alive* (BBC 2) to put down once they'd taken it up, but it was nothing to do with the programme. The four coloured immigrants interviewed by the sympathetic Esther Rantzen were not seeking God; they'd got one. What the programme was really about was their difficulties in keeping hold of their own culture, of which their religion is one branch, in an England that expects them to conform to English culture.

The young Pentecostal Christian, Elaine Foster, seemed on particularly good terms with her god, who is the object of devotion of a sect which even for Birmingham sounded rather stuffy. No dancing, no parties, no hand-holding, no drinking or smoking, smiled the bright and evidently happy teenager, whose idea of a good time is to go about singing hymns and evangelising her pink neighbours. Dancing, she explained is sinful because it's something the body lusts after.

It didn't sound much of a life until the cameras took us to look at one of the interracial Pentecostal services, and then you saw that with its piercingly tuneful and exciting singing, the stamping and clapping, laying-on of hands, giving of tongues, transports and possessions, it was probably far more emotionally gratifying than anything else going on in Smethwick that day.

CONTEMPT

The Hindu girl, Vijay Malik, presented with unanswerable justice that while she has studied Western ways and adopted what she can of them, the English are contemptuous and indifferent to hers.

The Moslem girl from Coventry, Rehana Rafik, said she couldn't see how her children, when she had them, could be Pakistanis. To me this was the saddest thing anyone said; for it forced you to realise that the kind of integration they are expected to make, which means the acceptance by the weaker culture of the stronger one is not only dull, it really amounts to an extreme of intolerance.

It will be objected that these girls were all taken from the middle class; but they had to be articulate because the programme was discussing complicated attitudes.

If one thing emerged more strikingly than another it was that all religions are man-made, and have as at least one of their main objectives the subjugation of women.

PROBLEM

Now in its 23rd hour, Granada's *A Family At War* has got up to January 1942, and a decisive breach between Sheila Ashton and David, the philandering sergeant pilot. Last night's script, by Geoffrey Lancashire, got a good deal of variety of pace and style into it; quotes from John Donne, if memory serves me right, and a glimpse of a corner of a Southport dance hall on a Saturday night.

It attacked the problem the serial is stuck with; how to be serious without being dull. But it still dives into implausible and therefore the dullest, dullness when it is chez Ashton. It's a puzzle how the writers have failed to humanise the old Ashtons.

ANIMAL CRACKERS
By WILL SPENCER

'What on earth gave you the idea I was a bookworm?'

Golf course death

A man with shotgun wounds was found dead on a golf course at Romsey, Hampshire, yesterday. He was Mr Frederick Tear, of Northlands Road, Southampton.

Bank picketed

About 20 people protesting against the involvement of Barclays Bank in South Africa picketed the bank's annual meeting in London yesterday.

Figure 4.2 Sample Peter Black TV review in 1971

Elaine was probably the best off of the four because the others had to fit eastern ways into westernised lives.

CONTEMPT

The Hindu girl, Vijay Malik, presented with unanswerable justice that while she has studied Western ways and adopted what she can of them, the English are contemptuous and indifferent to hers.

The Moslem girl from Coventry, Rehana Rafik, said she couldn't see how her children, when she had them, could be Pakistanis. To me this was the saddest thing anyone said; for it forced you to realise that the kind of integration they are expected to make, which means the acceptance by the weaker culture of the stronger one is not only dull, it really amounts to an extreme of intolerance. It will be objected that these girls were all taken from the middle class; but they had to be articulate because the programme was discussing complicated attitudes. If one thing emerged more strikingly than another it was that all religions are man-made, and have as at least one of their main objectives the subjugation of women.

Sample Peter Black column: 'The Non-permissive Society Was the Best Thing on in Smethwick', *Daily Mail*, Thursday 14 January 1971.

It is worth mentioning, to understand the immediate context of the situation, that to reach the preceding page 3 story, the reader would have had to pass front-page stories about a bomb attack on the home of then Home Secretary Robert Carr and about the break-up of a former star athlete's marriage; and page 2 stories about Singapore welcoming Russian ships and the death of a Nazi general who was on the point of arrest and trial as a war criminal. For the average reader, turning to Peter Black's column may have felt like relief, from the presentation of weighty, remoter matters. The average reader in middle England, I suspect, was more interested in what was going on in Smethwick than in Singapore. Besides – and whoever composed Black's headline was surely aware of this – the name *Smethwick* still had a powerful resonance to British readers, as the name of the political constituency with a large Indian immigrant minority which (Wikipedia reports; see https://en .wikipedia.org/wiki/Smethwick_in_the_1964_general_election, last accessed 19 July 2018) 'gained national media coverage in the 1964 general election when Peter Griffiths of the Conservative Party gained the seat against the national trend amidst controversy concerning racism'.

I wish neither to overstate nor underestimate Peter Black's covert influence on how *Daily Mail* readers viewed the world in 1971 (and for many years before). But here, by contrast with the faceless leaders and editorials, was a flesh-and-blood individual, with a breadth of understanding of television and the 'real world', delivering a steady stream of opinion not only about what in his estimation made for high-quality television but also about what he believed to be reasonable values in 1970s Britain. It might be different if he came across as a dogmatic right- or left-winger, tending to rant. But no such characteristics are apparent. He does not write about directly party-political matters and it is not easy to determine, from his 150 or so stories in the *Mail* in 1971, if he inclined more to Labour, Conservative or Liberal politics. He is the reasonable middle-class person of that time, the moderately well-off 'white-collar' professional, even-handed even in his criticism of programmes he found unsatisfactory. Writing in a *Sight and Sound* TV column a decade earlier (Brien 1960: 98) Alan Brien described Black as 'easily the most professional and least gullible of the daily paper critics'; for Leonard Miall of the BBC History Unit, Black was 'the outstanding television critic of his generation' (Miall 1984: 100).

I collected a large sample of the stories written by Black in the *Mail* in 1971 (nearly all of them are TV programme reviews), as one potentially revealing expression of the newspaper's broadest socio-political values at that time. And with a view to using CADS to measure continuity and change in values, I sought a comparable sample of TV review/criticism stories by a named writer, also in the *Daily Mail*, in 2011 – thus exactly forty years later. But a search of the *Daily Mail* in 2011 revealed that, along with some other newspapers and perhaps influenced in part by the fragmentation and decline in TV viewing, this newspaper had no regular TV critic/reviewer in that year. There were several options for selecting a broadly comparable corpus (e.g., building a 2011 corpus of TV reviews by a journalist on a different tabloid newspaper), but all would have introduced some unlikeness of forum or genre relative to the 1971 corpus. I decided that the precise year of the second sample was not critical, and that since at the end of 2012 the *Daily Mail* resumed the publishing of TV reviews, by Christopher Stevens (henceforth often CS), these reviews continuing throughout 2013, a comparable corpus of his stories was my best choice.

Christopher Stevens turned out to be just as interesting a figure as Peter Black. He joined the *Mail* in 2012 after nearly thirty years in journalism, first on provincial papers and then on *The Observer*. In addition to writing for the *Mail*, he has produced a well-received book about the TV sitcom writers Galton and Simpson (*Masters of Sitcom*), a biography of the psychologically complex actor-comedian Kenneth Williams (*Born Brilliant*), and a poignant account of how his own family coped with one of the children being born profoundly autistic (*A Real Boy*). As he says on his website (http://christopher stevens.info), he writes a daily review of the previous night's viewing from Monday to Friday. This reflects a change of direction in the *Mail* editorial office in late 2012, after a few years in which no regular reviews of TV programmes had been published at all: Peter Paterson, who had been the *Mail* TV critic for nearly twenty years, seems not to have been replaced when he retired in September 2006 (Ellis 2008: 231). It is as if the *Mail* realised anew that there was, after all, a significant mass audience for particular programmes watched at or around the same time (via view on demand), as the viewing figures for *Downton Abbey* and several talent competitions would suggest. The analyses that follow relate to two small corpora. That of Peter Black's items was laboriously compiled from stories made available for research in the *Daily Mail Historical Archive*, which has OCR-scanned each issue of the newspaper and is fully searchable by keyword. I compiled a PB corpus of approximately 53,000 words and 100 stories – all of the substantial TV reviews published under Black's name in 1971. Alongside this, the CS corpus of Christopher Stevens's TV reviews from 2013 is of approximately 62,000 words and comprises just 46 stories. Thus the 2013 stories are considerably longer than those of 1971: PB's average story length is just over 500 words, CS's 1,350 words.

4.2   General Topics in Black and Stevens Compared

While this chapter's central purpose is to compare the socio-political values of Peter Black and Christopher Stevens by corpus-analytic means, some initial impressions, based on the titles and ostensible main content of stories may be useful. Such a survey finds Black writing evaluations of a number of plays for television, together with a very few columns on soaps and sitcoms. All these were ostensibly fictional and mostly explored interpersonal relations, while treating such serious topics as adultery, arms dealing, industrial pay disputes, Irish republicanism in the 1940s and parent-child neglect. But even more frequently Black reviewed factual programmes or documentaries covering a vast range of serious contemporary concerns, of which the following is just a sample: the troubles in Northern Ireland, government-imposed censorship of TV broadcast of IRA leaders' voices (Black firmly opposed this), permissiveness versus censorship, the world of children's comics, the American war in Vietnam (including the My Lai massacre), UK airport expansion into adjacent residential or green-belt areas, drink-driving, dropping out of the consumerist 'rat race', the life experiences of people with dwarfism, the UK's civil defence preparedness, xenophobia in Switzerland and the harms and cruelty of factory farming.

In the Stevens columns of 2013, by contrast, there are very few reviews of factual, documentary or current affairs programmes. The nonfictional programmes reviewed were mostly full-column profiles (often 2,000 words long) of TV actors or celebrities such as Joey Essex, the late actor James Gandolfini, the late Mel Smith, actor David Suchet, Delia Smith (the cook), David Walliams, Benedict Cumberbatch and Olivia Colman. The very few factual stories that happen not to be built around a celebrity include one on a documentary about Liberty, the upmarket London furnishings store; one on a fly-on-the-wall documentary called 'Educating Yorkshire', which was set in a northern state school;

one briefly assessing *Gogglebox* and a programme about the Hutterites and one about obsessive hoarders. But much the larger number of Stevens's reviews are of non-factual, non-documentary programmes – in other words, mostly of soaps and fictional crime, adventure, or comedy series. Topics included the following: *Dr Who, The Great British Bake Off* (twice), the rape scene in *Downton Abbey, Downton Abbey* again, *Broadchurch*, violence against women in a fictional crime series, *House of Cards* and the decline of structured family-based viewing (displaced by random, Netflix-style binge-watching), Miranda Hart's feeble comedy, Ben Elton's feeble sitcom, reminiscence about *The Professionals*, denunciation of the 'censoring' of the ritual violence and racial insensitivity in early *Tom and Jerry* cartoons and 1970s sitcoms, Coronation Street as too pc and sordid and Agatha Christie's *Miss Marple*. The credibility and plausibility (psychological or social-realist) of plays and soaps, in particular, seems to have been much more of a concern in Black's columns, while in Stevens's reviews the interest is more in the entertainment value of the programmes discussed: mostly, the idea that the programmes might entail social commentary on the way we live now does not arise.

4.3   Methodology

In light of the particular kinds of text studied in this chapter, only a few of the various means of analysing discourse linguistically to identify speakers' ideology are applied here. Little use is made of Hallidayan transitivity or van Leeuwen's social role analysis, for example, because in these corpora of TV reviews there is not sufficient continuity of named, unnamed, or elided protagonists to warrant their use. In both corpora (the 2013 corpus especially), much of the ideational representation was at one remove – a reporting of what some programme showed happening – and enormously diverse – what happened in this particular scene in *Downton Abbey*, or how the judges reacted to this particular failed culinary creation in this episode of *The Great British Bake Off*. For the same reasons of heterogeneity of topic and treatment, an extensive consideration of metaphors was not undertaken. This chapter study mostly follows the key stages of a corpus-assisted CDA, as outlined in Baker et al. (2008), and briefly discussed in Chapter 1. The qualitative stage involves formulating intepretations, which I try to cast in a clausal (or propositional) format initially, wherever possible, since any characterisation of a person's (or polity's) values and ideology ultimately must be propositional: a set of statements about the *desiderata* of a decent, moral life. Propositional formulations are only a starting-point, however, being disjunct and with the potential of coming into conflict with each other. More powerful and persuasive than separate values-expressive propositions is the weaving of these into a unified, coherent and (importantly) evaluation-bearing narrative – a covert 'story' about what has happened, is happening, may happen, or ideally ought to happen, and (the evaluation part) why that sequence of events is admirable or deplorable or something else.

4.4   Peter Black on *Class*

Since the overarching interest is in what Peter Black's and Christopher Stevens's stories reveal about their and the *Mail's* attitude regarding economic inequality, my underlying question is: What do the two journalists have to say about class, poverty, being poor, being rich, inheriting and inheritance and wealth in the Britain of their day? But that question is almost never answered directly; it has to be approached through identification of candidate passages and analysis of suitably contextualised excerpts; and identifying all and only those sentences or paragraphs in discourse that are 'about' inequality or class or being poor when fellow citizens are rich is a far from straightforward exercise. A simpler corpus-linguistic question must be answered first: How often do Black and Stevens use specific words reflective of these topics? Wmatrix found these frequencies, in the PB corpus, for all forms of the following items: *class* (46), *poverty* (5), *poor* (16), *rich* (22), *inherit* (4) and *wealth* (2). The counterpart frequencies in the slightly longer CS corpus (where frequencies accordingly should be roughly one-fifth higher) are: *class* (38), *poverty* (5), *poor* (14), *rich* (9), *inherit* (4) and *wealth* (1). The comparatively high frequency of expressions containing the word *class* (in CS as well as PB) suggests that further consideration of these should be a priority.

It may be objected that the discourse pertaining to wealth inequality (in PB and CS) may be entextualised by many other means than the uses of *class* in multiple contexts. But no other relevant term was remotely as prominent, when a search was undertaken of the PB and CS corpora for other words from the same UCREL semantic categories as those to which *wealth, income, (in)equality* and so on are assigned. Those semantic categories are I1.1+ (Money: Affluence), I1.1 (Money and pay) and A6.1 (Comparing: similar/different), respectively. When all thirty-one words in PB that are semantically tagged as I1.1+ are examined, for example, only *rich* (sixteen instances) is frequent, and several of these are unrelated to wealth, reducing the wealth-denoting instances to twelve: a strikingly lower frequency than that in PB for *class* (46). Thus focus on the use of *class* here has strong quantitative justification, supported by examination of the KWIC lines of the less frequent wealth-related terms. A final point to make about (socio-economic) *class*, as distinct from the other 'core' sociological categorisations upon which people's identities are assumed to be founded (race, ethnicity, religion, age, sex, gender, sexual orientation, etc.) is that unlike them it intrinsically entails inequality.

Roughly a quarter of the forty-six words or multi-word expressions in PB containing the *class* morpheme can be ignored, being unrelated to any social-stratificational sense of the word (e.g., *classical music, classics, first-class* and *in the Muggeridge class*), leaving thirty-five from the initial forty-six instances of *class* relating to socio-economic class. It is customary to display the instances of a targeted expression in a corpus in a Key Word In Context (KWIC) format, e.g.:

1. one gathered, only to vocalise the **class** struggle). She wouldn't allow the
2. ostly professional and middle/upper **class**, only two wore slightly masculine g
3. ed up by Billy 's sons, waging the **class** struggle under the cry of: One day

Such concordance lines enable collocational analysis and the noting of any patterns of frequently co-occurring lexical uses or grammatical forms immediately before or after the target item; some of the analysis reported (see the following) is indeed based chiefly on evidence from the KWIC restricted window of co-text. But particularly bearing in mind that these KWIC lines are far from random since they all come from the same author writing the same kind of journalism in a single twelve-month period, a variant kind of immediate co-text is more worthy of attention, namely the graphological sentence in which each of these uses of the word *class*, in this socio-economic sense, occurs. Accordingly I reproduce here the full sentential contexts of the identified thirty-five examples. This presentation means that words close to the target or keyword but separated by a period are ignored. A sentence-based listing is less automatic and certainly generates varying length samples, depending on the size of the enveloping sentence. But a search and capture based on the preceding and following period punctuation is arguably no less automatic than the assembling of KWIC lines; rather it is a form of discourse search that enables greater attention to sentences. The sentential-co-textual presentation also makes it easier to add, in square brackets, a brief note about the story from which the sentence comes, and of whether multiple uses of *class* appear in the same story; this in turn will indicate the dispersion of the thirty-five uses.

PB'S 35 Uses OF *Class* (in the Social Stratification Sense, Bold Added), in Their Sentential Context, with Source Story Annotations in Square Brackets

1. Her vision of folk music is as something solely political, a form of cultural expression reserved for the working **class** (as long as it uses it, one gathered, only to vocalise the class struggle). [profile of Peggy Seeger]
2. Of the eight women, mostly professional and middle/upper **class**, only two wore slightly masculine gear. [a study of lesbians]
3. The failing torch, we gathered, would be picked up by Billy's sons, waging the **class** struggle under the cry of: One day we're going to stand up and screw them first. [review of Neville Smith's play, *After a Lifetime*]

4. *The Harder They Fall* was about the highly paid directorial **class** who've lost their jobs.

5. Jeremy James's *Excuse Me, Your **Class** is Showing* (*Man Alive*, BBC 2) pinpointed some fascinating examples of change, coming up with two conclusions.

6. The **class** structure is best dealt with either by ignoring it or contentedly accepting it. [also from review of *Excuse Me, Your Class Is Showing*]

7. His wife, however, snobbishly defended her self-awarded status of 'working **class'** and would deeply resent, she said, being called middle class. [also from review of *Excuse Me, Your Class Is Showing*]

8. Next to old Parsloe the most serene was an artist who had totally rejected **class**. [also from review of *Excuse Me, Your Class Is Showing*]

9. East Anglia appears to be immovably associated by some TV playwrights with **class** distinctions of the most obnoxious sort. [review of Robert Holles's play, *Michael Regan*]

10. Programmes about **class** distinctions have an endlessly guilty fascination for us British. [also from review of *Excuse Me, Your Class Is Showing*]

11. Finlay had everything: The mystery of medicine, a triangular relationship which could change from doctor-housekeeper- doctor to father-mother-son; the nostalgic appeal of the recent past; and all in impeccable, **class**less Scots accent. [review of *Dr Finlay's Casebook*]

12. The genius of the three [profiled aesthetes: Aubrey Beardsley, Oscar Wilde and Ernest Dowson] was reasonably well suggested (for Wilde and Dowson there were recitals from the works), but the complicated motives that propelled them towards ruin boiled down to little more than reaction against the overstuffed middle-**class** prosperity of their Victorian milieu. [programme about the fin-de-siecle aestheticists]

13. The middle-**class** innkeeper Oxlade ('I try to run a civilised place') mistook Michael and his wife for a pair of bog-trotting Irish, though Michael had been his neighbour's farm manager for five years and his wife, to judge from the accent Anna Calder-Marshall gave her, had clearly been born thereabouts. [also from review of Robert Holles's play, *Michael Regan*]

14. It then became a melodrama about a decent middle-**class** chap with a good war record and an obviously correct attitude towards such things as long-haired psychiatrists, BBC plays, and the questioning of the Army by TV news men; who, after demonstrating how firmly he put down attempts to lower his standards, rescued the police from an awkward situation by a cool display of courage in the face of an armed opponent. [further description of Robert Holles's play, *Michael Regan*]

15. It will be objected that these girls were all taken from the middle **class**; but they had to be articulate because the programme was discussing complicated attitudes. [programme about young black women in the Midlands]

16. The play was every bit as cosy in its own way as Esther McCracken's accounts of the quiet weddings of the southern middle **class**. [review of Neville Smith's play, *After a Lifetime*]

17. Moreover he had a girl, middle **class** and black. [review of Carey Harrison's *The Private Sector*]

18. His wife, however, snobbishly defended her self-awarded status of 'working class' and would deeply resent, she said, being called middle **class**. [also from review of *Excuse Me, Your Class Is Showing*]

19. She wouldn't allow the middle **classes** – 'the bank clerks and professors' – any share in its comforts. [critical profile of Peggy Seeger]

20. Former IRA leader Peadar O'Donnell told how he tried and failed to change the IRA from a terrorist organisation to a genuine working-**class** movement. [about the Irish Republic, at fifty]

21. I've never been able to take to the glum, working-**class** secret agent myself, though it is a purely personal quirk. [review of *Callan*, crime detective series]

22. She identifies completely with the working-**class** struggle. [critical profile of Peggy Seeger]

23. Clearly it is not possible for a man who has climbed out of a comfortable Southern working-**class** background to become Tory Prime Minister to be dull. [profile of Ted Heath]

24. The Birthday Run (Granada) had the simplest of plots, designed to bring the close-knit working-**class** family of bicyclists into collision with the working class novelist who's escaped. [review of Arthur Hopcraft's play, *The Birthday Run*]

25. A carafe of water now stands on Annie Walker's table instead of the bottle of tomato sauce that directors used to introduce as a kind of dramatic shorthand to indicate a working-**class** situation. [Review of *Coronation Street*]

26. The author's heart was clearly in the right place, and a good play about the gap between the educated generation of working-**class** and their elders, and about the loneliness of an old widower, unused to rest, lay somewhere alongside it. [review of Peter Hankin's *The Pigeon Fancier*]

27. The Sinners play, taken by Hugh Leonard from Frank O'Connor's story *The Holy Door*, showed the effect of these thunderous sexual taboos on the lower-to-middle working **class**.

28. Her vision of folk music is as something solely political, a form of cultural expression reserved for the working **class** (as long as it uses it, one gathered, only to vocalise the class struggle). [critical profile of Peggy Seeger]

29. See second mention of *class* in item 24. [review of Arthur Hopcraft's play, *The Birthday Run*]

30. If you weren't as moved by it as you felt you should have been, it was because the author jumped cheerfully into the trap that threatens working **class** playwrights, tempting them to write with an indiscriminate affection for the working **class** which is a kind of sentimental snobbishness. [review of Neville Smith's play, *After a Lifetime*]

31. See second mention of *class* in item 30.

32. Armed with a tape recorder and a sympathetic manner, Seabrook once did a very good radio series about working **class** attitudes in Blackburn, and the observation of facts in a modern Midlands cosmetics factory in Skin Deep rang equally true. [review of O'Neill and Seabrook's *Skin Deep*]

33. The only family that is still defiantly working **class** is the Ogdens, Hilda and Stan and daughter Irma – and Hilda is pestering Stan to install a shower. [Review of *Coronation Street*]

34. Now, said the script, the policy is to industrialise further; and as this cannot be done without creating and depending upon a skilled working **class** it may be that the Lisbon docker we saw may get more than £6 for a 60-hour week. [review of documentary *Portugal – Dream of Empire*]

35. Once again the political theme was the working **classes'** exploitation by the Tories, betrayal by Labour, and in the case of these Liverpool Irish, the oppression of the Church. [review of Neville Smith's play, *After a Lifetime*]

4.4.1   Peter Black's View of Class in General

The first thing to note is simply that class is important to Black: consider how often *class* appears in the relevant sense, compared with the infrequency of relevant uses in PB of these other social categorizers: *race* (1), *gender* (0), *ethnicity* (0), *religion* (5) and *age* (12) – even *sex* (32 instances; mostly *sex* [13 uses] and *sexual* [10 uses]) is less prominent. By contrast, *sex* is far more frequent than *class* in the Stevens corpus. While none of the other terms just listed, including *sex*, has any significantly frequent collocates in PB, *class* has *middle* (2.23) and *working* (2.82) as left-hand collocates and *struggle* (1.73) as a right-hand one (T-scores in parentheses). In the CS corpus, among the listed terms (*race, gender*, etc.), only *sex*, in the collocation *sexual violence* (T-score of 1.73) and *age* (in *all ages*, T-score 1.72) have any significantly frequent collocate (just one, in each case).

If class is important to Black, the working class seems of particular interest, since approximately half the mentions have *working* as the immediate leftward collocate: talking about class is mostly talking about working-classness, but also, to a lesser extent, middle-classness. There is another stratum besides working and middle, but it is more vague – those who are *professional* or *middle/upper* (both in item 2) or *directorial* (in item 4): these categories are each mentioned once only.

Class entails *distinctions* (this is explicitly mentioned twice: in items 9 and 10) or *structure* (item 6). Some of the class distinctions are *of the most obnoxious sort* (item 9), which implies that many if not all class distinctions are on a continuum of unpleasantness with 'most obnoxious' as an endpoint. Whether for this or other reasons, in example item 10 PB avers that these class distinctions are endlessly fascinating to us British, and the fascination is a guilty one to boot. Black seems to be analogising an interest in class differences to some kind of transgressive prurient interest. Presumably middle-class himself, it is unclear whether Black sees the fascination as shared by both classes, or chiefly experienced by one, in its supposed relations and contrasts with the other.

4.4.2   Black on Middle-Classness

On the basis of the immediate collocates of *middle class* in the PB corpus, we are also given to understand that middle-classness may go along with prosperity and 'overstuffed-ness' (both in item 12), innkeeper/proprietor status (item 13), decency and being a *chap*, having a good war record (item 14) and southern-ness (item 16). Interpreting the collocational evidence in this way is open to challenge, I recognise. But I suggest that the implication (in item 14) is that *decent* and *chap* tend to associate with *middle-class*, while 'having a good war record' is so strongly associated with middle-classness that one hardly ever reads of a working-class person having one. A quick search of the Bank of English online confirms these intuitions. There is no exact match for *good war record*, but 89 matches in its 717 million words for *good war*, with these examples being indicative:

1. They were young, energetic, of good family, well-educated with **good war** records
2. 'He's an old Harrovian, my dear, and a superb bridge player,' while their husbands closed one eye because 'He had a damned **good war**, and is a member of the MCC.'
3. The captain was Vincent Cartwright, a great rugby man, Oxford, Blue, Barbarians, president of the RFU, a solicitor with a **great war** record.

While we can suspect that in item 14 Peter Black is deploying some of these associations ironically, so as subtly to criticize the playwright for resorting to melodrama and stock attitudes towards BBC plays and long-haired psychiatrists (who are male, presumably), he can do this only because the primed associations are themselves well-established.

In a later column (item 19) it is surprisingly asserted that the middle classes are exemplified by bank clerks and professors; but Black puts this claim within quotation marks and attributes it to the American folk-singer Peggy Seeger, whose views he clearly finds eccentric and unreliable (the idea that class has a different meaning for Americans is echoed in *class* sentence 10 in the CS corpus). So this case is just one example of the pervasive need, in 'ideology mining' of the kind attempted here, to look at examples in sufficient context to be able to judge whether the writer is averring on their own behalf or reporting the view of someone else, perhaps in a spirit of assent but equally possibly intending to reject or rebut it. The review from which item 19 comes, about a programme profiling folk-singer Peggy Seeger, contains a good example of a more oblique but still reasonably clear evaluation from Black: 'The clarity of her [Peggy Seeger's] political thought was well expressed by her blanket damnation: "I take pleasure in not being liked by policemen, liberals, and bank managers".' Here, the initial subject noun phrase presupposes that Peggy Seeger possesses clarity of political thought. But we are invited to treat that presupposition as ironic, with Black insinuating incoherence and foolishness in Seeger's politics, both by the content of the following direct speech (Black seeks our agreement that it is ridiculous to derive pleasure from being disliked by policemen, liberals and bank managers) and by the phrase *blanket damnation* (which the reader is likely to take as a variant of *blanket condemnation*). A *blanket* kind of any nominalisation (*approval, promotion, praise, denunciation*) carries a negative connotation: a *blanket* action is almost always an over-general and indiscriminate one.

4.4.3   Black on Working-Classness

As for the working class as represented in PB, individual members may be *glum* (item 21), but the working class also contains close-knit families (item 24). It has sometimes experienced rapid, *gap*-creating (item 26) change, in educational and other respects, between the younger generation (*educated*: item 26) and the older one, who by implication are not educated at all even though, in some cases, *skilled* (item 34). We can assert that distinction because in PB and recent recorded UK discourse more generally, one almost never reads of *the skilled middle class*, only of an *educated* or a *professional* one. Bank of English data (mostly from the 1990s, admittedly) would seem to confirm this:

> *skilled middle(-)class*, 2 instances
> *skilled working(-)class*, 10 instances
> *educated middle(-)class,* 37 instances
> *educated working(-)class,* 1 instance
> *professional middle(-)class,* 13 instances
> *professional working(-)class* 1 instance

The final single instance, of *professional working class*, strikes an odd note until on closer inspection one finds that it comes in an American National

Public Radio broadcast, and like the Peggy Seeger quotation reflects the different US conception of class. Black is thus reflecting widespread assumptions that *educated* is a common attribute of the middle class and a rare one in the working class, while *skilled* is an attribute of some in the working class and almost none in the middle class.

The strong, quasi-paraphrastic association of middle-classness with education helps explain item 15. The reasoning behind Black's phrasing here seems to be that middle-classness enabled these girls (but not working-class ones) to be articulate; the unstated intermediate link between middle-classness and articulacy is very probably education. Thus *middle class* means, roughly, both 'educated' and 'articulate'. You cannot expect the working class to have these qualities, item 15 implies.

More can be said about *articulate*: it is used by Black on four occasions in the 53,000-word selected corpus, always referring to women, and on two of those occasions it collocates with *intelligent*: 'Rachel Kempson's embittered but intelligent and articulate woman; including the intelligent and articulate ones [viz.,Women's Liberation campaigners] we saw'. So for Black *articulate* means, roughly, 'intelligent, female' and as we have seen, normally 'middle- or upper-class' and educated (the single use of *articulate* in CS in 2013 describes a twenty-one-year-old philosophy student said to be outraged at her treatment on *The Great British Bake Off* programme: *Ruby is intelligent, articulate and forceful*). This helps explain Black's wording when he reports a comment, about their quality of life, made by one of the evidently *working*-class women resident in a council-owned, high-rise housing estate comprising twenty-eight tower blocks in Battersea: 'The most articulate of the women wondered if the architects would design such places for their own families to live.' The subtext is that, among a group where from their class you would expect neither education nor intelligence nor articulacy, one of their number nevertheless said something worth reporting.

This is not quite the whole story, however, since PB evidently regards educational opportunity as the key enabler of a better, fuller life for younger Britons, and the means by which class division can be reduced and exclusion by background from meritocratic opportunity can be ended. In his 'Five Lies about the British' on 15 July, he writes:

First, one has to recognise that there appear to be two apparently quite different types of British, separated by World War II. The division is between a generation that hadn't much and one that's seen the ironing out of differences in incomes, education, opportunities.

In the second sentence, the post-war generation (denoted by the pro-form *one*) is logically one marked by a working-class/middle-class distinction, while the first generation mentioned in this sentence appears to refer to everyone in the pre-war generation, but must be chiefly referring to the working classes. Black cannot mean that the pre-war middle class 'hadn't much' in the same way as the pre-war working class. In the post-war period the working class have done much better thanks to some 'ironing out of differences' in the three named areas, the most instrumental of which was undoubtedly education. It is education, Black either states or implies, that empowered the angry young working-class playwrights, Ted Heath, Callan, the 'articulate' Battersea council house resident, young Parsloe of the Oxford Union (the son of old Parsloe, in item 8) and Ken Barlow in *Coronation Street*, in the stories from which the thirty-five reported sentences come.

4.4.4   Class Struggle

A struggle between the classes exists, in the world of PB: *class* and *struggle* are close collocates three times here (items 1, 3, 22), and the frequencies noted in the previous section might suggest that the antagonists are the working and middle classes. The struggle is implicitly asymmetrical, in that those in the working class are struggling against the middle class, but not the reverse. Accordingly one can have or hope to create a *working-class movement* (to advance the struggle) (item 20) – but the collocation *middle-class movement* sounds rather unnatural (although not entirely unheard of). Whether or not working-classness surrounds you as a 'movement', it can be a constraining container and therefore something that only with effort one can *escape* (item 29). Evidently Prime Minister Ted Heath broke free (item 23), but in his case the unspecified figurative pit or valley which he *climbed out of* was not constricting but *comfortable*: Black believes there are contented working-class Britons as well as struggling, discontented ones. He champions Mr Heath in arguing that he cannot be dull because he had the talent to *climb out of* his working-class origins; by contrast the fictional Callan (item 21) has stayed put, class-wise, and reaps the reward of *glum*-ness. By implication, anyone with talent can 'climb out' if they choose to, and it's Callan's own chippy fault if he decides not to.

The working class is in some respects under siege, then, and sometimes can only survive by means of acting *defiantly* (item 33). At the same time Black is critical of those he judges too strident in their proclaiming of working-class credentials. Of these people he twice complains that they are 'snobbish': playwright Neville Smith is found guilty of 'sentimental snobbishness' (item 30), while in a different column the wife of a servant/housekeeper who defends her 'self-awarded' working-class status is said to be doing so 'snobbishly' (item 7). The class struggle is understood by PB sometimes to be quite vigorous and heated; for example, item 3: *waging the class struggle under the cry of: One day we're going to stand up and screw them first*. In context the reader sees that PB reports this 'cry' with detachment if not irony and disbelief, but the reported cry presupposes that the middle class does screw the working class and never the other way about. Likewise item 35, which comes just a few lines earlier in the same story, reports as presupposed *the working classes' exploitation by the Tories.* The fuller context, however, makes it clear that PB is reporting what he understands to be the values espoused by the TV play he is reviewing, and not his own views. Moreover, he accuses the playwright of 'a kind of sentimental snobbishness' and 'indiscriminate affection' for the working class – predominantly negative qualities.

Perhaps most strikingly Black ends his review of Neville Smith's play (the source of items 16, 30, 31 and 35) with the remark *It was at least a personal view.* Not only has he spent valuable space reporting ideas about class that he is unpersuaded by, he has also implied that such sharply different views are to be welcomed. There is an open-mindedness about this engagement with others' different assessments of life in Britain which we may find contrasts with what emerges nearer the present day in the realm of TV reviewing, where journalists may be more inclined to reject or simply ignore views or themes they regard as aberrant. Vehement rejection is Stevens's line in his review of a BBC five-part crime series called *The Fall*, about a serial killer (*Why Does the BBC Think Violence against Women Is Sexy?* 10 June 2013): in his opening sentence he calls it 'the most repulsive drama ever broadcast on British TV'. There is no mention of any positive qualities in this series, which seems to have attracted Stevens's attention because of what he sees as its sadistic and demeaning representation of women and female sexuality: these, and not class, will be found to be among the prominent discussable themes in CS's 2013 TV reviewing.

4.4.5   Collocation as Reformulation

An explanation of the interpretive method being applied in this chapter to the PB and later to the CS sentences containing the word *class* is appropriate at this point. It can be discussed in relation to item 11 in Section 4.4, which carries the interesting presupposition that sometimes in 1971, rather than exchanging one class for another, one could avoid class altogether. Item 11 approves of the way the three main characters in the fictional drama *Dr Finlay's Casebook* speak in what Black calls *impeccable, classless Scots accent.* I interpret this as saying that if you have a *Scots accent* your speech, at least, can be and perhaps will be both *classless* and *impeccable.* In declaring that the three main characters of *Dr Finlay's Casebook* deliver everything in *impeccable, classless Scots accent* (no indefinite article, for some reason), PB is not explicitly declaring that to speak in a Scots accent is to be classless or to speak classlessly. But his phrasing encourages the inference that to speak Scots is to speak classlessly. This covert claim works in *classless Scots accent* since (perhaps especially to Southern

Britons) that description does not seem immediately implausible. But if the reference had been to *a classless Oxford accent, a classless Dublin accent* or *a classless Brooklyn accent*, we would immediately question the writer's judgement (or ear).

This process of semantic association lies close to the heart of what makes collocation interesting. I suggest it applies quite generally in evaluative narrative journalism such as reviews, except where there are adjacent signals implying negation, irony or contrast. Thus, to give one example of the process: the collocational patterns of the kind noted here can be understood to be not only associating the two terms severally with a third one (e.g., a head noun denoting a referent) but also directly with each other. An accent can be Scots and it can be classless, as distinct and potentially contrastive qualities (*classless, but Scots; Scots, but classless*), but when we are told about *a classless Scots accent*, we are given some encouragement to think of 'classless Scots' as a unified quality comprising two attributes. There is an implying of a paraphrase, elaborative or reformulatory relationship between *Scots* and *classless* (and likewise, between *classless* and *impeccable*). Just that alternative condition would characterize such possible (wordier, it may be noted) but non-occurring versions as these:

> all [was spoken] in an impeccable but classless Scots accent
> all [was spoken] in an impeccable Scots but classless accent
> all [was spoken]in a Scots accent that was both classless and
>   impeccable

There are connections between my interpretive procedure and those set out in Teubert (2010), as the basis of his interpretative use of corpus evidence in discourse analysis (see also Dilts 2010, who reports research on semantic preference that found a strong tendency of collocating words to share or converge upon a unified meaning). For Teubert, the uncovering of the meanings of words and phrases in a given discourse is an hermeneutic (interpretive) process, relying principally on intertextuality and paraphrase. In both cases the varied co-texts that accompany the uses of a target phrase (such as *civilized world*) are examined to determine whether there is repetition with variation, conscious echoism, in the different occurrences (suggesting intertextuality) or whether the occurrences are free-standing instances and non-echoic (in which case each carries its own potentially distinct paraphrased meaning). In looking at the co-textual accompaniment of a selected phrase, Teubert calls paraphrastic those 'text segments that attempt to explain, affirm, modify, reject or merely elaborate on the discourse object corresponding to the expression in question' (Teubert 2010: 204). Later he summarises:

Meaning is what the entirety of the paraphrastic content available for a given lexical item, a phrase, a text segment or a full text within a given discourse (which may well be the discourse at large or a sample thereof) tells us ... Meaning is paraphrase, explicit paraphrase and paraphrastic content taken together. (2010: 207, 220)

In this study of PB and CS, there are few occasions of explicit paraphrase (such as equative sentences of the form *class is x*), but plentiful instances of what I am treating as disclosing paraphrastic content. Paraphrastic material taken from diverse sources will typically contain divergent, even contradictory material, but when all samples come from a single newspaper and even as here from a single author, considerable convergence can be expected. Not everything smoothly fits the epithets-as-paraphrastic principle proposed here. Whereas I have argued that classifiers and (especially) epithets often co-occur because they are mutually reinforcing, the collocation of *middle class* and *black* in item 17 runs somewhat counter to this (there was only a small African-Caribbean middle class in the United Kingdom in 1971: *black* didn't normally 'mean' *middle class* – or vice versa – at that time). The fact that, structurally, these are classifiers and in predicative position after the head-noun *girl*, rather than attributive and before it, may be a reflection of this atypicality. The wider context helps explain the phrasing here, the play under review being about an American girl, Lulie (no race is mentioned: we assume she is white, and an internet check for actress Barra Grant who played Lulie confirms this), who 'followed her coloured boyfriend to London to find that he'd been softened up by the genial tolerance of the place and was no longer the sinewy militant. Moreover he had a girl, middle class and black.' In other words, the context includes the bitter struggle for the recognition of African Americans' civil rights, seen by the playwright or by Black as in contrast with the 'genial tolerance' (of what, is not specified) supposedly to be found in London circa 1971.

The reader also needs to be alert to irony and humour, where this seems to be suggested. Thus in the observation about the Ogdens being the only family still 'defiantly working class' in upwardly mobile Coronation Street (item 33), Black adds 'and Hilda is pestering Stan to install a shower.' Taken at face value this implies that owning a shower unit in 1971, and not merely a bathtub, is strongly indicative of comfortable middle-class amenity, except that it is surely something of a joke, even though Black will not say how much of one.

4.4.6   Final Thoughts on Class in Black

The foregoing sections draw directly on the wordings in Black's columns, or the presuppositions of the wordings, in order to develop an account of his values and convictions, his ideology. There is little subjective or interpretive intervention on my part, beyond the selecting and marshalling of the textually given evidence.

While a few stories perhaps inevitably use *class* several times over (e.g., the stories on Peggy Seeger, Neville Smith's play *After a Lifetime* and the documentary *Excuse Me, Your Class Is Showing*), the word is quite widely dispersed, suggesting that it is a recurring consideration. In those stories where class is discussed at length, there is fairly consistent criticism of those judged to be making too much of it, and in particular of the idea that the working class suffer any disadvantage or exclusion. In his 4 February column (the review of *Excuse Me, Your Class Is Showing*, which appeared under the title *You Can Even Get by Now without a Rich Daddy*) Black declares that meritocracy is on the rise, and that '[t]he class structure is best dealt with either by ignoring it or **contentedly** accepting it' (emphasis added). The latter options – neither of which is congruent with Black's previous suggestion that class structure is giving way to a merit-based hierarchy – entail two different presuppositions. The first is that class can (in 1971) be ignored – but this is belied by all of Black's mentions of it in his columns, and his choosing to write about programmes where it is central. The second presupposes that it would be reasonable ('best') for those disadvantaged by class structure nevertheless *contentedly* to accept it and the disempowerment, hierarchy and exclusion it entails. In a similar way, women and black and minority-ethnicity people were once advised by some voices in public life to ignore or quietly accept gender- or race-based unequal treatment. As for Black's counsel of downplaying class conscious- ness, it is evident that he is principally thinking of this as a coping strategy not for the working classes, but for the middle classes – as evidenced by his best exemplar of someone who has 'totally rejected class' (item 8): the successful pop musician Mike d'Abo (educ. Harrow and Cambridge). There is no question, in Black's world-view which unembarrassedly regards middle-class life as preferable to working-class, of someone as middle-class as d'Abo needing to 'climb out' of his class (in the way that working-class Edward Heath was represented as having to, strug- glingly). Only the upper classes can 'reject' their class and (some of) its advantages, just as 'rejecting' race and gender privileges is only open to the societally advantaged: white males. What remains unmentioned, as if unthinkable, is the idea of a whole society rejecting class through its democratic institutions, including its tax arrangements and a fully demo- cratised educational system.

4.5   Class and Other Values in Christopher Stevens, 2013

While the shorter PB corpus has thirty-five relevant uses of the *class* mor- pheme, the CS corpus has just fourteen instances of *class* in the relevant sense (most of its thirty-eight uses carry other meanings, including fifteen uses of *classic*). Thus mentions of *class* as a social category comprise only 0.02% of the CS corpus, less than one-third of PB's counterpart frequency, which is 0.07%. As for the other identifier terms (all forms) briefly computed earlier for the PB corpus, the frequencies in the CS corpus are as follows: *race* (2), *gender* (3), *ethnic* (0), *religion* (2), *age* (27). Therefore with the interesting exception of *age* (*aged, middle-aged*, etc.), these terms are neither more nor less prominent than in PB.

While *sex* was present in PB (32 instances), as expected it is much more prominent in the CS (71 instances, not including the proper name *Sex Pistols*). On the evidence so far presented we might surmise that where Black frequently ponders class concerns as explored in the 1971 programmes he watched, these are far less salient in Stevens, who dwells more on the sexual concerns he finds in the 2013 programmes. What might be the implications of this? Is it too speculative to suggest some shift of attention, over the years, away from 'struggle' of a social and economic nature and towards 'pleasure' (and perhaps prurience, or gossip) of a more personal or individualised kind? This was suggested of American television at least, as long ago as 1985 in Neil Postman's *Amusing Ourselves to Death*, which argued that network TV was increasingly designed as a 'self-medication' and commodification which satisfies us as consumers while dismantling our sense of ourselves as responsible citizens. An interest in other people's sex lives is removed from the realities of wealth inequality in ways that an interest in other people's comparative socio-economic status is not.

Here are the fourteen relevant uses of *class* in the CS corpus, in their graphological-sentence contexts. While three stories contain two instances each, the remaining eight uses are in a further eight stories, so there is a reasonable dispersion in this small sample.

1. Thomas Barrow again, holding forth on **class** injustice: 'I get fed up seeing ...' (a) How our lot always get shafted'; (b) How it's always the same old, same old'; (c) How it's the rich what gets the pleasure and the poor what gets the blame' [quiz item about anachronisms in the *Downton Abbey* script, 6 May 2013]
2. Such accurate social and **class** satire was the joy of Clarke's scripts. [nostalgic appreciation of Roy Clarke's 1970s–1980s sitcom *Open All Hours*, 9 September 2013]
3. South Africa's **class** divisions are vast. [programme about a group of South Africans, whose lives have been traced every seven years since 1992, 12 May 2013]
4. When she was introduced to Matthew's mother, she uttered a classic line that defined the chasm she hoped to maintain between the **classes**. [*Downton Abbey* review, 27 December 2012]

5. In the Seventies we had *Upstairs Downstairs*, the double story of two **classes** in one house, aristocracy and servants. [item on the top 50 TV shows of all time, 19 April 2013]

6. The working-**class** people in South-East London and Kent, pictured here, had just survived six years of war and night-time air raids. [background to *Call the Midwife!* 4 February 2013]

7. How could a soap opera about an ordinary British working-**class** street have blundered so far from its origins? [critical review of *Coronation Street*, 20 August 2013]

8. Nearly half of working-**class** viewers watched for four hours a night – a level gauged by sociologists to be 'addictive viewing'. [book review by Stevens of Joe Moran's *Armchair Nation: An Intimate History of Britain in Front of the TV*, 20 August 2013]

9. Played by emerging heart-throb Dan Stevens, his Manchester lawyer character was the symbol of a rising 1920s middle-**class**, bridging the old divisions of aristocracy and servants. [*Downton Abbey* review, 27 December 2012]

10. 'I have a big, healthy affinity for the middle **class** and the blue-collar, and I don't like the way the government is treating them.' [quotation from US actor James Gandolfini, in obituary/appreciation, 21 June 2013]

11. Born in 1946, he never felt he belonged among his upper-**class** school-fellows. [profile of Poirot actor David Suchet, 9 November 2013]

12. He also thinks we should feel sympathy for Stephen Ward, the go-between who procured showgirls for upper-**class** sex parties at a Thameside stately home. [programme about Andrew Lloyd Webber and the 1963 Profumo scandal]

13. The **class** system has been turned inside out, unions have held the country to ransom and have been vanquished, the workplace has changed beyond recognition and women have won equal rights. [book review by Stevens of Joe Moran's *Armchair Nation: An Intimate History of Britain in Front of the TV*, 20 August 2013]

14. Though he rarely read crime novels, he sat down with a stack of Agatha Christie books, almost everything she ever wrote about this former Belgian police inspector who became the most celebrated private detective by appointment to the British upper **classes**. [profile of Poirot actor David Suchet, 9 November 2013]

4.5.1   *Working-Classness and Middle-Classness in Stevens*

What do these fourteen items suggest Stevens thinks about class and its significance in 2013 Britain? Taking them in order they imply that *class injustice* (item 1) existed at the time depicted in the *Downton Abbey* serial

(1910–1920), although the mention of it in a gently mocking quiz question, attributed to a particular speaker said to be *holding forth again* (with its implication of tiresome haranguing of addressees), all suggest irony or qualified assent even to this historical claim. Item 2 presupposes that at an earlier time at least there were class practices and pretensions worthy of satirical mockery. Item 3 implies that the United Kingdom is unlike South Africa (where the class divisions are *vast*) even though formerly, at fictional Downton Abbey, there was a *chasm* between the landed gentry and the upper-middle professional class (item 4). But considering items 1, 2 and 3 together, notwithstanding differences of time and place, a picture emerges of British class divisions of the past (so different from the vast ones of South Africa) as something to be observed and laughed at, rather than as a current problem to be addressed. A seemingly alternative typology of class (item 5, also 9) focusses chiefly on the aristocracy and their servants. But item 9 somewhat questionably suggests that the division between aristocrats and servants can be *bridged* in some cases, for example, by someone who is a lawyer, from Manchester, rising, and a heart-throb (this claim is confused, however, since the Dan Stevens character is actually only bridging the middle- to upper-class *chasm* mentioned in item 4).

Working-classness was a property of some of the people in London and the South-East who survived the Second World War (item 6), but it is or was also a property of *streets* (item 7), and there is something *ordinary* and *British* about such working-class streets. A search for either *working(-)class* or *middle(-)class* followed by either *road* or *street* in the 98 million word BNC corpus yields no matches other than four, for *working(-)class street*. The same searches in the CQPWeb Bank of English found five uses of *working-class street* and two of *middle-class street*. But it was not just certain thoroughfares, ordinary British streets, that projected working-classness. Some of the people watching television could be classified as working-class – there was such a thing as the *working-class viewer* (item 8) in the period that Moran's book discusses, and half of these watched far too much TV (they were addicts), a debility not reportedly affecting viewers from other classes. As for item 10, this chiefly reminds us that the United States is another country, where assumptions are different; for James Gandolfini there is no contradiction between *middle class and blue-collar* (implicitly co-referential).

Item 11 reports a different kind of near-contradiction. It describes actor David Suchet as a person who attended an independent fee-paying school filled with upper-class pupils (it is hinted that schools, as well as their pupils, can be upper-class) but who claims not to have *belonged* with those schoolfellows: he was among them but not of them. This outsiderhood may have made it all the more useful that the profiled actor read all of Agatha Christie's Poirot books, about the fictional detective who acts *by appointment to the British upper classes* (item 14), now understood to be plural. Readers of the quoted phrase are expected to recognize the echo of a phrase about elite, and sometimes secret, service to a court or monarchy, reinforcing the idea that anything to do with *the British upper classes* entails exclusivity. Just as schools and private detectives could be upper class or not, so could *sex parties* (item 12), and their upper-classness might be evidenced in part by a *stately home* venue and the presence of *showgirls*.

Two important things emerge from the small set of *class* mentions in the CS corpus. First, the scant references to the *working class* (just three, making it no more frequent in the CS corpus than *mother-in-law* or *Ibiza*, compared with sixteen mentions in PB). Second, the emphasis on class is mentionable only in relation to Britain's past, but not its present.

4.5.2   'The Past 60 Years ...'

Item 13 of *class* in CS is arguably the most revealing of all, particularly when considered not just in its framing sentence but as part of the entire paragraph in which it sits:

The past 60 years have seen the greatest social upheaval in Britain's history. The class system has been turned inside out, unions have held the country to ransom and have been vanquished, the workplace has changed beyond recognition and women have won equal rights. Same-sex marriages and single-parent families are now the norm.

Here is a social history of Britain since 1963 in just four lines – one version, a partial history. The shaping influence on readers of the *Daily Mail* of just such compact histories, sufficiently repeated, could be considerable; in time, Stevens's narrative(s) could become his readers'.

And yet we must also remember that Stevens is not a political scientist but a journalist, aiming to entertain a diverse readership. Thus his final claim, that single-sex marriages and single-parent families 'are now the norm', clearly absurd if interpreted literally, is better understood as a loosely rhetorical way of saying that these situations are now widely accepted, rather than seen as illegal and shameful, respectively, as they mostly were in Britain circa 1963. The rhetorical looseness may also hint at the speaker's covert antipathy: the use of *is/are now the norm* to refer as here to changed socio-cultural practices (as distinct from more neutral reference to new technological or material resources) usually implies that for the speaker/writer the practice may be legal but is still unwelcome or regrettable.

Similarly rhetorical is the claim that more social upheaval has happened in the last sixty years than ever before. These having been noted, Stevens's metaphors, constructions and word choices in the reproduced paragraph invite several comments.

First, the clause *The past 60 years have seen the greatest social upheaval* is a classic 'ideational metaphor' in Hallidayan terms (i.e., a construction that is overtly expressed as one kind of process – here, a mental one of seeing – but underlyingly entailing a different kind – here, a material one about unnamed people changing social relations, with the sixty-year time span being a circumstantial adjunct). Indeed essentially the same construction is one of Halliday's textbook examples (Halliday & Matthiessen 2014: 717). Both Subject and Object, or Senser and Phenomenon in semantic terms, are vague nominalisations that avoid specifying human actors and affected parties. The adopted wording puts the passage of time itself in subject/agentive position, rather than any human groups or historical forces. And even if done by people rather than by the past sixty years, 'seeing' is a significantly more passive process, a powerless witnessing, than a material process such as 'causing' or 'achieving'.

Second, in *The class system has been turned inside out*, the precise meaning of the metaphor of 'turning inside out' is obscure (more so than 'turned upside down'), and possibly strategically so. The source may be football match commentary, where a skilful attacking player who flummoxes the defender is said to 'turn them inside out'. It implies fundamental change to the class system but does not specify its nature.

Third, *upheaval* (in the first sentence) always has a negative semantic prosody: 'an upheaval is a big change which causes a lot of trouble, confusion, and worry' (*Collins Cobuild Advanced Learners Dictionary*, p. 1603). So beyond saying that recent years 'saw' great social change, Stevens is expressing the view that these sixty years of social change have been far from an unqualifiedly good thing.

Fourth, regarding the phrase *Unions have held the country to ransom and have been vanquished*, a narrative in which specified agents *hold to ransom* but are also *vanquished* would appear to be self-contradicting. But perhaps these predicates are tacitly time specific, the alleged ransoming occurring in the 1970s and the alleged vanquishing occurring in the 1980s. Again Stevens's evaluation is clear, since holding anyone to ransom is by definition criminal, and *vanquished* associates the victor with heroism and moral justification. We are not told who vanquished the unions, but there is a suitable textually adjacent candidate, which readers may interpret as implied: the unions have been vanquished by *the country*. This would only reinforce a simple opposition expressed in the first clause – the unions versus the country – as if these were well-defined and mutually exclusive groups (whatever 'the country' denotes, it does not include the unions). There is a danger, in the interpretation of this paragraph, that the highly questionable separation of 'the country' from 'the unions' will be extended, as a cancellable presupposition, to the other large groups named in the paragraph, as if they too are separately named here because they are quite separate groupings with no overlap: unions, women, same-sex marriages and single-parent families. Those most seriously misrepresented by such a faulty classificatory extension are women, if they are interpreted as being separate from rather than instrumental within trade unions, same-sex marriages and single-parent families.

Finally, the phrase *the workplace has changed beyond recognition* is a further highly condensed formulation, where *workplace* is a stock metonym, not to be taken literally but rather alluding to all kinds of working conditions (hours, rest times, paid holiday leave, maternity leave, sick leave, pension, work injury compensation, outlawing of sex and race discrimination in hiring and promotion, TUPE rules, etc.). And *beyond recognition* logically cannot be literally true either. But the most important effect stems from the sentence's verb, *change*, used here in a one-participant structure of the kind some linguists call 'ergative', to distinguish it from commoner transitive uses of verbs which have Active and Passive counterparts (*I changed the arrangement* / *The arrangement was changed (by me)*). In the 'ergative' use of *change*, an underlyingly transitive process (X changed Y) is recast with the affected or theme/medium participant in Subject position, and mention of any agent or causer (the X) is completely elided – to the point that it cannot be reintroduced grammatically: for example, *The arrangement changed* (see also the discussion of the ergative verb *change* in Chapter 5 on *Luddite/s*). Thus for the purposes of concealing agency or initiating causes, ergative constructions are much more effective than agentless passives. In the case of workplace change, Stevens has decided it is either inappropriate or unnecessary to specify who caused the radical changes, implying that in relation to this part of British history it is more important to note the change than to draw attention to who or what (but behind most *what*s there is a *who*) brought it about. Given the space pressures in journalism, the wording is defensible; but it is often interpreted as saying 'it just happened', things change, the world moves inexorably on, propelled by forces far beyond human control, and there is no alternative to our making the best of changed circumstances. It didn't just happen, however; the workplace changed because employers and employees adopted changed terms and conditions of work and reward, including new technology, and none of this happened spontaneously or without agentive effort. Stevens's ergative construction means that no causers of change need be mentioned at this point, although one key agent of workplace change has already been named in this typographical sentence, albeit only to be shamed: trade unions. In short, *the workplace has changed beyond recognition* tells the story in a way that avoids crediting the unions or any other agency with effecting this change.

4.6   *Equal* and *Fair* in CS and PB

The close reading of *class* sentences in the CS corpus highlights how peripheral the word and concept is to the 2013 reviews compared with those forty years earlier. And while the numerous engagements with the topic in PB relate to representations of class around 1971, the mentions in CS nearly all entail a harking back to a much earlier period, usually fictionalised, such as the *Downton Abbey* soap opera set in the 1910s, the 1920s and 1930s of Hercule Poirot or the 1950s of *Call the Midwife!* There is no use of the word *class* in relation to contemporary Britain at all in the CS corpus: the two contemporary uses relate to South Africa and the United States, respectively. This could be because class and class-based inequality do not exist in contemporary Britain, or if they do, are no longer judged by programme makers to be worth discussing. And yet other forms of inequality (e.g., those rooted in perceived differences of sex, gender, sexuality, race, religion or physical or mental ability) have mostly reduced over the years since 1971 without ceasing to be addressed in television programmes and newspaper reviews of these. Besides, economic inequality in Britain – the essential underpinning of class – has not lessened but increased across the past forty years.

Are the Stevens stories and TV programmes on which they comment addressing this inequality but using some other vocabulary than that of *class*? The answer seems to be no, and that instead, intimate interpersonal relations, especially sex, have taken centre stage in the 2013 TV reviews to a far greater extent than in 1971. One small index of this is what happens when a search of the CS corpus to find all the uses of words such as *equal, equality, unequal, inequality* and *(un)fair* is undertaken. This uncovers no instances of *unequal* or *inequality*, and just four occurrences of *equal*, only one of which carries the 'fairness, parity' sense and comes in the paragraph discussed in Section 4.5.2 (*women have won equal rights*). The single use of *equality* concerns sexual equality in the context of satirical fiction – and in a highly questionable way. Finally, *(un)fair*: while twenty-five instances of the string *fair* are detected, on closer inspection they are found mostly to occur within the word *affair*, as many as eight of which are of the sexual rather than the financial or current type: *an affair with one of his tutors, The affair with Scott, The on-off affair between . . ., A lesbian affair, an affair with Valladolid, an early love affair, the love affairs, carrying on a brazen affair.*

Again a contrast with the frequencies and uses of these items in the PB corpus is apparent. In PB, there are thirteen instances of *equal(s/ly)* – mostly nothing to do with socio-economic equality of course, but including this sentence in the course of a review of a programme about women's pay: *Equal pay for equal work and bigger homes where more families could live among communal possessions.* PB also has twenty-five instances of *fair (affair, unfairness, fairly*, etc.), mostly in the bi-gram *current affairs* or the degree word *fairly*. There are only two mentions of sexual *affairs,* plus Elizabeth I's *odd affair* with Robert Dudley. Most notable is a use of the negated form in a description of the harsh treatment of striking workers in a docudrama based on the (real) Pilkington glassworks strike: *It* [the treatment] *was of course 'unfair',* Black writes.

4.7   *Coronation Street, Sex* and *Race*, Then and Now

Despite the differences, there are some intriguing shared concerns in the Black and Stevens reviews. One is the fact that, despite the forty-two years separating them, both critics upbraid *Coronation Street* for moving away from its work-ing-class roots, albeit in different ways. The clever headline of the PB story in July 1971 – *That Street Is More a Mews* – suggests there has been an unsettling rise in living standards for its characters. For Stevens, writing forty-two years later in August 2013 – *A Tide of Scandal, a Feuding Cast and the Political Correctness That Could Kill Off Corrie'* – the soap is at risk of disappearing altogether as its ratings slide, 'sunk by a combination of scandal, political correctness and dire plot lines'. The long-running soap (fifty-three years in 2013) has erred in dwelling on 'sordid and nasty' story lines rather than the simple homely fare of earlier years. Now it requires viewers 'to slog through yet another portrayal of racial angst or transgender anxieties'. Stevens also quotes the actress who once played Hilda Ogden as declaring that the number of homosexual characters on the show has become excessive. As for Black, in 1971 he mostly reports on the 'upgrading' of the street: 'This probably reflects the flattening out of the social alps and crevasses and the general rise in living standards in the real world, but there it undoubtedly is.' Much of his 22 July report on *Coronation Street* is about the narrowing of the class gap that once made the characters and their depicted neighbourhood unambiguously working class and restricted in material cultural terms. On 20 August 2013, Stevens's diagnosis is that collapse of the show's ratings (viewing figures were down to a third of a previous high) stems from story lines that focus on race, sex and gender conflicts which, purporting to speak for the general viewer, he finds extreme, clumsily handled or unengaging. As he concludes in a sentence which appears to have been worded with libel-averse lawyerly caution (the factive *aware that* undercut by the subsequent *is said to*), 'It's a chore [for viewers] to slog through yet another portrayal of racial angst or transgender anxieties, especially when you are aware that a festering atmosphere of factional friction and sexual slurs is said to poison the atmosphere backstage.' The implication is that race- or gender-based difficulties do not interest 'most viewers'. If, by contrast, class and economic differences do, they are not proposed by Stevens; rather his recommendation seems to be for a return to material that is camp, comic, exaggerated or melodramatic (in short, non-serious), along with moments of small human drama.

4.8   Key Semantic Domains in Black's and Stevens's Journalism: A Comparative Analysis

Using Wmatrix, and BNC British English 2006 or BNC Written as reference corpus (as appropriate), analyses of the PB and CD corpora were undertaken to identify their most frequent lexical items, their top keywords, their key (disproportionately frequent) parts of speech categories, and their high-frequency n-grams. A very few distinctive characteristics emerged, some of which seem most likely to be personal stylistic preferences of the two journalists, rather than having a deeper discursive significance.

For example, it emerges that Black makes frequent use of the phrase *a kind of* to preface and hedge a variety of evaluative judgements, an optional (structurally deletable) signalling that the judgement is admittedly approximate rather than precise while also implying an avoidance of absoluteness of judgement. Examples include *a kind of sympathy sprang up, a kind of nasal whinny, a kind of affectionate pity, a kind of moderation* and *a queer kind of double-think*. Such modalising hedges have been extensively studied for their wide evaluative potential; Davidse et al. (2013: 157) comment of similar examples in *The Times*: 'At face value, the qualifying string conveys that the description is only approximate, but its real rhetorical value is often the opposite, viz. that the categorization is carefully chosen and worded.' They also invite the addressee to engage in the process of specifying the sense; as Mauranen notes, perhaps deliberately using *a kind of* in her own formulation, 'What the uses of hedges in epistemic roles seem to have in common is a kind of openness' (Mauranen 1997: 122). Black's frequent use of *a kind of* is arguably indicative of his open-mindedness (and by implication the *Mail's* comparative open-mindedness at that time), his making of judgements but his tempering of them also, so as to invite the reader's response, in a way that is not present in the CS corpus forty-two years later.

In general, however, revealing trends (including the one just noted) are more likely to be found if priority is given neither to a word-based nor a parts-of-speech-based analysis of the two corpora, but a Wmatrix-enabled semantic analysis that might identify prominently contrasting semantic domains. (Semantic trends can then be cross-referenced with the keywords and parts-of-speech analyses, where useful.)

When the semantic domains in the PB corpus are computed against the BNC Written English sampler (using Wmatrix's set of UCREL semantic tags) the twenty-two domains listed in the left-hand column of Table 4.1 emerge as

Table 4.1 *Key Semtags in the PB and CS Corpora, in Order of Keyness, with Outliers Bolded*

Key Semtags in PB Corpus	Key Semtags in CS Corpus
The media: TV, radio and cinema (LL 817)	The media: TV, radio and cinema (LL 1716)
Drama, the theatre and show business (LL 483)	Drama, the theatre and show business (LL 1027)
Degree (LL 467)	**Personal names (LL 362)**
Alive	**Seem**
Pronouns	Pronouns
Light	Happy
Unethical G2.2-	Degree
Foolish	**Relationship: intimacy and sex**
Existing (LL 102)	Alive
Happy	Existing
People	Time: general
Evaluation: True A5.2+	Crime
Evaluation: Bad A5.1–	Violent/angry
Thought, belief X2.1	Light
Time: General	**Entertainment generally**
Failure	**Kin**
Personality traits	People
Violent/angry	Unethical
Negative	**Like**
Degree: Boosters	Foolish
Smoking and non-medical drugs	**Impolite**
Judgement of appearance: Ugly (LL 50.47)	**Music and related activities**
	Sad
	Other proper names
	Evaluation: Good
	Personality traits
	Darkness
	Emotional actions, states and processes
	The universe
	Unexpected
	Judgement of appearance: Ugly (LL 51.3)

Note: BNC Written Sampler is reference corpus

the most key categories, down to a still high log-likelihood of 50 (with some of the specific LL scores noted in parentheses). When the same calculation is done for the CS corpus, thirty-one domains are identified as the key ones (i.e., disproportionately prominent), again down to a LL of 50, and these are listed down the right-hand column of Table 4.1. In the table, those semantic domains identified as key in PB but not CS (there are seven of these), and conversely those that are key in CS but not in PB (there are sixteen of these), are high-lighted in bold, since they will be of chief interest in what follows.

Not all of these categories are equally ideologically significant, but it is reassuring that the two corpora do overlap extensively in terms of the most prominent semantic domains from which lexis is drawn, since this is some confirmation of generic commonality and of these discourses' genuine compar-ability. While it is unsurprising that the most key semantic domains in both corpora are 'The media' (*TV, film, television, documentary, radio* are the most frequently used words in this category) and 'Drama, the theatre and show business' (with *play, script, performance, producer* and *scene* the most fre-quent words), it is intriguing how many of the other key domains are also shared – including 'alive', 'light', 'unethical', 'foolish', 'existing' and 'happy'.

Turning to where the corpora differ in key semantic domains as noted in Table 4.1, just seven of the original twenty-two categories are highly key in Black but not so in Stevens, while sixteen of the thirty-one highly key domains in Stevens are absent from Black. These twenty-three domains can be regarded as highlighting semantic areas where the corpora differ most. But here too we must decide whether comparative presences and absences are all equally significant discursively. The lexical contents of each of the twenty-three semantic tagsets from the corpora are now briefly described and reviewed in note form, in order to help determine this significance and, given my research question, to direct attention to the most relevant tagsets (and their KWIC lines). The display options in Wmatrix make such an exercise straightforward. At a click I can view, as a list or in KWIC format, all 187 words in the CS corpus that are tagged semantically as expressing 'relationship: intimacy and sex'. The list view reports *love, sexual* and *gay* as the most prominent terms, comprising 75 of the 187 items, and – a necessary 'manual' check – there are no erroneous assignments to this semantic category among the 187 items.

The Seven Key Semtags Present in Peter Black, 1971 Only

1. Evaluation: True. Stems from high frequencies of *fact, truth, true* and *facts*: more precisely, *the fact (is) that, the truth is that, can(not) be true*, etc. These are a rhetorical staging of PB's declarations of what he judges to be truth, or the facts, which is not prominent in CS; they are an index of argument discourse used to emphasise a most important point.

2. Evaluation: Bad. (More specifically, classed as A.5.1– in the Table 4.1, words meaning 'superlatively bad'.) Few in number, but an index of PB's critical evaluations, using adjectives and nouns such as *worst, fatal, cata-strophe, disaster*.

3. Thought, belief. Probably significant: 375 uses of cognitive projecting verbs (*think, believe, thought, feel, felt*), nouns and adjectives. Plenty of *I (don't) think, some/others etc. think, I (can't) believe that* . . .

4. Failure. Less significant, since only sixty-nine items in all, twenty-one being *lost*, mostly as verb rather than adjective. Possibly reflective of PB's compassion for those who have lost something, failed at something or are coping with defeat.
5. Negative. 619 items, including 430 of *not or n't*: again, like 'failure', perhaps reflecting PB's attention to those who lack something.
6. Degree: Boosters. Of marginal significance; high use of *more, so, very, much, really* suggestive of more qualified evaluation, or discriminating or contrastive judgements, in PB than in CS
7. Smoking and non-medical drugs. Numerous mentions of *smoking, tobacco, smokers* . . .; these reflect PB's pronounced antipathy towards smoking, and concern at the health damage that in 1971 smoking was increasingly recognized as causing.

The Sixteen Key Semtags Present in Christopher Stevens, 2013 Only

1. Personal names: Significant. This keyness tallies with the prominence, among Parts of Speech categories in CS, of singular Noun Phrases. The LL keyness of 360 is very high, indicative of a pronounced focus on names (singular). These turn out to be television actors and celebrities of today or those who have recently died or the fictional characters they have played: *Chapman, Tom, Smith, Jerry, Miranda, David, Cleese, Joey, John, Lady Mary, Collins,* etc.
2. Seem. Not significant: a false high reading, caused by inclusion of *show(s)* in this category; when its uses here are overwhelmingly as a noun, synonymous with *programme*.
3. Relationship: intimacy and sex. A significant interest in the CS stories, reflected in high use of a range of nouns, verbs, and adjectives: *love, sexual, gay,* etc.
4. Crime. There are some false inclusions here also (e.g., *plot*, when it actually means 'story', not conspiracy), but this keyness reflects another prominent interest of the corpus. Frequent words are *crime, rape, suspect, gangster,* etc.
5. Entertainment generally: Significant. The most frequent items are *play/played* (mostly meaning 'act/ed the part of'), and this category reflects the corpus's focus, in fictional series, on actors and the characters they play rather than discussion of documentaries or factual programmes, where there would be no call for 'X plays Y' or 'Y is played by X' structures. Collocationally there is some interaction between this category and the 'Personal names' category, since a very frequent string is the following: 'Personal name (NP1) (BE) *played by* Personal name' [e.g., *Isobel Crawley (played by Penelope Wilton); Rev Paul Coates played by Arthur Darvill*; etc.].

6. Kin: Possibly significant, since this key domain reflects a far greater interest in *family, wife, father, son, mother, parents*, etc., than in Black or the BNC sample. We might read this emphasis on kin as relating to the more domestic and personal themes in CS, by comparison with PB. If kin/family implies a contrast with society or the wider world (as in Mrs Thatcher's comment in a 1987 interview that 'there's no such thing as society. There are individual men and women and there are families.'), then CS's turning towards discussing kin could be read as a turning away from commenting on society.

7. Like. Although this category (intended to denote 'love, affection') is a little unstable – the most frequent word, *like*, is here mostly in its irrelevant preposition or conjunction functions, rather than as a verb – the uses of *likes, love(d), fan, popular, enjoyed, applause* perhaps reflect CS's accent on positive things and approved things, by contrast with the keyness of 'Negative' and 'Failure' semantic tags in PB.

8. Impolite (adjectives and some nouns): *rude(ness), offensive, cheeky, bawdy, obscene* ... again reflective of the greater focus on interpersonal relations, intrafamilial or otherwise, rather than the clash of belief systems where 'rudeness' would be too slight or trivialising an evaluation.

9. Music and related activities: *music, songs, musical, opera, band, pop* ... the entertainment emphasis again, thus linked with domains 1 and 5.

10. Sad. This is quite a small sample; most of emotion terms – *suffered, sad, sadly, cry, grief* – are sometimes used formulaically, so probably insignificant.

11. Other proper names. Of minor significance: some of these names are simply those of television channels (*BBC2, ITV*, etc.), but others can be seen as an extension of the impulse to use personal names, domain 1 – an interest in the celebrity or commercial value of cult series, brands, titles, etc.

12. Evaluation: Good. (More specifically, classed as A.5.1+++, words meaning 'superlatively good'). Significant: the frequent words in this category are *best* (esp.), *greatest, brilliant* and *perfect*, and they arguably reflect the same broadly upbeat, positive tenor of CS that also underlies domain 7.

13. Darkness. A sample that is too small to be taken as significant or reliable.

14. Emotional actions, states and processes. cf 'Sad' (domain 10), with which this clearly overlaps, but likewise probably insignificant (and a small sample).

15. The universe. The phrase *the world* provides nearly half the 126 instances of this category, meaning 'situation, milieu'. Insignificant.

16. Unexpected. Again, too small a sample to be significant or reliable.

To achieve high semantic keyness in as many as sixteen domains suggests that the CS corpus focusses heavily on all those themes, whereas the PB corpus diverges markedly from the reference-corpus ordinary with respect to just a few domains. The glossing of the seven domains exclusive to Black suggests his columns emphasise what he believes to be the truth, or the facts, on diverse topics (formulations that lend themselves less easily to the celebrity profiles and entertainment reviews that CS offers). Alongside these 'categorical' judgements come very many subjective or modalised ones, using projecting cognitive verbs and Black himself as senser: *I think, believe, thought, felt*, etc. Because of all these projecting cognitive verbs, the Black discourse could strike the reader as reflective and critical, rather than simply descriptive. The overlap between Black's tags 2, 4 and 5, suggests some marked attention to failure, loss and unhappy outcomes, in ways which appear to contrast with the positive and upbeat emphasis in the CS corpus, reflected in the latter's key semtag domains 7 and 12. Where Stevens does touch on emotions and sad things, these seem to relate mostly to the personal or intimate, rather than some societal setback or frustration. But you have to get down to domain 12 to find an 'Evaluation' key semtag in Stevens, whereas the top two key semtags in Black are 'Evaluations'. In Black a representatively sharp contrast with the Stevens would be a sentence which included instantiations from the first three of the listed exclusive semtags [i.e., a sentence which combined Evaluation: True (e.g., *fact*), Evaluation: Bad (e.g., *worst*) and Thought, belief (e.g., *think, believe*)]. Here is one of the best exemplars I could find (using the Advanced Search facility for non-adjacent collocates in Antconc). It includes two of the first three exclusive semtags in PB, while *least* is an instance of 'Degree: Minimizer' semtag; the sentence comes from a review of a programme about fifty years of the Irish Republic:

Watching the seemingly inevitable curve of events as his programme had traced them, it was impossible not to **think** that the next huge **fact** is that partition will be ended; the huge question is how to do it with the **least** damage. [semtag exemplars in bold]

But it is the CS corpus that is the more semantically distinctive, with its preoccupation with television's celebrity performers, named individuals, its attention to sex and love, to crime and to family, but all these often in the context of performed entertainment (including music) with an emphasis on reporting on what was *enjoyed, brilliant* and *successful*. Sentences from the CS corpus that would most vividly show its difference from the PB corpus would report in enthusiastic terms on how two or three celebrated named actors played, with aplomb, characters who were family-related and/or sexually entangled, possibly in some way that involved rudeness or even crime. The closest exemplar I could find (again using Antconc's Advanced Search facility) is the following:

A lesbian **affair** between **Sophie Webster** and **Sian Powers, played by Sacha Parkinson**, has also been a regular fixture prompting one much-loved Corrie veteran to protest that there was too much emphasis on gay rights.

4.9   The Meanings of *Britain* and *the British* Then (in PB) and Now (in CS)

Since this study's focus is wealth inequality *in Britain*, it is worth exploring whether Britain and the British seem to be understood differently in the two corpora, judging by their uses of the words *Britain* and *the British*. Does Stevens tell a noticeably different story about Britain and the British from that told in 1971 by Black? Corpus evidence was gathered concerning *Britain* and *the British* in the two corpora. Partly to depart from the convention of always considering the PB data first, and partly because there are considerably more instances of *Britain* in the (admittedly slightly larger) CS corpus, the evidence in the Stevens corpus is discussed first.

There are forty-four occurrences of *Britain* in Stevens, and these have been extracted in their full sentential contexts and numbered chronologically; in the interests of brevity they are not reproduced here in their full sentential contexts, but the following discussion will reference these numbered instances. A first evident trend is that when Stevens mentions Britain, he is overwhelmingly talking about the past, or distant past. It is as if Britain's having a favourite sitcom, comedy duo or sitcom dogsbody was important then but is perhaps not so now. Congruent with this focus on the past, many of the clauses in which the word *Britain* occurs are also in the past tense.

There are several reminders of a 'bad' or 'failing' Britain in this remembered past. Back then, Britain was overtaken technologically (item 20); burdened by austerity but also bristling with violence (items 17 and 19); and characterized for twenty-five years by urban deprivation mitigated by district nurses and the NHS (item 5). It was distrustful of other countries (item 1) and ignorant of cranberries (item 7), 'compulsively' gripped by a political drama that seemed to chime with the era of political infighting at the close of the Thatcher era (items 8–10). But with half of adult Britain watching, we really were all in the living room together, and this 'created a communal feeling' (item 10). Britain was also in need of awakening in the taste-bud department (item 12) and with regard to homelessness and, arguably, visual explicitness (items 35 and 36: *Two years earlier, the drama* Cathy Come Home, *directed by Ken Loach, had woken Britain up to a homelessness crisis. But it was not until 1976, and the Roman epic I, Claudius, that nudity was shown. TV had come a long way in 20 years, and so had Britain.*) Perhaps British torpor stemmed from our 'addiction' to television (item 32: story title: *How Britain Got Hooked on the Gogglebox*).

These variegated glimpses are what *Britain* means, for Stevens, in 2013. It is somewhere with a chequered, often comical past – but then Britain is impliedly the home of 'classic comedy'. Most things were pretty grim back then (a vague era extending from the 1950s to the 1970s), when only very few TV personalities breached the codes of deference and reserve, and when they did (item 37), *[t]hat candour and recklessness were a revelation in stuffy, know-your-place Britain*). As for Britain in the present, it is fed up with mollycoddling by the state or its agencies (item 2); it is blessed with Ant and Dec and their talent and celebrity shows (item 11), and it is a good place for an actor to go on 'a demo' (item 22) – note the trivialising characterisation of this political activism; beyond these, according to the CS reviews, little more needs to be said about it.

As for *the British* in CS, there are thirty-seven occurrences of this, mostly describing properties that the British have, rather than who or what they are, or do. Roughly in order of mention in 2013, they report that the British have many TV series; bad behaviour; formerly an empire; much-loved TV dramas, crime and action series and sitcoms. The British also have pop music, a TV history, sitcom stars, actors, films, a Bake-Off programme (several mentions), traditions such as that Dr Who must be male, institutions such as the law and academia, TV audiences, behaviour influenced by TV, upper classes, scapegoats and formerly distinguished department stores like Liberty. Almost the only thing in the corpus that *the British* do is love anarchic humour. In CS the British are represented as neither doing much nor much done to.

Back in 1971 in the PB corpus, a scant nineteen mentions of *Britain* occur (thus fewer than half the CS total). These contrast with the ones in CS in several respects. To begin with and despite the lower number, a much wider range of topics is involved, with much less focus on Britain in the past and much less talk of Britain as if it were itself of the past. The word is more frequently used in discussion of serious topics than in CS; for example, defence, bankruptcy, poverty, permissiveness, and Irish nationalism. There are also some implications that the Britain of the present day (i.e., 1971) has flaws and weaknesses [e.g., in relation to sexual difference and tolerance (item 2) and cuisine or diet (item 9)] including its hostile treatment of its star celebrities (item 13) – a clear contrast with the admiration of their 2013 counterparts in CS. PB noticeably often mentions *Britain* in the context of foreigners or foreign countries, to focus on some phenomenon or other which is not always to the home country's credit. And items 5–7, taken from a review of a programme about the fee-charging Chetham's School of Music, link *Britain* with the political question of how to make the best musical education available to the most talented youngsters, without costs becoming a barrier.

What about *the British* in PB in 1971? There are thirty-five mentions, thus a similar frequency to that in CS. With regard to what the British are or have, the stories report that the British had an occupation (of Ireland), public opinion, troops and (military) services in the Second World War. The British are also said to have noise, a railway system and formerly propaganda; they also have the BBC, a sea coast, a government, a branch of women's lib, a camera (TV documentary powers), TV viewers, a long history and a point of view (e.g., of Albania) that contrasts with that of others (e.g., the Swiss). As to what they 'are', the British are fascinated by the last wilderness, are no longer sure Rhodes was a hero and are fascinated by class distinctions; they also realise they were deceived on some occasion. There is some 'doing' by the British in the PB columns: they sank to a low level of anti-German hatred during World War I and then disbelieved the truth; they sometimes cannot stand the Swiss; they worry about smoking; they accept financial comparisons but don't really believe them and they might send up sighs of relief if tobacco marketing was de-glamorized. On only two occasions in the PB corpus, both interestingly related to the truth of things, are they clearly Affected/Recipient (the 'done to') of a process: they received anti-German propaganda in World War I, and were lied about (on some occasion).

While frequencies for *British* are similar in PB and CS, there is much less mention of *Britain* in the earlier corpus. The high frequency of *Britain* in CS (the 0.07% frequency in CS compares with a 0.03% frequency in the BE2006 corpus, and one as low as 0.0002% in the much larger Bank of English) is coupled with a narrow focus on the past and on entertainment past and present. By contrast in 1971, Black is frequently alluding to present-day concerns when those words are mentioned. Black writes about present-day Britain and the British seemingly on the assumption that important, review-worthy TV programmes ought to reflect on the state of the nation and its citizens, their values and identity. His reviews continue the conversation about these concerns, implicitly aware that change (social, political, attitudinal) is possible.

4.10   Conclusion

A mass of details have surfaced in the course of the analyses discussed in this chapter, but I believe some headline trends can be identified. Peter Black emerges as in many respects – not all – a liberal progressive, albeit in favour of state intervention against antisocial or self-destructive behaviour. He is critical of certain kinds of materialistic progress (e.g., of building more airports at the loss of large tracts of countryside), clearly concerned about the societal and health damage caused by alcoholism and smoking and the latter's recently established link with lung cancer, hostile to knee-jerk racism and anti-immigration attitudes and mostly tolerant of diverse sexual orientations. He is prescient and passionate in his denunciation of intensive farming ('Cheap food is being produced at an ever increasing cost to the animals, by processes that are a blasphemy against the creation of life by any god you care to name',

25 March 1971). And he is no fan of Rupert Murdoch. In his column on 20 April, reviewing a play about an unpleasant Welsh business tycoon who aims to buy his way into Fleet St, Black remarks that 'it would have been better if they'd made [him] an Australian'.

For PB, class has undoubtedly been important, and middle class life is clearly represented as more desirable than working class life, in terms of material comforts, education and articulacy. But being one of the working class is 'not their fault', Black recognizes, and is rather a consequence of the cards life has dealt them; indeed, class distinctions are often distasteful. Furthermore, nowadays (1971) the talented can 'climb out', and into the middle-class. Snobbery and inverted snobbery are both to be deplored. Class is still important enough for several stories to be centrally about it, but in some respects Black treats class as *passé*. There is plenty of evidence that he is conflicted: on some occasions he half believes class 'no longer matters' or that the barriers are coming down; on other occasions he treats it as a persistent social reality in modern Britain. He shows no sympathy for the more militant forms of class struggle, but over and over again his phrasings reflect an awareness that differences and contrasting identities (of class, race, politics, sexuality and nationality, among others) are real, merit recognition and need sensitive renegotiation. His columns become a forum in which some of these tensions, differences and perceived and real inequalities are reflected upon, in an inclusive and undogmatic way.

When we turn to the CS columns, the conversation is along different lines and offers a different kind of interest and entertainment. It is chiefly about *Downton Abbey* and *Poirot* (in a romanticised past) or *Strictly, Bake Off* and *I'm a Celebrity* (in the talent shows of the present). The latter programmes invite discussion as successful televisual contests aimed at entertaining us, perhaps inspiring us (to cook, dance and bivouac, at least), and bringing us to a state of emotional empathy, as witnesses (sometimes judges, with a vote) to all the striving competitors who are baking, dancing, surviving on toasted grubs in the jungle, answering the jackpot-winning quiz question or otherwise undergoing some post-modern *rite de passage* within the televisual village. The key themes are entertainment, celebrity, glamour, fantasy, fairytale fame and rewards. Television's examination of ordinary people's lives – insofar as CS is a guide – has shrunk markedly.

In CS in the *Daily Mail* of 2013, class has disappeared from the discursive agenda of contemporary Britain, like black-and-white film, and with it any extended attention to the wealth and income inequality, and the material, social and educational disadvantages, with which it is bound up. It is only mentioned in relation to other countries, or to Britain in the past. Nor is there some other vocabulary with which social and wealth inequality is discussed. Union-powered class strife is gone, we are assured, and women have equal rights.

If anything, the upheaval and new norms (same-sex marriages, etc.) have taken us too far. Nor is there mention of the United Kingdom in 2013 as meritocratic (as there was in PB) or, generally, a land of equal opportunity for all. We might conclude that these things now go without saying, or we might wonder whether these ideas are so far from the reality for a significant number of readers that it would be inappropriate and 'demoralising' to mention them. In the CS reviews, celebrity performers are a major focus of attention. These are profiled via a prototypical narrative that is not far removed from the formulaic narrative structure of recurring basic stages of plot that Propp famously identified in the Russian folk tale (Propp 1971 [1928]). In Stevens's TV celebrity profiles, we are often told first of their wayward youth or a failing early career; then comes an addiction or a period of depression or low self-esteem; later and fortuitously there is a 'breakthrough' to huge fame, wealth and acclaim. The celebrities mostly come from comfortable or ambitious families, rarely emerging from 'nowhere'.

As the foregoing analyses have confirmed, it would be hard to read Black's columns in 1971 without thinking from time to time about the differences of life chances that followed from differences of economic background, and the complex interaction of characteristics contributing to that economic standing: your class, gender, race, age, nationality, education, talents and personality, to name just some. But in 2013 it would be hard to read Stevens's columns and turn your thoughts to contemporary wealth inequalities and the differences with which they are bound up (education, housing, race, diet) because – if these reviews are our guide – mostly the viewers' attention (hence the readers' also) is being turned away from those everyday matters and towards the jungle, the dance floor, the *Bake Off* kitchen, the sports arena, the talent show studio and the fictional landed gentry of *Downton Abbey* circa 1915. In short, a range of fantasy or fictional screens, stages and masques, where viewers can marvel at elite, gifted or privileged individuals doing things in extreme or exceptional ways, and enjoy the often escapist spectacle.

But why *should* the *Daily Mail* devote space to the deeper socio-political questions that Peter Black once addressed, least of all in its television reviews, when it is fighting for advertising revenue in a changed and ever more competitive marketplace for news and journalism? This objection would carry more weight were it not for the fact that the *Mail* does emphatically continue to see itself as a political campaigning agency, as quick as any broadsheet to expose and denounce any political action or inaction that it claims to be harmful to its readers' and the nation's interests.

Methodologically the chapter has presented a variety of corpus-analytic methods by which to compare and contrast two small corpora, predicted to be indirectly revealing of a shifting zeitgeist in relation to British wealth inequality. Are these two journalists authoritative and fairly representative of the *Mail* in those two years? I believe these single-author corpora may have been more influential on ordinary *Mail* readers than similar quantities of editorial comment (composed by diverse authors). It is more important that Black and Stevens have been influential (on readers) than that they have been 'representative' (of the newspaper); my interest is less in profiling the *Mail* itself than in exploring the possible ideological effects of its discourses on its readers.

If these *Daily Mail* TV reviews can be regarded as in some ways symptomatic and representative of changes in the national newspapers' values and norms, they are still only a small sampling of an immense shift. The persuasive function of the changed ways of representing economic inequality, as normal, inevitable and reasonable, is deeply embedded and widely dispersed, developed gradually over many years. As a result, to readers themselves the feeling of being persuaded to consent to something is imperceptible; they do not feel they are being 'persuaded' and are therefore not aware that they are consenting to anything. Rather they believe they are accepting the way things are. Collectively those in a position to determine the newspapers' content and to control its 'mirroring' function have managed the shift to a discourse more critical of restraints on economic inequality and more accepting of steep inequality.

5   Forty-Five Years of *Luddite* Behaviour

5.1   Ned Ludd and Robin Hood

Luddite/s, in its non-jokey contemporary meaning, has long been popular with journalists as a negative evaluation of workers judged to be unreasonably resistant to embracing new technologies and the changed working practices that arise as a consequence. Has this use of *Luddite/s* in the press modulated over the past forty-five years, alongside shifts in those papers' thinking about the acceptability of inequality? This chapter is linked to the one that follows, which looks at patterns of use of the name *Robin Hood* in political and economic contexts in the selected newspapers. Both names are moderately frequent items in *The Times* and the *Daily Mail* across the decades of interest, but they are more than moderately significant socio-political keywords. Each has a clear general narrative associated with it, even if the details an interpreter invokes may vary from one context to the next. Moreover Ned Ludd and Robin Hood are more linked in the collective conscious than is sometimes recognised.

> Chant no more your old rhymes about old Robin Hood
> His feats I but little admire
> I will sing the Atchievements of General Ludd
> Now the Hero of Nottinghamshire
>
> (from 'General Ludd's Triumph' in E.P. Thompson
> *The Making of the English Working Class*, p. 598)

The Luddite story contrasts with that of Robin Hood in several respects, but there are convergences too. Robin Hood flourished in medieval and feudal England, whereas Ned Ludd emerged in the era of industrialisation and the rise of factories. Both acted against those with power (old power in one case, new power in the other), adopting unlawful means for the alleviation of hardship. This acting in extremity and out of necessity was widely felt, by recipients of the Robin Hood story, to justify Robin's violent robberies. But opinion as to whether Luddite damage and violence had moral justification was quite mixed at the time and has remained so since. The balance of sentiment has been condemnatory: the Luddites 'went too far', Robin didn't. Criminal acts were done in both their names, but the law itself in both eras was in some respects arguably inadequate or worse: a framework for injustice or tyranny. The law was part of the problem, in need of wholesale reform, lacking the intrinsic humane authority to command the consent of the people so governed. If actions in modern Britain are severally interpreted as Luddite or Robin Hood–style activity, similarly the disturbing possibility is raised (in more minds when the action is called *Robin Hood–like* than *Luddite*) that the unfitness of extant legal arrangements justifies extra-legal action.

Several further characteristics make Robin Hood and Ned Ludd discursively relevant and comparable. Both are quintessentially English, more narrowly than British: it is doubtful that Ned Ludd and Robin Hood resonate with the Scots, for example, who have their own semi-mythical heroes such as William Wallace and Robert the Bruce. A newspaper which describes a contemporary political leader as either a *Luddite* or a *Robin Hood* is evoking an imaginary, mythical England which – while not quite timeless – still tends to be vaguely placed temporally and spatially: a pre-modern England of dark nights and dark woods, where justice required heroic direct action because the powers of law and order were wielded by oppressive barons or mill owners, taking from the poor (or those of modest means) to benefit themselves, the rich. But neither rebellious group is perceived as advocating mass revolution, in which the poor or disenfranchised permanently secure better conditions.

Alongside the similarities in our modern Hood and Ludd cultural scripts are several differences; for example, in most people's Robin Hood script the hero escaped, but the Luddites were caught and punished severely. Another difference is that Robin Hood and his merry men inhabited a romantic world in which the poor and oppressed received justice thanks to the nearly magical emergence of a warrior-hero who fought the cruel sheriff and barons selflessly and 'merrily'. The Luddites, however, were craftsmen whose skills were abruptly devalued by the adoption of the recently invented weaving machines (gig mills and shearing frames). Rather than wait for a hero-leader to emerge (notwithstanding the probably mythical Ned Ludd), they formed a secret brotherhood for the protection of customary employment conditions. Although we know Robin Hood to be as fictional as Ned Ludd, and Robin's merry men equally so, the Luddites were not. Robin Hood still connotes romance, manly heroism and fearless bravery, so that a coastal feature, an airport and numerous streets happily adopt his name, but there is no Ned Ludd Parkway, let alone a Luddite Airport.

Names such as *Robin Hood* and *Luddite* are interesting too in terms of their place in the lexicon of modern English. On the continuum that runs from grammatical to lexical items, these names carry evaluative connotations in excess of many other names, without being sharply delimited in sense (as might apply to *Marxist* or *Thatcherite* or *Blairite*, for example). Like *Elizabeth I* and

Victoria, they are personal names that are unlikely to disappear from British English, whereas *Gladstonian, Churchillian, Chaplinesque* and even *Marxist* could conceivably dwindle in frequency of use and familiarity to ordinary speakers. Because both names are strongly associated with a 'folk' and direct action challenge to the unfairness of the powerful and wealthy, their use in newspapers, with their own evolving narrative about the acceptability of wealth inequality, is of considerable interest.

5.2   The Luddites

Who, 'in history', were the Luddites and Ned Ludd? Some have suggested that strictly speaking they never existed, in the sense that possibly no group self-identified as *Luddites*. But there were groups of men who worked in the weaving trade mostly, some of whom named themselves followers of 'Ned Ludd' and, importantly, were so named by the press, politicians and social commentators in the early nineteenth century in the industrialising England of the Midlands and the North. They protested against the mechanisation of cloth-making factories (in 1811–12 especially, but there were outbursts of machine breaking decades earlier and decades later too), sometimes by means of damaging and disabling the new machinery that mill owners had invested in, dispensing with much skilled labour as a consequence. It is undeniable that the adoption of the new machines, often sited in new work-places called factories, led to the unemployment and impoverishment of large numbers of skilled workers. What is more open to debate is the morality of those proprietors who abruptly discarded their workers (no organisations resembling modern trade unions were legal in those days), and the morality of the sometimes violent reactions of the workers affected. So the Luddites can be characterised in many different ways: as a resistance movement, machine breakers, anti-capitalists, anti-modernists, revolution-aries or in a sense counter-revolutionaries; but each of these descriptions requires qualification. Most protesters were not particularly hostile to capital, but only to a radical change in worker-proprietor relations which, for example, abandoned the 'putting-out' of work that was to be completed by the family unit in their own home in favour of a factory model, which brought all hired hands to the entrepreneur's worksite. Some protesters or those sympathetic to them wrote pamphlets or more literary works (see Binfield 2004). Hilton (2006) offers a readable overview of the period, while E.P. Thompson's *The Making of the English Working Class* (1963) remains a profound account, combining penetrating analysis with absorbing narrative (see especially chapter 14 on the Luddites, aptly titled 'An Army of Redressers').

If we turn from historiography to lexicography to find out what *Luddite* means, we meet the following, given in the *Oxford English Dictionary* online as definitions 1a and 1b:

1a. A member of an organized band of English mechanics and their friends, who (1811–16) set themselves to destroy manufacturing machinery in the midlands and north of England.

1b. *transf.* One who opposes the introduction of new technology, esp. into a place of work.

Thus the OED characterises the original Luddites as organised to destroy machinery – very much the factory owners' perspective – whereas the weavers and croppers themselves would presumably have said they aimed to protect and preserve their livelihoods. The Macmillan online dictionary is more helpful in recognising the transferred sense of *Luddite* (someone who dislikes and avoids using new technology) to be for some time now the dominant one, but it is also a little more informative as to the word's 'story': 'From the name given to workers in 19th-century Britain who destroyed machines in factories as a protest against modern working methods.' The *Collins Cobuild English Dictionary for Advanced Learners* succinctly explains, 'If you refer to someone as a **Luddite** you are criticizing them for opposing changes in industrial methods, especially the introduction of new machines and modern methods.'

But for the purposes of my study of press representations of wealth inequality over the past half-century, the most interesting thing about the word *Luddite* and the concepts it evokes is its longevity – since its emergence 200 years ago up to the present day. As Jones (2006) shows, the *Luddite* label has continued to feed the collective imagination across two centuries in a range of writings and artefacts propounding ideas that critique the narrowing or monopolising of ownership and capital, or resist the loss of manual skills and crafts (i.e., a more literal notion of manufacture, making by hand, than we now recognise) in the face of cheaper machine-based production and increasingly complex technologies that need far fewer workers to operate them. In public discourses such as news media, *Luddite* has become a touchstone socio-political evaluative label, only loosely linked to any origins, just as *Robin Hood* has, for other purposes; both phrases bear on questions of social relations and stratifications and the distribution of wealth and power. Indeed as Adrian Randall notes in his foreword to the Binfield collection, for some radicals of the early nineteenth century, Ned Ludd displaced Robin Hood in the pantheon of champions of the underdog:

Robin had famously robbed the rich to give to the poor and defended the weak against arbitrary baronial power. But Ned Ludd epitomized the right of the poor to earn their own livelihood and to defend the customs of their trade against dishonourable capitalist depredators. While Robin, a displaced gentleman, signified paternal protection, Ned

Ludd evidenced the sturdy self-reliance of a community prepared to resist for itself the notion that market forces rather than moral values should shape the fate of labor. (Binfield 2004: xiv)

Some modern uses of *Luddite*, very clearly, no longer carry such connotations. For example, when the journalist Jane Wheatley interviewed the actor Richard Briers in *The Times* on 1 August 2009, she reported using no sound recorder but 'just my Luddite notebook (which he [Briers] approves of, being a bit of a Luddite himself)'. In fact wherever *a bit of a* prefaces *Luddite*, a strictly personal and mildly self-deprecatory favouring of 'the old ways' over some new technology is implied. This usage seems strictly recent: in the entire run of *The Times Digital Archive* (1785–2011), *a bit of a Luddite* occurs only six times and only in 1996 and later, whereas the OED's first example of *Luddite* in this transferred sense is from 1970.

Nevertheless, the darker connotations seem to have persisted even when unjustified – particularly those of a secret organisation bent on undermining the state (at least in its functions as protector of the propertied classes) and the freedom of capital to adopt new instruments and abandon customary arrangements. This in part may be because there are some parallels between the industrial disputes of the 1970s, the deregulation of labour and industries of the 1980s and the spread of neoliberal globalisation thereafter, on the one hand, and the clashes between workers and machinery owners in the late eighteenth and early nineteenth centuries, ranging from the 1779 Lancashire riots against mechanised cotton looms to the 'Swing' riots at the introduction of threshing machines to crop harvesting in 1830s, on the other. But the 1811–12 Luddites disabled or destroyed machines and did so in secret; these characteristics do not apply to the modern referents of the term, and the analogy is strictly speaking attenuated.

Consider, for example, particular associations of workers in the modern period, such as the 5,000 NGA print workers who were in dispute with Rupert Murdoch's News Group International in 1986, having been summarily displaced by the sudden introduction of electronic typesetting: they vehemently opposed the new technologies and their job losses, but there is little evidence of them resorting to systematic damage or conspiracy. And calling someone a Luddite for occupying trees or the green belt with a view to preventing their destruction by a new road or housing estate is invoking the 'determined protest' meaning of the original term but not, except perhaps by insinuation or intentionally damaging association, the 'violent prevention' meaning. In the earlier period as in the near-contemporary one, the state-sanctioned mainstream discourse was that 'technological progress', a seemingly agentless and unaligned force akin to gravity, could not and must not be halted, lest markets move elsewhere (another part of the country, or overseas entirely). But Luddism was more than an objection to technology and markets; as Randall (1986) emphasizes, it was also an ideological struggle to defend customary rights and arrangements against the deracinating onslaught of a purely 'rational' calculation of economic growth and progress; it opposed those modernists who asserted that innovation ensured there would be more work (of a sort) for more hands, albeit to the detriment of those workers with now-superseded skills.

5.3   *Luddite* and *Luddites*: Grammar, Meaning and Frequency

For a name whose origins lie in a movement from long ago with limited historical depth and breadth, *Luddite* is impressively frequent in modern newspaper discourse. Using Nexis to search UK national newspapers for the two decades from January 1991 to December 2011, as many as 1,722 uses of *Luddite* were returned. Most were in *The Guardian, The Independent, The Times* and *Sunday Times* (nearly 1,200 of the total), so it seems to be much more a 'broadsheet' word than a tabloid one: there were only thirty-six hits in *The Sun* and *The Express* combined.

How is *Luddite/s* used in *The Times*, and with what meanings? *Luddite* (without number marking) may be used as an adjective (mostly attributively, with a following noun, but sometimes predicatively) or as a noun and head of the phrase – in which case it is often also at the end of the clause, thus just before a major sentence-structure boundary. A striking presentational difference in *The Times* is that almost exclusively in the early years was *Luddite* used with warning quotation marks around it, as if to make absolutely clear that the term was being used evaluatively and not with a historical reference intended.

5.3.1   Luddite *as Adjective*

In its adjectival use in *The Times*, collocational analysis reveals that *Luddite* is often followed by an implicitly negative abstract noun, such as *battles, opposition, distrust, impulse, backwardness, tendency, crusade, attitude, thinking, objections, campaigns, rebellion, fetishism* and *behaviour*. Of these, *impulse* and *behaviour* in particular need not always collocate with adjectives implying something undesirable (e.g., when preceded by *generous*), but with *Luddite* as modifier, a negative sense is always established in the co-text. Here is a nice example of such contextually negative prosody: *would profoundly disagree with their Luddite, eco-fascist Utopianism* (8 July 2010): *Utopianism* is not intrinsically a term of criticism, but here it clearly is. In contrast to the abstract head nouns, the concrete ones following adjectival *Luddite* are infrequent and diverse; in one random sample they included *luvvies, layabouts, schmucks, author, union leaders* and *Prince of Wales*.

As for predicative adjectival uses (usually following a form of the verb *be*), the epithet is often followed by a *to* + infinitive complement specifying the scope of the 'Luddite-ness'. This is evident in the first two of the following indicative examples, where the scope-specifying complement is underlined.

> *It would be Luddite to resist the BBC's case for technical changes*
> *Some middle-aged managers may have been too Luddite in their thinking to be able to adapt.*
> *Without being Luddite or hysterical, we should certainly be worried.*
> *The Bill was not luddite and was not intended to shackle this technology.*

5.3.2   Luddite *as Noun*

In the second structural pattern, where *Luddite* (mostly singular) is the head of a Noun Phrase, the Subject is often a third party but may be the speaker (hence *I*), and the verb is usually a form of *be*:

> *These scientists are not romantics or Luddites. They simply know that*
> *I'm not a Luddite or anything, but it was better in the old days*
> *Don't get me wrong: I'm no Luddite. But the point is that*
> *We are such Luddites in this country, so suspicious of*
> *I am not a grumpy Luddite. As a musician, I couldn't tour as I*

As reflected in these examples, when *Luddite* is the head of the noun phrase there is usually a negation marker on the governing verb.

5.3.3   Meanings of Luddite

Two most common ways of using *Luddite/s* emerge from the data:
1. Uses related to employer–employee industrial relations, sometimes involving so-called restrictive practices, where the organised opposition (e.g., by a trade union) to proposed changes to terms and conditions sometimes leads to a strike; here management or politicians, unsympathetic to the protesters, denounce the latter as Luddite/s.
2. Uses entirely unrelated to industrial relations, where a person or group is described (or self-described) as *Luddite/s* on account of their dislike and rejection of some innovative technology, which they usually feel needlessly pressured to adopt in the name of progress.

These two uses and broad meanings (the denunciatory and the deriding or self-deriding) are markedly distinct, and as indicated my interest is in the first only. But the second meaning may affect the impact of the first, possibly muffling without really weakening the sharply denunciatory first meaning. While strict secrecy was a defining characteristic of the historical Luddites, this does not very evidently apply to the workings of modern unions and strikers, even if some uses in the press may be suspected of intending to insinuate this. A broader connotation that tends to attach to most op-ed press uses of *Luddite/s* and *Robin Hood* is the implication that whoever is so described is 'living in the past', subscribing to attitudes that fit a bygone age. Reflecting this, both phrases are sometimes preceded by *latter-day,* implying a need to signal a surprising contemporaneity of an identity or attitude that 'really' belongs to or in the past.

5.3.4   Luddite/s: *Indicative Frequencies*

In the five most politically relevant sections of *The Times* newspaper, for the years 1971 to 2011, there are 355 instances of *Luddite* in the digital archive, thus an average annual frequency of nine occurrences, with frequencies per section as follows:

> Editorials/leaders (26)
> Feature articles (aka opinion) (185)
> Letters to the editor (42)
> News (85)
> Politics and Parliament (17)

The greatest diversity of uses is in the feature articles, ranging from Conservative minister Norman Tebbit imagining union leaders nostalgically recalling 'the Luddite sagas of Grunwick, Saltley Coke Works and the busting of British Leyland' to Griff Rhys Jones's humorous piece about men in small boats, British amateur yachtsmen who are 'like real beer *aficionados*: Luddite fantasists'. To the 355 hits for *Luddite* can be added 179 instances (in the same newspaper sections) for *Luddites*, at an average annual frequency of four occurrences. Low though these numbers are, they are much higher than those recorded in *The Times Digital Archive* for the entire 1811–1971 period: 87 for *Luddite* and 143 for *Luddites* (perhaps unsurprisingly more used than *Luddite* in the early nineteenth century). Table 5.1 shows the distribution of the two forms for each year in the period studied. No parallel table of occurrences in the *Mail* was compiled, since *Luddite* and *Luddites* were simply too infrequent in the relevant news/editorial sections: from 1971 to 2004 there were just seventy-eight and forty-one uses, respectively, at an average of just three per year.

Even the *Times* frequencies in Table 5.1 are too low to be suggestive in themselves; instead it is the particular uses that the words *Luddite* and *Luddites* are put to in specific articles in different years that may prove important. And since the newspaper has grown in size over the period, rather higher frequencies in more recent years are only to be expected. Taking the two forms together, there is an average of no more than ten uses of *Luddite/s* for more than twenty years, from 1971 to 1994, with 1982 (seventeen uses) as a solitary early peak year. From 1995 onwards the frequency averages around 15 and

Table 5.1 Luddite + Luddites Tabulated by Year (1971–2011) in Selected Editorial and News Sections in The Times

1971	1972	1973	1974	1975	1976	1977	1978	1979	1980	1981	1982	1983	1984	1985
4 + 5	7 + 5	1 + 2	3 + 0	0 + 7	4 + 0	7 + 4	8 + 4	0 + 1	9 + 2	1 + 1	10 + 7	5 + 7	8 + 3	7 + *3

1986	1987	1988	1989	1990	1991	1992	1993	1994	1995	1996	1997	1998	1999
7 + 1	5 + 0	5 + 4	7 + 1	8 + 4	4 + 2	3 + 7	12 + 3	6 + 3	11 + 5	8 + 5	14 + 8	18 + 5	21 + 13

2000	2001	2002	2003	2004	2005	2006	2007	2008	2009	2010	2011
16 + 4	17 + 6	4 + 7	8 + 3	14 + 10	11 + 8	18 + 2	16 + 5	7 + 3	9 + 6	16 + 5	16 + 3

never falls below 10, with a peak of sorts in the early years of New Labour, 1997–2001. Thus initial numerical indications are that both the early Thatcher government years and the first Blair government were periods involving a surge in *The Times*'s use of *Luddite/s*. Closer examination of the uses in the 1997–2001 period however, to be discussed later, reveals that those uses are rarely 'political' and denunciatory and applied to industrial relations, as they are in the Thatcher-dominated early 1980s. Accordingly, uses of *Luddite/s* in the early Thatcher years are the focus of several sections of this chapter. They are preceded by a 'scene-setting' survey of uses of *Luddite* and *Luddites* in the pre-Thatcher 1970s (i.e., up to the general election of May 1979); this aims to explain the contrast between how the *Mail* and *The Times* use these words, and the political ideology they seem to represent in those pre-Thatcher years – the years of Heath, Wilson and Callaghan: three mixed-economy centrists.

5.4   *Luddite/s* in the Early 1970s in *The Times*: A Preliminary Survey

In the early 1970s, the seven uses of *Luddite* in 1972 are noteworthy; they are mostly in letters to the editor, in which one or another trade union is criticized as *Luddite*. On its own behalf, *The Times* of 1972 seems disinclined to stigmatise the unions with this term, and the one mention in a leader in that year is negatively framed and includes old-style scare quotes: *Traditionally Miners Have Never Done Anything That Could Conceivably Be Called 'Luddite' – That Is, Sabotaging Machines* (28 January 1972). The uses of *Luddite* in readers' letters to the editor are less circumspect: a 2 June letter from a TGWU member who is highly critical of over-powerful unions ('the unions cling to the Luddite mentality and turn their backs on progress'); a 22 August letter arguing it is odd for socialists to decry technological change and the material progress it brings ('Such is a Luddite, not a Marxist, notion') and one on 22 November from Lord Balogh rejecting the anti-growth argument of union leader Clive Jenkins as 'irrepressible Luddite fallacy'. The final *Luddite*-using letter of the year is further confirmation of some difference of view between the *Times*'s leader writers and those readers whose letters it publishes. This letter of 1 December takes issue with a *Times* leader of the previous week, which had suggested that the train drivers' union ASLEF was not really acting irresponsibly. Disagreeing, the letter writer declares, 'For a union in a fit of childish and Luddite pique to disrupt the industry and commerce of the country, and the lives of its citizens, is irresponsible in the extreme.' Remarkably, on the same day *The Times* publishes a long article (as news; not a mere letter) by the rail union leader Ray Buckton, in which he is defending the train drivers' stoppage in that earlier dispute:

During the past months many words have been bandied about and one epithet given to my society is 'Luddite'. No adjective has been more ill-used. We welcome change but it is the responsibility of a trade union leader to do his utmost to ensure that the interests of his members are adequately safeguarded.

So in the early years of interest, while *The Times* is prepared to publish readers' letters denouncing various unions as Luddite, it does not adopt this evaluative label on its own behalf. This distinction between the editorial view and corresponding readers' views (and variations in the detectable 'gap' between these two) is of importance throughout this study, and can be related to the difference between writers who aver on their own behalf and those who report views that are attributed to someone else (discussed as 'epistemological positioning' by some discourse analysts: see, e.g., Bednarek 2006).

The few uses of *Luddite* in *The Times* in the next few years are mostly without political resonance. Rare exceptions are a letter from the Conservative shadow minister Sir Keith Joseph, on 11 November 1976, criticizing Labour government industrial relations laws as 'Luddite legislation' and a 3 August 1977 report on submissions to the Windscale inquiry into use of nuclear power stations to meet the UK's energy needs, where Arthur Scargill declares his opposition to nuclear power but adds that, '[f]ar from being a Luddite with a narrow, vested interest in the coal industry', he would welcome the development of solar energy.

Luddites (plural) is usually infrequently used in the 1970s, but it has an early peak in 1975, when it mostly occurs in the news section and concerns conflicting industrial relations. The first of these, characteristically, comes in an article entitled *Yorkshire Miners Threaten Overtime Ban on Smokeless Fuel Concession* (28 January 1975) and reports the Yorkshire coal miners' president, Mr Arthur Scargill, at length:

> Mr Scargill said: 'We are not behaving like Luddites. Negotiations at national level are under way and we feel that we on our part are showing good faith by intimating to the coal board that while we are very committed on this question we are prepared to give them time to negotiate a satisfactory solution.'

Another use comes in the report (26 April 1975) of a clash between the Engineering Workers Union and the chairman of the (nationalised) British Steel Corporation (BSC), who had outlined plans to cut 20,000 jobs from the BSC workforce: 'Mr James Reid, of Clydeside, said the delegates were not modern Luddites, but they refused to accept economic arguments implying that decisions could be abstracted from their social consequences.' A profile of the new steelworks union leader, Bill Sirs, by Paul Routledge (19 May 1975), includes a lengthy quotation from Mr Sirs himself:

Responsible workers will not abuse their power by halting technological progress so long as it can be demonstrated that technology will not destroy the industrial and social lives of the workers. The Luddites would have been unheard of if joint consultations had been established effectively much earlier in the history of industrial relations.

Like Scargill and Reid, Sirs mentions Luddites to emphasize the inapplicability of the description to his union and modern industrial relations. Perhaps realising that it is becoming a 'dog-whistle' word, these unionists may be trying to modify its impact by using it themselves.

A final example from 1975 again concerns industrial relations: a 12 November *Times* report of a statement in Parliament by Labour Prime Minister Harold Wilson about business difficulties and industrial unrest at the car manufacturer Chrysler UK interprets the prime minister as describing both the workers and the bosses as 'Luddites': 'He said: "It was not until last week that we realized there were Luddites on both sides of the situation – management and ownership as well as on the other side," presumably a reference to Chrysler workers.' Mr Wilson's 'a plague on both your houses' criticism skilfully drains the word – on this occasion – of its power to have a strongly contrastive effect, a denouncing of one side and approving of the other. It is a fine example of Mr Wilson's political adroitness in maintaining some degree of control of conflicting interest groups. Twelve years earlier, in his famous 1963 speech envisioning a new Britain forged in the 'white heat' of new technology, Wilson had implicitly sided with C.P. Snow and his critique of the British ruling class, in Snow's influential 1959 Rede Lecture entitled 'The Two Cultures'. There Snow complained that the Establishment was packed with arts-educated intellectuals who were 'natural Luddites', unappreciative of the importance of science and engineering. Now in 1975 Wilson reiterates that there is 'no room for Luddites in the Socialist Party'.

Wilson's use of *Luddites* in criticizing both sides is also reported in the *Mail* on the same day. It is one of just three uses of the word in the *Mail* in the pre-Thatcher 1970s, the other two also occurring in 1975: on 15 September, a comment calls the steel workers' strike 'monumentally irresponsible' but also emphasizes that 'the blastfurnacemen are not latter-day Luddites setting out to smash new machinery', and on 3 December, following Chrysler's decision to pull out of car manufacturing in Britain altogether, with the loss of thousands of jobs, a feature article by Anthony Shrimsley contests the narrative he believes the Labour government will attempt to tell as to who is at fault. He contends that Chrysler's American management 'have been branded as Luddites – industrial wreckers given to smashing machinery to prevent progress', but argues this is sheer government myth, and the truth is more probably that both management and workers have failed to adapt to new market conditions. For present purposes, what is most notable here is that *Luddites* is again *not* being applied by the newspaper to the workers or the unions.

The singular form, *Luddite*, also appears in the *Daily Mail*, but in just three stories in the later 1970s, when sentiments are shifting. The first is a 9 August 1978 sarcastic comment, seemingly more in sorrow than in anger, about a Bethnal Green railway signal box, said to be overmanned by engineers who deliberately take their tea break during London commuters' rush-hour, thereby delaying many people. The engineers' work to rule is 'cosily Luddite, quintessentially English', the *Mail* complains, and reflects the decline of 'a once great nation'. A second caustic comment on 22 November 1978 deplores the 17% pay settlement with the Ford car workers, after a nine-week strike. It sees this as hugely damaging to the government (whose target for pay rises was 5%), the unemployment rate and the country: 'It must underline Britain's pathetic role as the querulous also-rans of the Common Market, an inefficient, Luddite and still relatively low-wage country.' Finally an Andrew Alexander feature article (30 November 1978) is doubtful that the government can now impose meaningful penalties on Ford (for its breach of pay guidelines): the 'aid' the government might withhold was always mostly for the government's own benefit, an inducement to firms to build factories in, for example, 'some God-forsaken parts of Merseyside where there is urban decay, a Luddite workforce and an appalling record of industrial relations'.

In the pre-Thatcher 1970s, then, there is no evidence of *Times* leader articles or feature (opinion) articles using the forms *Luddite* or *Luddites* in explicit denunciation of unions, union leaders or workers. The words are infrequent and used by reported others, quite often where the suitability of the label is denied. As for the *Daily Mail*, application of the *Luddite/s* epithet to the unions is rare in the pre-Thatcher 1970s, but it begins to emerge in hostile uses in 1978.

5.5   *Luddite/Luddites* Used Politically in *The Times* and the *Daily Mail* during the First Thatcher Term

Advertisements are little discussed in the present study, given their usually narrow commercial purpose. But the following item in the *Daily Mail* of 18 May 1979 can hardly be ignored, since it constitutes a powerful early advocacy of neoliberal market economics and is also the first mention of *Luddite/s* in the *Mail* after Mrs Thatcher became prime minister. The Conservative government commenced on 4 May, and this advertisement appeared exactly two weeks later, occupying the whole of page 8 (see Figure 5.1). Dominated by its approximately 160 words of text, it is illustrated by an image of a smashed alarm clock and a small IBM logo, with the headline *You Can't Stop Time by Smashing Clocks*. The text recounts how early nineteenth-century textile workers responded to the threat from new machines by smashing them up. It

You can't stop time by smashing clocks.

Between the years 1811 and 1816, a band of textile workers had just the answer to the threat of technology.

They literally threw spanners into the works.

And smashed up the new machinery which they blamed for their unemployment and distress.

If this attitude had prevailed, weaving would still be a cottage industry.

Ploughs would never have exceeded 4 horse-power.

The steam engine would have lost out to the cart driver.

And Britain would never have become the economic power it was in the nineteenth century.

Yet the action of the Luddites carries a very instructive lesson: it's not progress itself which is the threat, but the way we adapt to it.

For without technology, a nation's progress would undoubtedly falter.

Machines bring down the cost of production.

Which in turn either creates greater profit for reinvestment, or holds down the costs of the product, so providing greater purchasing power for the pound.

The result is greater wealth – the ideal climate for increased employment.

And machines that relieve man of the tasks that limit his personal fulfilment.

Smashing the clocks might destroy the mechanism of progress.

But it will never delay tomorrow.

IBM

IBM UNITED KINGDOM LIMITED, P.O. BOX 41, NORTH HARBOUR, PORTSMOUTH PO6 3AU.

Figure 5.1 IBM 'You Can't Stop Time' advertisement (*Daily Mail*, 18 May 1979, p. 8)

suggests 'the action of the Luddites carries a very instructive lesson: it's not progress itself which is the threat, but the way we adapt to it' – although nothing is said on the latter question (what adaptation might require or from whom).

There is more than a suggestion that adaptation simply means 'acceptance' because clock smashing 'will never delay tomorrow'. Technological innovation and progress are here cast as simply a matter of time and moving with the times; what is progress is assumed to be incontestable, like the passage of time, rather than requiring consideration of the implications for everyone affected. Similarly, smashing things up is assumed to be unquestionably and invariably bad. Instead the emphasis is on the benefits of machines, such as lower costs and higher profits: 'The result is greater **wealth** – the ideal climate for increased **employment**' (bold added). The nominalisations (bolded) are referentially vague since they include no mention of human Actors and Affected participants; only with effort can the reader register that the 'greater wealth' accrues to those making, owning and using the new machines, and drains away from those similarly reliant on the outmoded technology. This is presentationally rather in contrast with how the advertisement begins, with the workers unambiguously named and criticized for the personal agentive interventions (throwing spanners, smashing machinery), represented as destructive and irrational:

Between the years 1811 and 1816, a band of textile workers had just the answer to the threat of technology.
They literally threw spanners into the works.
And smashed up the new machinery which they blamed for their unemployment and distress.

It would have been difficult to have cast this introductory exemplum mostly through nominalisations: it uses only a few, most notably *technology* and *unemployment*, since this would have immediately prompted the reader to ask '*Who* did this smashing of machinery?' It could also be argued that figuratively speaking the factory owners smashed up the old machinery and ways of working. But one of the few nominalisations at the opening is perhaps strategic: the workers are said to have blamed *the new machinery*, when it would be truer to say they blamed those proprietors of the new machines and factories who summarily disregarded long-established customs and conventions. IBM's promotion of its products makes its case on the basis of two dubious equative identifications: new technology is progress, and progress comes with the passage of time; since the last of these, time, cannot be halted, neither can the preceding two. But a moment's reflection reminds us that progress is far less inevitable, far more questionable, than the passage of time or, indeed, the emergence of new technologies.

In the period of Mrs Thatcher's government, the next industry-related mention of *Luddite* in the *Mail* is in a speech from Keith Joseph (18 December 1979), warning that high pay claims threaten jobs. The story's first paragraphs run:

Union leaders are pricing their members out of jobs by insisting on big wage demands, warned Industry Secretary Sir Keith Joseph yesterday.

And he added that the Luddite activities of some unions were seriously holding back Britain's industrial recovery.

While relevant use in the *Mail* is sparse (just two mentions of *Luddites*), 1980 constitutes a peak year for uses of *Luddite/s* in worker-related contexts in *The Times*. On 25 February, a political news story reports Tory backbencher Edward du Cann foreseeing a 'new industrial revolution' along with the public expenditure cuts that Mrs Thatcher was shortly going to itemise: 'Workers all over the country are repudiating extremists' leadership, with its mixture of Luddite and self-destructive tendencies, and demanding the right to work.' Then a 14 March item on the views of a leading analyst of the car industry reports him hoping for a changed climate with regard to pay disputes and industrial relations, and asking, 'Do we at last mend our ways or continue down the dreary Luddite path of overmanning, dispute ridden, unproductive performance?' Two months later, on 10 May 1980, comes a short news item entitled *Minister Is Saddened by 'Luddite' Nalgo*, about how Mr Heseltine, the Secretary for the Environment, is frustrated at the Nalgo (local government) union's refusal to help with providing staffing figures in local government: 'It is typical of the negative and hostile, almost Luddite, attitude that so many people criticize local government for.' As we have seen in the discussion of council housing in Chapter 2, the Thatcher governments mounted a concerted campaign to reduce the power and costs of local authorities (most notably the Greater London Council, dissolved in 1986).

On 11 July 1980, it is Sir Keith Joseph's turn again: a *Times* report on Parliament includes part of his speech, as Secretary for Industry, reminding the House of the 'poisons or handicaps' which he had listed a year ago as those the new government must grapple with: 'nationalization, fiercely progressive direct taxation, deficit financing, a large Luddite and politicized trade union movement, and egalitarianism'. On 12 July a letter to the editor turns the spotlight on MPs themselves, suggesting their pay should be performance-based, to combat 'the lack of motivation ... absenteeism ... the Luddite rejection of all aids to efficiency'. A 26 July news item reports the Education under-secretary making a speech in which he claims that '200 years ago the Luddites lost out in their struggle for the preservation of an outdated domestic production system in Britain. Their defeat brought an explosion of production and higher living standards.' A 28 July letter to the editor about the industrial dispute at *The Observer* claims to speak for its long-suffering readers, inconvenienced by the quarrelling management and printers: 'The survival of the [*Observer*] paper is more important than any Luddite or reactionary principles.' A feature article on *Business Efficiency* on 6 October reports Mr Barrie

Sherman of the white-collar trade union ASTMS using irony in confessing he may have to become an 'unwelcome Luddite' when discussing the introduction of office technology, unless a larger number of technology agreements are reached and managements change their attitudes. The final 1980 mention of *Luddite/s* in an industrial context is on the last day of the year: the writer Anthony Burgess is given generous space in the *Mail* to air his opinions about the past year and the likely shape of the coming one. He predicts that unemployment will remain high, with new technology entailing 'a diminution of the workforce' which the trade unions are intent on resisting. He observes that '[t]he Luddites broke the machines; the typographical unions permit millions of pounds worth of new equipment to rust in Fleet Street' – before contemplating the possibility of *The Times* disappearing in the coming year, symptomatic of the 'sickness' of British syndicalism. It didn't; but the paper had recently been silenced during an industrial dispute lasting nearly a year, from December 1978 to November 1979.

Before advancing further through the instances of *Luddite* in *The Times* in the first Thatcher years, it should be noted that in those years *The Times* also published an ongoing series of humorous articles set in the fictional village of Great Grimpen where the word *Luddite* appears as the family name of one of the characters: a Mr Kevin Luddite, shop steward of a union with the acronym NASTI, whose members work in the local business called Allied Elderberry Wines. The first such stories appeared as early as 1974 and 1975, but they were most frequent in 1980 (and therefore greatly increase the frequency of the word *Luddite* in that year). These stories appear under the byline of a Francis Kinsman and aim at droll descriptions of the squabbles in this fictional village involving the local gentry, random do-gooders and the unionised workforce. These instances of *Luddite* cannot be set aside as entirely inconsequential, however, regardless of whether readers found them entertaining. While they bolster the idea that unionist activism is laughably reflex and predictable, and equate a Luddite mentality with unconstructive militancy, the management and shareholding gentry of Great Grimpen fare no better in these reports. Perhaps, harking back to the sentiments expressed in 1975 by both Prime Minister Wilson and the *Mail* columnist Anthony Shrimsley, there is a message of 'a plague on both houses' in these lightly satirical entertainments; if so, this is at variance with the emerging more hostile representation.

That more hostile and vehement use of *Luddite/s* is apparent in a *Mail* Comment of 5 August 1981, *The Buffers of Lunacy*. This condemns a proposed national strike by railway workers – and also singles out for criticism Lord McCarthy, who had chaired the pay negotiations. The British Rail (BR) Board – and the *Mail* – now want the workers to accept productivity and other conditions ('de-manning' is mentioned) in return for the already-agreed generous pay award. The workers want the pay deal without those strings attached.

But a Luddite, something-for-nothing strike that compounds the losses of British Rail will only serve to strengthen the influence in Cabinet of those Ministers – almost certainly the Prime Minister among them – who fear that BR is not and never will be anything other than a rusty bucket with a hole. . ... Hardly worth repairing. [ellipsis in original]

Meanwhile in *The Times*, in its report of the House of Commons debate on the Queen's speech, 10 November 1981, Mr Tebbit (Secretary for Industry) is found commenting on the dangers of rising unemployment and the need for there to be more settlements like the recent British Leyland car workers' one, reflecting 'a growing understanding of the facts of economic life'. For there to be higher productivity, new technology has to be accepted rather than feared: 'The opposition to new technology today was not openly luddite but a sort of reasoned luddism with an attempt to hide behind a cloak of reasonableness' [sic]. On 10 December 1981, *The Times* prints a news feature about a few Labour election candidates who are supporters of the controversial Militant Tendency, advocates of widespread nationalisation, and extra-parliamentary action; such mobilisation, the article contends, puts them 'in a long and honourable tradition in the Labour movement which encompasses such groups as the Luddists and the Chartists who believed in direct action . . .'.

Turning back to the *Mail,* on 30 December 1981 comes its next relevant use of *Luddite*, again in a comment: *Would you pour more money into Buckton's bucket?* This concerns those of the railworkers who are more highly skilled (e.g., train drivers) and who are members of the ASLEF union, led by Ray Buckton; they are still resisting the Rail Board's productivity/flexibility conditions, whereas the larger NUR union by this point has agreed to them. This uses the same 'holed bucket' metaphor as was noted in August, in the headline and the body text – the phonetic similarity with the union leader's surname clearly being an invitation. The comment suggests that the government might subsidise the railways more generously, at European levels, if there was evidence of the employees being committed to improving efficiency and productivity, so that the money was well spent rather than like pouring water into the leakiest of buckets. But 'Ray Buckton and his Luddite locomen personify the clinching counter-argument'. Men who were once 'the aristocrats of the footplate' have been misled by Buckton (the *Mail* argues) into becoming 'the saboteurs' of the yearned-for modern railway system.

The stream of delegitimising and distancing uses of *Luddite* continues in 1982, in both newspapers. Soon after the *Mail's* comment (just discussed), a short letter in *The Times* (15 January 1982) declares that 'Mr Buckton's open letter to commuters (January 11) merits only one conclusion: he is a hair-splitting Luddite.' Just a day later, *The Times* prints a letter from the chairman of something called the Independent Secretarial Training Association which questions a recent article's very low estimations of the expected *per diem* productivity of a competent typist: 'on the face of it, this formula could have been devised by a committee of luddite trade unionists seeking to provide more jobs for one-handed keyboard operators'. Around this time, a *Times* news item (14 January 1982) criticises some teachers and school administrators for a 'general Luddite reaction to new technology which you do not understand and which may threaten your job'.

The next *Mail* use, another comment, is again on the rail dispute (17 February 1982). This time, a third party, chairman of British Rail Sir Peter Parker, is particularly lambasted and urged to resign if BR settles on ASLEF's terms. However, Mr Buckton is also criticised: he is 'a Luddite who sees no further than the sanctimonious tip of his own nose', in leading a resistance to reform which will ultimately destroy a great many railway jobs. More than four months later, ASLEF are again threatening a strike rather than accepting the flexible shift-work conditions demanded, with government support, by the Rail Board. A *Mail* Comment on the situation (30 June 1982) is expressively titled *Suicide Bid* and argues, 'The locomen do a skilled and responsible job. But they live in the past. They are Luddites. They prefer to smash the rail system rather than modernise it.' *The Times* had expressed a similar view nearly three weeks earlier. In *BR Progress 'delayed by Luddites'* (12 June 1982), the Transport minister is reported blaming union members for 'pointless Luddite disputes' in delaying the proposed government-financed electrification of various routes. But the report of a debate in Parliament ten days later (22 June 1982) has a Labour MP objecting to this specific description:

When the Secretary of State, in a speech recently, accused the rail workers of being Luddites he was not only being unjust but insulting to men who had tried hard to reflect the determination to work with the board in order that the country could have a modern railway system.

A long feature article shortly after (*The Times,* 14 July 1982) describes Labour leader Michael Foot's speech at the Durham miners' gala. Described as courting cheap popularity, it claims, '[H]e lined up the Labour leadership with the Luddites and tipped the balance back towards the ASLEF executive, with an intemperate assault on the British Rail board.' Public and rail workers alike will pay dear for this, the article warns.

Earlier in the summer, a *Times* news item (12 May 1982) reports Mr Tebbit warning that 'Company managements were sometimes as Luddite as unions in their refusal to accept new technology and working practices', in particular failing to adopt a modern worker-informing consultative managerial style (again perhaps echoing Mr Wilson from 1975). But a month later (12 June), a trade union is once more the sole target of invective, when the Transport Secretary Mr Howell blames the NUR for the damage caused by 'pointless

Luddite disputes' at British Rail. Five days later the report of proceedings in Parliament shows Howell being challenged on this point by a Labour MP: 'Will the minister authorize major investment programmes, such as the one for the East coast main line, instead of making ludicrous luddite charges against the unions which only inflame the situation?' A further five days later (22 June 1982), in a parliamentary debate on the crisis in British Rail, the Labour Opposition spokesman is reported saying that 'the reasons behind the dispute were not the trades union Luddite approach, but were far more complex and deserved to be treated seriously'. As the dispute dragged on, we find that at Prime Minister's Questions on 14 July 1982 Mrs Thatcher is asked a 'helpful' question by one of her own MPs, concerning Mr Foot's declared sympathy for the ASLEF train drivers' campaign: 'Has she noted that the Leader of the Opposition had yet again put the interests of a small luddite union in front of the interest of commuters and of the national interest?' A *Mail* comment of 8 October 1982, *Competence with Conviction*, is an encomium to Mr Norman Tebbit, the Employment Secretary, for what the *Mail* regards as his compelling speech at the recent Tory party conference.

His hammering of union extremists was also vintage Tebbit. It was a telling indictment, but yet he held out sober hope from the very fact that it was from the rank and file who are abandoning Luddite practices that improvements in the economy are coming.

On the same date, *The Times* summary of parliamentary debate on unemployment reports Mr Tebbit's closing speech on behalf of the government at length. One of the points he is noted making is that '[d]espite their Luddite leaders, many trade unionists had cast off the shackles of restrictive practices'.

The established trends continue in 1983, with a *Mail* political sketch by Andrew Alexander of speeches in Parliament (27 January 1983), which reviews the Transport Minister's presentation of the Serpell report on a possible future 'rationalisation' of the rail system (although never acted upon, it caused alarm by contemplating a drastic reduction in the network, so as to achieve solvency). The sketch includes the observation that 'Labour has a vested interest in keeping the rail network as long as possible and the railway unions as large and Luddite as possible.'

As before, alongside representations of Labour and trade union purposes as 'Luddite', there are periodic declarations that other participants in the economy, who may be proposing qualifications or restrictions with regard to some innovative practice, are doing so for non-Luddite purposes. Thus in a *Times* report of speeches in the House of Lords (21 January 1983) Lord Hailsham is found assuring the House that the new Data Protection Bill 'was not luddite and was not intended to shackle [information] technology'. And a *Times* editorial of 28 March 1983, *Streaming the Channels*, gives a guarded welcome to the BBC's planned switchover to VHF and well-spaced broadcasting frequencies:

'It would be Luddite to resist the BBC's case for technical changes: listeners on certain frequencies still find programmes barely audible.'

By way of an *in memoriam, The Times* reprints (on 8 April 1983) two articles from 1950 by George Schwartz (recently deceased), its one-time economics columnist. The first is titled *Luddite Smoke,* and both question the comments of a tobacco workers' union leader, responding to factory trials of a new and faster cigarette cutting and packing machine. Workers should get 'their share of the profits' generated by the new machine, the union leader had declared. Schwartz inspects and dismantles this claim in both reprinted columns, in ways which *The Times* judges 'as relevant today as when they were written 23 years ago'.

With the preceding examples, this survey of *Luddite/s* in *The Times* and *Mail* during the four years of the first Thatcher government concludes. It reveals that, over and over again, the words *Luddite/Luddites* are used chiefly and strategically to characterise the more outspoken union leaders as destructively backward-looking and protectionist. These words are reported when used by a very few powerful leaders of the government, chiefly those with responsibility for industrial relations, and most particularly Sir Keith Joseph, first, and Mr Norman Tebbit, later.

The narrative of 'what is going on in Britain' is always a contested one, with disparate versions competing for acceptance and each version shaped by a multiplicity of co-tellers. *The Times*'s and *Mail*'s editorials and their reporting of Joseph's and Tebbit's words cumulatively contribute to the government's narrative of what has happened, is happening, and of what needs to be done concerning industrial relations, the actions of employers and organised labour and employment practices more generally. The recurrent message is that employees need to accept the reality that adoption of the latest technology and higher productivity targets in all industries is essential for them to stay efficient and competitive, even when this leads to the loss of certain types of job: no one can afford to do otherwise. Embedded in this message is the conviction that the duty to be economically competitive and profitable is more compelling than any responsibility towards employees.

5.6   *Luddite/s* after June 1983

The recurrent deployment of *Luddite/s* in political commentary in *The Times* and *Mail* in the first years of the Thatcher period is sharply denunciatory of particular union leaders and memberships, representing them as extremist, at least figuratively violent, and behaving in ways that were unreasonable, remote from common sense and destructive. By emphasising these alleged characteristics, the newspapers promoted just that understanding of the unions involved.

This usage may have peaked in the first Thatcher administration, but it continued in the following years. Thus a *Mail* comment of 3 January 1984,

No Rest Cure, rejects the Trade Union Council's call for longer holidays and shorter hours and recommends that the TUC campaign for higher productivity instead, and a welcoming of the new technology, rather than 'fighting it with Luddite stubbornness'. And in 1985 various *Mail* comments or news features tell readers:

- that while Sir Keith Joseph's Better Schools White Paper fails to promise teachers much-needed pay increases, 'the teaching unions have been blinkered, even Luddite, in their total unwillingness to accept formal assessment of their work in school';
- that a threatened postal workers' strike in April 'would be a Luddite strike – aimed at barring the use of new technology, more than half the benefits of which are intended to go to the workers';
- as if 'to encourage the others', a *Mail* Comment on the nationalised telephone company, British Telecoms (*Don't Hang Up on B T Despite Crossed Lines*, 2 June 1985) suggests that BT 'is beginning to look like one of the more striking success stories of the 1980s', having shaken off a previous reputation for 'lack of salesmanship, lack of financial control and Luddite working practices'.
- that according to the lead front page story on 15 August 1985, *BR Boss Gets Tougher Still*, Sir Bob Reid would sooner close the rail system down than compromise in the face of rail union strike threats: 'His view is that without productivity improvements, there is no future for the railway industry, and that management cannot live with a "Luddite" attitude on the part of organised labour. While the union might feel bound by the ballot result, BR management does not.'
- that (a Comment of 4 September 1985 declares) a set of TUC demands concerning the coal miners, to be made of any future Labour government, constitutes 'a charter for the law breaker and the Luddite'.
- that (a Comment of 28 October 1985 warns) the miners' leader Arthur Scargill might still run for re-election, despite the failure of his strike and the many defections to the rival UDM union: 'it is still entirely possible Mr Scargill could win such a vote of confidence in the Luddite rump of the NUM [National Union of Mineworkers]'.

In short, in the space of a few short months, the *Mail* has deployed the Luddite verdictive to colour its readers' understanding of the alleged work grievances of the teachers, the postal workers, the railway workers, the TUC and the Scargillite coal miners. A Comment of 12 November in this same year indicates that the list could have been longer. Entitled *There's a Hole in Britain's Bucket* (thus again using the 'holed bucket' metaphor to encapsulate the idea of state funds being poured pointlessly into inefficient and unprofitable industries) and reporting how pay rises in the manufacturing industry are double the rate of inflation, it warns, 'Some of our unions are still Luddite and over-politicised compared to those in Europe, the United States and Japan.' Interestingly, this Comment triggers one of the very few letters, across the entire forty-five-year period, which uses the word *Luddite* while vehemently disagreeing with the *Mail*'s position on workers' pay and conditions (22 November 1985). It is from a toolmaker who works long hours for modest pay and believes that teachers, nurses and local authority workers are rather better off than those employed in manufacturing industries. His opening sentence is bitter in its irony: *So it's the greedy workers and Luddite unions to blame once again.*

By 9 April of 1986, a *Mail* Comment feels hopeful enough to turn from the stick to the carrot, reporting some industrial recovery and informing readers that '[a]ttitudes to work are no longer so Luddite or bloody-minded'. But before any such emergence of a changed governmental and journalistic tone, the country experienced or at least witnessed the profound industrial confrontation known as the Miners' Strike. At the very mid-point of this year-long strike, a *Times* opinion piece by Kenneth Fleet on the economy and the weakening stock market (5 September 1984) declared:

The harm is in what the miners' strike, even if it does not lead in the end to Mr Scargill's coronation, signifies about attitudes and priorities in unionized Britain. Perhaps after all, there has been no fundamental change: politically motivated Luddites still rule, despite a lengthy recession and Mrs Thatcher's brisk experiment in economic realism.

Perhaps this comment reflects the newspaper's collective thinking as succinctly as any other brief formulation in that critical period and concerning this most prominent clash between industry and government, the coal miners' strike, to which I now turn.

5.7   The Miners' Strike of 1984–85

In these years of Conservative government (1979–97), no industrial dispute was more critical to the government and the trade union movement than the year-long miners' strike (6 March 1984 to 3 March 1985). This was led by Arthur Scargill of the National Union of Mineworkers (itself quite divided over strike action), against the government-appointed management, the National Coal Board (NCB). Those miners on strike were protesting against the numerous pit closures and job losses that the NCB had embarked upon. The strike remained illegal because the NUM held no national ballot of members and a minority of men continued working; this in turn meant that other unions showed limited support. Despite these difficulties, Scargill and the striking miners hoped to restrict coal production (crucial to the power stations that created electricity nationwide) to the point that the government and NCB would agree to major cuts to their pit closure plans. Opposing them, the government relied on extensive coal reserves; supporting and protecting those miners who continued working; and an aggressive and comprehensive policing of strikers' and of secondary picketing (road blocs at motorway exits, and so on).

It is no surprise, in these circumstances, to find *Luddite* used in the *Mail* in reference to the conflict. A short editorial entitled *The Other Way* appears on 19 April 1984, six weeks into the strike and begins trenchantly: 'The Luddite pitmen will today be centre stage.'

It goes on to accuse the miners of a 'suicidal pantomime' at a time when 'the rest have learned their lesson' (British Leyland, British Rail, British Airways, and British Steel are cited). Five days later, the deputy leader of the Labour Opposition, Mr Hattersley, is condemned in a Comment for directing all his criticism at the government and the Coal Board: 'In this, the most bitter, the most potentially violent and Luddite of confrontations, Roy Hattersley ... bends over backwards to put party before country.' The strike dragged on throughout 1984 with little evidence of a major impact on industrial output (no power cuts, for example), several violent confrontations between the police and the pickets and considerable financial hardship for those on strike and their families. With no prospect of Coal Board compromise, Scargill and the NUM eventually had to accept defeat, presenting this as an 'agreement' to return to work. This 'agreement' was greeted in the *Mail* by a multimodal front page Comment, comprising an editorial, where again the *Luddite* word is used, and an accompanying cartoon; they merit closer scrutiny.

The Comment occupies the entirety of the front page, with this headline in very large, thick black lettering, occupying a full quarter of the page:

DON'T LET HIM TRICK US NOW

Above this headline, in smaller print, runs the observation: *After all the agony the only one who hasn't moved an inch is Scargill.* Below the headline on the left runs the story text, while on the right is a huge cartoon (Figure 5.2). The cartoon depicts Arthur Scargill's beaky-nosed head atop a dove-shaped body of plumage which on closer inspection is recognisable as body armour formed out of overlapping metal plates. That the 'bird' is an artefact is confirmed by its being positioned on a trolley with rudimentary wheels fashioned from wood or stone. Between Scargill's lips is an olive branch, and below the cartoon runs the caption *The Dove of Peace*. Nearby are the closed walls of a town labelled NCB, with the grizzled face of Mr Ian MacGregor, the Coal Board chairman, looking over the top, in place of King Priam watching from the towers of Illium. The clear cultural reference is to the story of the Trojan Horse, and we are to understand that we should trust Scargill's NUM no more than the Trojans should have trusted the Greeks bearing gifts. The body text not only fills the remainder of the page, but continues on page 6, where the following thoughts are included:

The Dove of Peace

Figure 5.2 Cartoon of Arthur Scargill as 'Trojan Horse' Dove of Peace

Arthur Scargill, the Marxist Luddite, would have the miners and their children and their children's children imprisoned for all eternity in the clapped out pits of yesteryear.
    He has to be defeated. He has to be seen to be defeated.
    Britain's best hopes for a democratic and a prosperous future depend on it.

All of this is in sharp contrast with a *Mail* comment of 15 January 1974, at the height of an earlier miners' pay dispute in a period of government-attempted pay-rise restraint (to combat inflation). Significantly, that miners' grievance was official and had the backing of the TUC, so the Comment's reference to union leaders is to the TUC, rather than more narrowly the miners' union (in which Scargill was already emerging as a leading figure). The title of the 1974 comment, *An Honourable Failure*, was evidently intended to apply to both unsuccessfully negotiating parties: 'neither side has acted dishonourably. Both union leaders and Government Ministers were more concerned with the interests of the nation than with political calculation.' Even throughout 1975, as shown earlier, neither newspaper is inclined to condemn any of the unions or their leaders as Luddite; but in the later 1970s those judgements hardened, and thereafter the *Mail* consistently represented Arthur Scargill as *Luddite* for the rest of his career. An item of 9 July 1987 includes the description 'Scargill [is] triumphant in his Luddite zeal', for example, while a comment of 26 September 1988 refers to 'Mr Arthur Scargill and his Luddite practices'. If a target of opprobrium is portrayed wearing a particular verbal cap frequently enough, the *Mail* seems to have reasoned, then its readers will be persuaded that it must fit. As recently as 28 November 2002 comes an article by John Macleod, an outburst of exasperation and mockery at what he sees as the myths and archaisms protecting the firefighters, who were then on strike. The romantic-heroic image of their work does not 'sell' with the public these days, he says, 'not since Scargill led the miners over a cliff'. And he complains also at what he alleges is the firefighters' '"Buggin's turn" promotion structure that would have gratified the Luddites'.

5.8   *Luddite/s* in the Last Three Decades

In the later years of the Conservative governments of Margaret Thatcher and then of John Major (1986–97), deployment of the Luddite/s epithet declines sharply. One *Times* editorial (*Labour in the Docks*) on 11 April 1989 is about Labour leader Mr Kinnock's generally moderate politics and his likely response to the government's proposed abolition of the Dock Labour Scheme; in principle, Labour might be expected to object to this, but the *Times* speculates that Kinnock will not want to be identified with *restrictive practices and 'Luddite' attitudes* which usually harm the party with voters. Generally, *The Times* leaders use *Luddite* on a diversity of topics, not worthy of note here since none is directly connected with industrial relations.

Similarly in the 1997–2001 period, while there is a comparatively high frequency of *Luddite/s* in *The Times*, extremely few have to do with industrial relations: almost all appear in what *The Times* archive classes as feature articles (i.e., opinion), and which concern reluctant adoption of new IT methods and equipment in the home or the office, where such adoption (or rejection) remains a secondary issue rather than job-threatening. A few uses concern genetically modified food and other areas of ecological debate. One partial exception is a *Times* editorial, *On the Beat* (17 December 2001), that chastises the Police Federation for being one of a few 'special interest groups whose Luddite approach to innovation or reform' does a disservice to their profession. One of the strangest is a feature article by future Tory minister Michael Gove (30 November 1999) prior to the greatly disrupted World Trade Organisation meeting in Seattle; although he notes that critics of 'the WTO and its model of global turbo-capitalism are dismissed as illiberal, isolationist and Luddite', he sides strongly with their defence of national sovereignty, directly threatened by the proposed variant of the recently abandoned Multilateral Agreement on Investment. That variant also failed, but by January 2015 and now a government minister, Gove endorses a similar initiative, the Transatlantic Trade and

Investment Partnership (TTIP), and rejects its many critics as scare-mongerers. But we have to wait until 9 October 2009 for a *Times* leader, *Lost in the Post*, that uses *Luddite* again in an industrial relations context. The leader roundly condemns the proposed pre-Christmas strike at *Royal Mail*, by the Communication Workers Union: 'Essentially the strike is Luddite: against machines.'

Employment-related uses of *Luddite/s* in the *Mail* in the post-1997 years are similarly few in number. *Turning the Tables* is a 10 February 1998 comment on the many tests that primary school children are now required to take, seen by the newspaper as a belated victory for Mrs Thatcher, a laudable emphasis on 'back to basics' teaching, and 'an indictment of the educational establishment which staged so long and Luddite a resistance'. The teachers are again targeted in a comment of 15 April 1998, entitled *They Never Learn*. The National Union of Teachers (NUT) had voted for a four-day week in the classroom (to give time for lesson preparation and administrative tasks); this is described as a 'wrecking strategy ... espoused by the Luddite tendency in the NUT – against the despairing advice of that union's more moderate leadership', and one which will alienate public sympathy. In the same day's paper Simon Heffer reiterates this message in a 1,000-word attack on the NUT – titled *Britain's Middle Class Luddites* – as needlessly and archaically militant: it 'still speaks the language of Arthur Scargill'. A Comment of 4 February 1999 outlines reasons for being sceptical about GM crops and food, but hastens to assure that its questioning attitude 'isn't a Luddite approach'. A commissioned feature article of 30 December 2002 protesting against IVF and the 'baby-making' cloning industry, *Call a Halt to This Ultimate Abuse of Mankind*, complains that '[t]hose of us who object to the burgeoning industry in human life have been ridiculed as Luddite, alarmist, or moral Fascists.' A long *Mail* article on the findings of a government-funded survey of popular sentiment concerning GM food, *Frankenstein Food Revolt* (25 September 2003), reports the survey's chair, Professor Malcolm Grant, at length. Grant noted how GM supporters, including Prime Minister Tony Blair, had tried to marginalise GM critics, 'suggesting they are Luddite and ignorant': 'Professor Grant said: "It is easy to sneer at the way people express their views. I would not dismiss them as Luddite. I would say they encompass a wide range of different issues".' Using Nexis as the database for the years from 2004 to 2016, very few hits appear for *Luddite/s* in the *Mail* and in the context of political or employment disputes. Most concern adjustments to the digital age, or objections to GM crops and food which the *Mail* actually endorses; and in very many, additionally, the point being made is that the speaker is 'far from being a Luddite' or 'not a complete Luddite' or in some similar way might be thought of in Luddite terms but really should not be.

One of the few employment-related serious uses comes in an article by leading Conservative politician Iain Duncan Smith, on 21 February 2012, defending his controversial Work Experience scheme (a voluntary work-fare scheme, previously noted in Chapter 2). He complains that the government's opponents 'constitute a group of modern-day Luddites' who are misleading the public in a 'deliberately malicious' fashion. And a 30 March 2012 comment supports the government's condemnation of 'the Unite union and its Luddite leader Len McCluskey' over their threatened strike action. On 5 September of that year, the new Planning minister, Nick Boles, is reported dismissing opponents of planning reform as 'hysterical, scare-mongering latter-day Luddites'. Almost the only *Mail* article in the entire twelve-year period that directly concerns industrial relations is an opinion piece of 8 December 2016 which expressed anger and frustration at the strikes that have brought misery to commuters, arising from a dispute between Southern Railways and its employees, who are members of the Rail, Maritime and Transport Workers (RMT) union. The *Mail* castigates both sides: 'a weak and incompetent management' and 'selfish, Luddite trade unions which put interests of their members in front of those of passengers'. This dispute also prompts a return to the use of *Luddite/s* in *The Times*: a news item of 8 August attributes the strike to 'the selfish Luddite aims of the RMT union', while a 16 December feature article by Philip Collins declares, 'The Luddites of the RMT are not only the scourge of passengers, they are ruining the reputation of trade unionism into the bargain.' Collins here plausibly presupposes that Luddism and unionism can be distinct, but as I argue in the next section, the dominant assumption repeatedly expressed in the *Mail* and *The Times* in the 1980s and tacitly maintained since is that they overlap largely.

5.9   Concluding Remarks: The *Luddite* Narrative

This chapter has concentrated on how the terms *Luddite* and *Luddites* have been used in *The Times* and the *Daily Mail* over the past forty-five years, when applied to jobs and strikes rather than to smartphones and other digital technology, and when used by or about politicians, or leaders of unions or businesses. As used here in the negative representation of union leaders, Labour politicians and others judged to be the newspapers' political opponents, *Luddite/s* powerfully contributes to the representation of those so described as unreasonable, dangerous, destructive, inflexibly hostile to innovation and still wedded to an approach that marred a dark period in English employment and industrial history. In the context of the norms of a democracy and the rule of law, where Parliament decides with the consent of the governed, *Luddite* is one of numerous epithets, such as *bankrupt, fascist, totalitarian, Maoist* and *Stalinist*, that are deployed to delegitimise people or their actions. But in British political journalism *Luddite* is in different senses weaker and stronger than many of these other epithets. It is stronger in being a distinctively British label (English, even), with a specifically British history, which the others cited lack. It is weaker in connoting violent attack on machines rather than their owners directly; and its carrying less extreme associations than *fascist* or *Stalinist* explains why 'nice' people will admit to being *a bit of a Luddite* about apps, or e-readers, where they might hesitate to self-describe as *a bit of a fascist*. This broader use of *Luddite* actually assists its use in newspapers' delegitimising characterisations. Use of a label like *Stalinist* or *fascist*, by the newspaper itself or a public figure it reports, might be rejected by *Times* or *Mail* readers as extreme and abusive, as 'going too far' and redounding to cast the users of such names in an unflattering light. That risk, when an editorial or politician calls another public figure a *Luddite*, is greatly reduced because of the word's range of uses over two centuries.

In Chapter 4 I proposed in evaluative journalistic op-ed writing, words used as co-epithets or in some other co-constructional relationship within the same phrase (noun phrase, adverbial phrase, etc.) can often be interpreted as in a paraphrastic or reformulatory relationship. Drawing on the collocates accompanying uses of *Luddite/s* in 1982 alone, we can derive the representation that (for *The Times* and *Mail*) those deemed *Luddite/s* are also hair-splitting; trade unionists; prone to form committees with ridiculous goals; sanctimonious; living in the past, system-destroyers; intemperate; sometimes company managements that resist new technology and practices; creators of pointless disputes; small interest groups at odds with larger groups; prone to hostile reaction rather than adaptive; associated with employment practices that some ordinary workers are abandoning; and union leaders, rather than their ordinary members.

These paraphrases of words are never fully mutually compatible, but local incompatibilities do not prevent a few clear predicative characteristics becoming prominent. Among the strongest are that Luddites are unionists and *vice versa*, and that a Luddite is a union leader and *vice versa*. When these generalisations take hold in the *Mail*'s and *Times*'s discourse, they have the potential to persuade their readers that trade unionism itself, regardless of any of its other aims and purposes, is regressive, pernicious and unfit for the modern world. Insofar as *Mail* and *Times* readers accepted this narrative, they must have understood Britain circa 1982 as being in a situation of recurrent conflict between the government and numerous management boards, on one side, intent on progress, innovation, adaptation and the larger (even national) interest; and unionized workers often led by a 'Luddite' and thus induced to be Luddites themselves, on the other side. There was only one side that readers could identify with – unless they were prepared to align with the hair-splitting and sanctimonious, the intemperate and pointlessly disputatious.

Even a brief scrutiny of the collocates and contexts of use of *Luddite/s* confirms that it serves as concise denunciation of any response that the speaker regards as negative, destructive, uncooperative, unreasonable and 'antimodern' (as reflected in such examples as 'thick-headed *luddites* railing vainly against the modern world': *The Guardian*, 18 August 2005). It is also increasingly evident that it is often a textually constructed opposite (Jeffries, Davies) of an intrinsically rather different word and concept, namely *change*. The concept of change, in the specific sense in which it is used as encapsulating the antithesis of Luddism, implicates a number of further attributes, such as adaptability, flexibility and perhaps especially, compliance, which are by no means inevitable consequences of being positively oriented to change. Orientedness to change, in some circumstances, is strongly associated with rejection of the status quo, explicit non-compliance, so change does not always entail compliance – but conceived as Luddism's opposite it always does. Compliance is importantly implicated in the discursively constructed schema of change that centre-right newspapers project as part of the representation of 'good employment relations and practices' which are invoked as the very opposite of Luddite attitudes. And compliance with change also importantly assumes and accepts that the underlying agent of change is external to the people who must accept the change. It makes no sense for people to instigate changes which they then 'comply' with: compliance only comes into the picture when you are subject to someone else's agenda for change, not your own.

This may be partly concealed by the grammar of the verb *change*, which as was already noted in Section 4.5.2 of Chapter 4 in discussion of the sentence *The workplace has changed beyond recognition*, is an 'ergative' verb. It is an ergative verb because it allows the thing that undergoes the change not only to occupy the Object role in the clause (the usual pattern: *The board changed the workforce*) but also, alternatively, to occupy the Subject role almost as if it were the Agent, not the Affected party, in that process: *The workforce changed*. This is at variance with normal transitive verbal processes (such as *pay, hire, fire, promote, welcome, reward,* etc.), where only the party doing the paying or hiring and so on can occupy the Subject role in an active voice clause. Who does what to whom is therefore more explicit in sentences about paying and hiring and so on, and more obscure in sentences about changing. A statement such as *The workforce changed* doesn't reveal who caused the change; conceivably it was the workforce themselves who were the instigating agent, willing to change; but then again it could well have been some other external actor that caused the workforce to change. Agency is not disclosed.

Change, as noun and verb, is a crucial socio-political process, reflected in modern organisations' preoccupation with 'the management of change'. But it is incontrovertibly a two-participant process involving an Agent and an Affected, notwithstanding the masking of this that ergative and passive constructions foster (*The policy changed; the policy was changed*). When the individuals involved as Agent or Affected are identified, a further question can be asked as to whether they have participated in the change willingly or not. The original Luddites resisted a compelled change, a change forced upon them by factory owners. Today the agent of change may still be a manager or business owner who controls by means of greater – unequal – power. Where they impose change rather than lead employees to agree to change, they are inherently part of an anti-democratic system. A good measure of whether anti-democratic forces, those of inequality, are spreading or shrinking in the modern British workplace is the degree to which people experience change as imposed upon them or agreed upon and consented to by them.

In a neoliberal, market-forces-driven, entrepreneurship-rewarding, small-state-friendly polity, change is definitionally desirable, necessary and inevitable. It is always 'time for change' – the slogan of many a campaigning politician. One of the most eloquent summaries of anti-Luddite sentiment comes in then Prime Minister Tony Blair's speech to the Labour Party conference in September 2005, urging renewed commitment to the reform of public services and 'change'. 'There is no mystery about what works', he declared; what works is 'an open, liberal economy prepared constantly to change to remain competitive'. A *Times* graphic on 25 September 2005 listing the buzzwords in Blair's speech identified *change(s)*, with twenty-three uses, as by far the most frequent. In his September conference speech Blair talked in the tough way characteristic of the later years of his premiership. First he warned, in a metaphor both awkwardly redundant and faintly menacing in its militaristic hints, 'Change is marching on again'. Time marches on or never stands still, but it is a redundancy or tautology to say that change does. If the subtext was that we in Britain needed to toughen up, Blair soon made it clear that the toughening would not be to enable us to combat the Change army as the previous metaphor might have led us to think, but to adapt to it, and even collaborate with it:

The character of this changing world is indifferent to tradition. Unforgiving of frailty. No respecter of past reputations. It has no custom and practice. It is replete with opportunities, but they only go to those swift to adapt, slow to complain, open, willing and able to change.

Sceptics remarked wryly that qualities such as being swift to adapt and slow to complain were not noticeably typical of most British people. But it is the earlier quoted characteristics, ascribed not to people but to some putatively agentless convergence of circumstances encapsulated in the nominalisation 'this changing world', that are of especial interest here: *indifferent to tradition ... No respecter of past reputations. ...* Could any phrases be more explicitly anti-Luddite than these, and Mr Blair's commending of the modern world as having 'no custom and practice'? If a constructive Luddism can exist at all, it does so by virtue of affording respect and attention to tradition and customary practices. But Mr Blair's 2005 speech expresses a deep antipathy to such values, viewed as barriers to profitable adaptability and 'gig economy' technologised enterprise. In the Blair blueprint, those affected by change are not supposed to question the terms or conditions of change, but simply submit to them for the greater good that is growth and profitability.

Insofar as Mr Blair's position prevailed (and even in the remaining Labour years, to May 2010, it did so only partially), the values of the IBM 'smashed clock' advertorial of 1979 had become thoroughly entrenched, to the point that there was no longer any significant call for the naming and shaming of people with 'Luddite' tendencies. There has been, however, a recent twist in this tale. As Andy Beckett (2017) noted, there were no dissenting voices, even within Labour, to Blair's 2005 change-embracing deregulatory prescriptions. But twelve years later, mired in the Brexit mud with a 'just about managing' Conservative government knocked on its heels by Corbyn's Old Labour near-victory in Mrs May's 'give me a mandate' June 2017 general election, free market neoliberalism is looking less secure. Beckett suggests that both main parties are turning away from unfettered capitalism, and a new economic order may be emerging. There is, however, little discursive evidence yet of parameters accordingly being reset at the *Daily Mail* or *The Times*.

6   Forty-Five Years of *Robin Hood*

As with the previous chapter, this one looks at how a name with a rich social and political history – *Robin Hood* – has been used in evaluative political discourse in *The Times* and the *Daily Mail* since 1971. The relevance of *Robin Hood* – as a name, an idea, and a story – to the unequal distribution of wealth in Britain scarcely needs explaining, as these newspapers recognise.

6.1   Powerful Names

In the course of a 'third leader' on 6 February 1995 celebrating the crime fiction produced by authors such as the late Patricia Highsmith, *The Times* declares that 'Sherlock Holmes has become the best-known English character in the world, with the possible exceptions of Robin Hood and Henry VIII.' In *The Times* of 2016, the phrase *Sherlock Holmes* occurs 57 times, *Henry VIII* has an impressive 144 hits, while *Robin Hood* is mentioned 43 times. None of the three will be mentioned as often in the mass media of 2016 as Donald Trump or Queen Elizabeth II or Kim Kardashian, but they have enormous staying power – especially Robin Hood. And two of the three are relevant to matters of wealth and wealth redistribution – especially Robin Hood.

6.2   *Robin Hood* in *The Times*: Preliminary Profile

A critical discourse analysis must select systematically, from the thousands of *Times* and *Mail* stories that use the phrase *Robin Hood* across the nearly fifty years of interest, to focus on those uses which bear at least indirectly on wealth inequality. *The Times Digital Archive* (for the years 1971–2011) and *Nexis* (for 2012 and later) return 5,826 and 211 uses, respectively, of *Robin Hood* – a total of approximately 6,000 mentions. Most of these are of slight critical discursive interest, other than to confirm that Robin Hood remains a prominent cultural 'meme' or marker, a lexical unit that is arguably a core item of British English. Roughly one-quarter of all these mentions (e.g., in TV schedules) refer to films, stories and TV shows about the legend of Robin Hood. Approximately 20% are toponymic, referring to *Robin Hood's Bay* in Yorkshire, or *Robin Hood Airport* in Doncaster (which opened in 2005), or a horse, pub, road or housing estate with that name (especially *Robin Hood Gardens* in Poplar, London, whose demolition was contested in the courts). About 10% of mentions are in stories classified as news, where the name may appear in the direct speech report of some individual worthy of note. In recent years a further 10% of uses, approximately, are in stories about two *Robin Hood Tax* proposals. In 2010, a '*Robin Hood*' tax on mining profits was mooted in Australia; and then came a campaign to apply one to financial transactions in the European Union. This was much discussed in 2010–12 in the United Kingdom and the European Union generally and was promoted by President Sarkozy of France, but it was vetoed by then UK Prime Minister Cameron. Representations of the Robin Hood tax are discussed later.

The most important uses of *Robin Hood* in *The Times* for critical discourse analysis purposes have occurred in the editorial and commentary section (leaders, letters, and feature articles). In the period covered by the digital archive, to 2011, there are 745 hits for *Robin Hood* in stories from this section. These comprise 31 editorials, 63 letters to the editor, and 651 feature or opinion articles; all occurrences in the first and second of these categories have been examined in detail, while instances of *Robin Hood* in the diverse set of feature articles have been more selectively noted, since they are only very occasionally relevant to my topic. A search in *Nexis* (for the most recent five years to the end of 2016), which has no distinct classification of stories into sections such as editorial and commentary and which does not include letters to the editor, returns 211 uses. Some stories are duplicates, most concern the Robin Hood tax, and there are no more than two or three opinion/editorial articles using *Robin Hood* in relation to wealth and redistribution; these have been included in my close 'manual' survey of the 651 feature/opinion stories from the digital archive. The upshot is that a small corpus of 162 stories (ninety-four editorials and letters as noted, and sixty-eight feature articles) was created, approximately 150,000 words in size and containing 271 uses of *Robin Hood* drawn from the entire forty-five-year period, where the phrase was judged to be used in an evaluative way.

A significant number of these 271 more evaluative uses, perhaps as many as a third, have the structure *a Robin Hood figure* (sixteen instances) or *a latter-day Robin Hood* or *a self-styled Robin Hood*. The stories in which these occur are typically about a 'colourful rogue' or not-so-charming criminal with however some good intentions or some affiliation with the downtrodden, in a range of countries or times. Thus we find a Croatian Robin Hood, a Carpathian one, and other ones in Mexico, Venezuela, India, Sicily and Scotland. There is also *an Albanian Robin Hood*; *a genuine Colombian Robin Hood*; one Tilka Manjhi, *an 18th century Robin Hood character* and another located *off the Somalian coast*. Quite often evaluating someone as a Robin Hood figure is hedged: *a kind of Robin Hood*, a *sort of Robin Hood*, an *almost Robin Hood* figure and so on. There is also an *Islamic Robin Hood* and even a *digital* one (a Latvian computer hacker). These 'exotic' Robin Hoods are never a politician.

The *Robin Hood* description encapsulates the referent's agency in some act of wealth transfer. These uses imply recognition that the 'genuine' Robin Hood flourished in Sherwood Forest in medieval times, so that these various others are only figuratively like the true Robin Hood in some respects. And the phrase is so entrenched in the language that it can be deployed in morphologically creative ways. Unlike the preceding cases, little if any criminality is apparent in these cases. One incident is described as *a proper Robin Hood moment*; on the strength of one incident of vigilante justice a gang of criminals won a *Robin Hood reputation*; a journalist reports on a blatant email scam sent by someone who *would like to do a little reverse Robin Hood-ing* and the actions of a man in a Cookie Monster costume who stole a chocolate biscuit company's giant logo and threatened to destroy it unless a particular children's hospital was given free biscuits are called *very Robin Hood*. This diversity of uses of the *Robin Hood* tag affects how the description is understood. The general idea remains: that a Robin Hood person or process bravely and cheerfully takes from the rich and powerful by force to aid the poor and weak. But additional suggestions are strengthened: that the person so described is socially disruptive or worse, often with something carnivalesque in his actions.

Where a modern public figure is *playing Robin Hood* or said to be *a Robin Hood figure*, the descriptions make explicit that the individual so described is not himself Robin Hood (and Robin is unequivocally male-gendered), notwithstanding the similarities. Being a pretend Robin Hood rather than the real thing, such people are not to be taken entirely seriously on their own terms, it is implied. These negative and mocking colourings apply particularly when the phrase *Robin Hood* is attached to an agentive individual, and rather less when applied to a process or action. Such factors must have been weighed up by the leaders of the *Robin Hood tax campaign*, when deciding that the implied promise in the title outweighed any insinuations of unreality, or self-dramatizing 'gesture politics'.

6.3   *Robin Hood* in the *Daily Mail*: Preliminary Profile

Paralleling the situation in relation to *The Times*, two separate electronic archives needed to be consulted for the *Daily Mail*: the *Daily Mail Digital Archive* for the years 1971–2004, and the advertisements-free, graphics-free bare text *Nexis* database for the period from 2005 to 2016. Between the two, more than 4,000 mentions of *Robin Hood* are recorded. For the archive years, more than four-fifths of these are in features, and mostly of minimal interest as in *The Times* (e.g., schedule listings of film, TV or radio programmes or reviews of these; references to Robin Hood's Bay, the Robin Hood Airport, or various street names). Only eighty-five are in the *Mail's* editorial and commentary section; just those eighty-five uses (divisible into twenty-three editorial comments and sixty-two letters to the editor) and a very few instances from a subcategory of features called feature articles, are relevant here. The main evidence for the following discussion, therefore, in which socio-political uses of *Robin Hood* in *The Times* and the *Mail* for any given time period (such as a year or a decade) are considered together, is eighty-five editorials or letters in the *Mail* and ninety-four editorials or letters in *The Times*.

6.4   *Robin Hood* in the 1970s

Editorial items mentioning *Robin Hood* relevantly in *The Times* in the 1970s are few – and they are letters only, not leader articles. The first letter, on 1 June 1972, questions the provision of extra financial support for people living on low incomes: 'The state may add a tithe to their sustenance by engaging in the sport of Robin Hood, but carried too far that game will surely destroy both nations, rich and poor.' This phrasing explicitly recognises that Britain is two nations: the rich and the poor. The letter is one of several responding to an open letter published a few days previously from a Mr Hugh Barry, addressed to the prime minister. The Barry letter had argued that living on a weekly wage of £20.50 – the minimum earnings offer then being made by the Railway Board to their workers in an ongoing pay dispute – was intolerable. The next relevant use is in a letter commenting on a *Times* proposal for a 'National Investment' compulsory savings levy (27 December 1973), which the correspondent warns could be grossly unfair unless it amounted to employee shareholding: 'It would be a reversal of the Robin Hood role'.

On 27 February 1974 – the day before the general election of 28 February – *The Times* publishes a letter from the Catholic Bishop of Southwark, defending the figures he had used in a recent commentary. In that commentary the bishop had questioned the morality of the present situation, where 'a disproportionate amount of the national wealth is in very few hands'. In the interests of national unity (a concept noted as prominent in several of the budget speeches discussed in Chapter 3), the bishop suggests it is essential that 'the ownership of capital, and the power that goes with it, should be more widely diffused'. He then reports how an acquaintance who recently made huge profits on a property deal has just donated a fifth of those profits to the Bishop's fund for the homeless: 'Perhaps I should have refused it, but Robin Hood has always been in my calendar of saints!' He goes on to hope that people might voluntarily move to a more sharing mentality so that 'the ethics of Sherwood Forest will no longer be necessary'.

Next comes a letter of 15 March 1974 about the freeze on housing rent increases being imposed by the new Labour government and the extra burden, in rates increases, it will impose on homeowners. The rates increases would be needed to cover local councils' shortfalls in revenue: in effect, a slight shifting of the tax burden away from renters, whose payments were frozen, and on to owners. The correspondent remarks, '[A]t first sight the Robin Hood attitude of the present government may have something to commend it to a proportion of the electorate', before asking 'how many millions per year will have to be paid by taxpayers and ratepayers to subsidize council house tenants?' In the next mention, in a letter of 16 October 1974 about the ethics of taxation, the correspondent discloses that he tries to see the taxman 'as an essentially kind-hearted and strictly non-violent Robin Hood rather than as a selfish and malevolent Dick Turpin'. A short tongue-in-cheek letter of 20 March 1975 suggests the Labour government revives an earlier tradition and declares 1 May 'Robin Hood's Day, in recognition of the national benefit from the capital transfer tax' (a tax on the transfer of capital by gift or bequest which was replaced, from 1986, by Inheritance Tax).

What of *Robin Hood* in the *Daily Mail*, in the 1970s, the Heath-Wilson-Callaghan years? There are a few barbed uses, of local rather than national political significance: the very first mention of *Robin Hood* in a *Mail* comment of 1971 comes in a short item about Nottinghamshire county council paying the rent of certain 'problem family' council tenants (how many is not stated) since this is much cheaper than evicting them and moving them to welfare homes. Although '[t]he Sheriffs of Nottinghamshire are playing Robin Hood with the best intentions', the *Mail* cannot approve of this encouraging of 'the feckless'.

By contrast with *The Times*, the *Mail*'s uses of *Robin Hood* (in comments and letters) across the forty-five years are consistently applied to the economic policy of one or another Labour government, or of a Labour politician, or of the party itself when in opposition. The uses always imply the policy so described is romantic and unrealistic, if not a kind of madness, in what is judged to be its extremism. A few uses, in the 1970s, buck that trend of application exclusively to Labour politics: in the earliest years of the period studied the *Robin Hood* label is also applied to a Conservative prime minister.

A *Mail* comment on 27 September 1972, reviewing Mr Heath's proposal for a moderate and controlled increase in wages and prices, hints that he may be revealing a Robin Hood tendency. The *Mail* says Mr Heath's proposed wages and prices policy is a handsome offer, deserving the support of business and the unions alike. 'Above all, it has the ring of fairness', the paper declares. But it goes on to wonder whether there might not be 'too much of the Robin Hood spirit in it for the [Ford] car workers of Dagenham to stomach'. The Ford car workers had proven united and militant in their demands for significant pay increases, so here the *Mail* implies that the 'greedy' car workers are less

interested in moderating the pay imbalance between rich and poor than Mr
Heath is. The Heath-as-Robin-Hood trope is repeated six months later in
a leader of 5 March 1973 about the hospital workers' strike for higher pay.
The *Mail* judges this strike as ill-advised, despite also seeing the hospital
workers as 'particularly deserving'. The editorial states that '[l]ast autumn,
Mr Heath tried to market his own brand of Robin Hood Socialism to beat
inflation. He proposed to hit the living standards of the rich to help the poor.'
It goes on to declare that the present difficulties stem from the unions' refusal to
compromise with the government, rather than the latter's inflexibility. In both
these examples, Mr Heath's conciliatory pay proposals aimed at placating
employees and unions, employers, and the Treasury, are repeatedly called
benign or 'Robin Hood' interventions. But as the *Robin Hood* epithet implies,
the approval is far from unqualified: there is veiled criticism of Heath as 'too
conciliatory', and perhaps even weak, in making so many compromises with
organised labour.

The *Mail's* first association of Labour with Robin Hood comes in an editorial
comment of 26 March 1974, titled *Robin Hood on Probation*, in which the
contents of Labour Chancellor Denis Healey's forthcoming budget, predicted
to redistribute from the wealthy to the disadvantaged, are guessed at and
critiqued. Although inflation was then running at around 15%, the *Mail* editorial argues against further deflationary measures. It is also unhappy, however, at
the prospect of reflation by redistribution, which it sees as an attack on those
who save (and hopefully later invest, supporting enterprise): 'if you take from
the better-off to give to the poor, then you are, in effect, transferring money
from those who save to those who spend all they can get'. In an extended
equating of Mr Healey with Robin Hood, the leader article ends with this
observation (albeit one hedged by the phrase *could threaten*):

When Robin Hood sips his brandy and water, and twangs his tax bow in the Commons
this afternoon, he must know that one rash gesture from him could threaten the well-
being not just of his own merry men, but of the whole anxious and watchful nation.

Just two days later the *Mail* decides that Healey isn't Robin Hood after all.
In a feature article it is tartly remarked of his economic policies that while he
may have 'set out to be Robin Hood' Mr Healey has ended up 'more like
a kindly version of the Sheriff of Nottingham'.

By 11 July 1974, the *Mail* is transferring the Robin Hood name as a jibe from
the moderate Healey to his left-wing cabinet colleague, Tony Benn.
An editorial derides his ministry's proposals for three new public bodies to
oversee public broadcasting funding, media ethics and press advertising revenues. The *Mail* denounces these as oppressive bureaucratic monsters,
announced in ludicrous jargon and pompous acronyms, and Maoist in their
intent on state control: 'Bow down before "An Advertising Revenue Board"

(ARB), to supervise and play Robin Hood with all Press advertising revenue. That is to say, taking from those who are making little or no profit and giving it to those who are even worse off.' On 30 November of that year comes a lengthy *Mail* comment – *So Was Robin Hood Just a Maladjusted Delinquent after All?* – on the pretext that two new television series about the hero are in production by ITV and BBC, with the BBC team declaring that their version would come with a strong sense of 'the political and social life of the time'. Purporting to assist the BBC project, the *Mail* comment offers its own suggested storyline for the series, in essence a laboured whimsical imagining of the merry men as petty or not so petty modern-day criminals (siphoning petrol and stealing groceries on the one hand, hijacking planes on the other). The scenario lacks internal coherence and is chiefly an opportunity for joking allusion to various kinds of 'rebels' of note in 1970s British popular culture (unemployed rock musicians, hippies, groupies, fugitive train robbers skulking in Brazil, etc.). It re-describes Robin and his men, but it does not describe acts to aid the oppressed poor. It also contains, unrelated to the Robin Hood motif, a satirical treatment of bureaucratic jargon. The final paragraph reads: 'And everyone lives happily ever after. Or to put it another way, total personnel maintain a maximum satisfaction-feedback quotient on an open-sided long-term basis.' This is perhaps intended as a further put-down of the BBC team, with their proposed 'sociological' treatment of Robin Hood. Read from today's perspective, the item jars since the genre it pastiches is strongly associated with management-speak rather than either countercultural or sociopathic tendencies. The *Mail*'s underlying motive seems to be to reiterate the irrelevance of Robin Hood and the 'sociopolitical conditions of his emergence' to the modern world, by encouraging derisive laughter at attempts (as in this comment, or by the BBC) to suggest otherwise.

In 1975 (6 February) comes a feisty letter from the owner of a small business denouncing Labour's proposal to raise the National Insurance contributions payable by the self-employed (an increase that the *Mail* had campaigned against). The headline for the entire letters page uses the writer's message: *This Robin Is Not Robbing the Rich*. It is noteworthy that simple puns on *robbing* and *hood* often feature in the *Mail*'s mentions of the hero. The letter writer comments: 'The Labour Government seems to have a misplaced Robin Hood complex as far as we are concerned. Self-employed is not synonymous with wealthy.'

In 1977 *Robin Hood* appears again, at the opening of a comment piece on 2 June, *How to Help and Not Feel Guilty*, about the North–South aid talks in Paris, where developing countries in the global South sought compensation for the many years of colonial exploitation. The *Mail* tells us that Robin Hood 'had it easy', and 'his form of economic aid was uncomplicated', whereas the danger today is that '[t]he taxes paid by poor people in rich countries can so easily end up in the pockets of rich people in poor countries'. The *Mail* particularly rejects the idea that the developed North should feel any post-colonial guilt or be prompted to act on that basis, and argues against restructuring the South's debts: this 'leads only to further Government extravagance (as we in Britain know to our own cost)'. Skimpy in its advice as to 'how to help' despite the promise in its title, the comment makes a powerful one-sided case against any international intervention motivated by moral responsibility. It characterises moral responsibility as a matter of Western leaders 'feeling guilty' and being influenced by 'an ugly element of moral blackmail'. This argument against international intervention extends to become also an argument against domestic intervention motivated by moral responsibility.

6.5   Grunwick

In the summer of 1977 one particular employer–employee dispute received enormous attention in the newspapers and elsewhere; it came to be known simply as 'Grunwick'. Touching upon many core dimensions of the social contract, it also triggered an allusion to Robin Hood in a letter to *The Times*, published on 12 September 1977.

The Grunwick dispute was a protracted strike by women, mostly Asian and recently immigrated from East Africa, working in a small photographic film-development company. They sought recognition of their union but were rebuffed by the owner of the business, Mr George Ward. Although affecting a relatively small workforce, the dispute developed enormous social and cultural resonance, involving moderate Labour and Liberal politicians and right-wing Conservative ones on opposing sides; fluctuating levels of support from the predominantly male and white trade union movement and a government-commissioned inquiry led by Lord Scarman. Scarman's report, urging moderation, was rejected by Mr Ward. Supporting him, Sir Keith Joseph, a prominent Conservative ally of Mrs Thatcher and a shadow minister on the Opposition front bench (he featured in Chapter 5 on *Luddites*) called the report 'either naïve or slipshod'. As for the key question concerning the legality of the owner's refusal to recognise the union, this was finally resolved in his favour by the Law Lords. In his outspoken attacks on Scarman and such moderate politicians as Shirley Williams and David Steel, Sir Keith was widely felt to have 'gone too far', with even Mrs Thatcher years later in her 1995 autobiography writing that his comments were 'too sharp'.

The 12 September letter is critical of Sir Keith Joseph's intransigent attitude, and spoke for many when it complained that Sir Keith's enthusiasm for the Law Lords' upholding of the employer's legal rights paid too little attention to the wider sense of unfairness in employment relations and disrespect for workers that the dispute seemed to suggest: 'Does Sir Keith Joseph really believe ...

that the law must at all times and in all circumstances be upheld? Has Sir Keith never heard of Robin Hood?' The foregoing contextualisation only begins to sketch out the implications of the Grunwick dispute, which has continued to attract extensive commentary, analysis and film documentary treatment. The confrontation raised questions about race and gender relations, fair employment terms, the respective rights and power of employers and unions and about what sort of Britain people were living in and wanted to live in. Sir Keith called the dispute 'a make-or-break point for British democracy' and insinuated that those sympathetic to the strikers were paving the way to communism, while more moderate Conservatives (the Opposition party at that time) regarded him as unhelpfully divisive. But his stance also expressed a major fault-line, separating moderates from right-wingers, within the party that was soon to embark on eighteen years of government, under Mrs Thatcher and later John Major. In the light of these high stakes, it is all the more striking that *Robin Hood* is invoked by *The Times* letter writer, as encapsulating principles of fairness which, for this writer, were more important than those of strict legality. Sir Keith and the hard-line Tories had moved too far away from Robin Hood values.

Grunwick is extensively treated in the *Mail* also, with no fewer than fifteen editorial comments in 1977 alone referring to the story. But it noticeably devotes most of its coverage not to the basis of the dispute itself – what the strikers sought and what the proprietor refused to allow – but to the alleged picket-line violence and the difficulties the mass picketing presented to the police, who are repeatedly applauded for upholding the law and protecting the right of non-striking Grunwick employees to continue working. But neither the *Mail*'s letters about the dispute – where the 'mob rule' threatened by the pickets is also mentioned – nor its comments invoke the name of Robin Hood.

Other than the comments and letters items, a very few of the news stories in the *Mail* in the 1970s and 1980s also deploy the Robin Hood label in strategic representations of 'excessive' and 'unrealistic' wealth-redistributive proposals. These include a 13 January 1977 news story titled *It's 'Robin' Crosland*, which begins, 'Foreign Secretary Anthony Crosland took the helm of Europe yesterday and promptly announced plans – like Robin Hood – to soak the rich nations and give to the poor.' On 8 March in the same year, a report that is critical of parliamentary debate on Concorde (headline: *Robin Hood in Reverse*) complains that the supersonic aircraft panders to the rich and wastes ordinary taxpayers' money, 'rather like a Robin Hood in reverse, taking money from the poor and giving it to the rich'. A 23 April 1977 report of a criminal fraud case describes 'the Robin Hood world of two wealthy philanthropists who got their money from a £1 million fraud'. A short news item on 22 June 1977 begins: 'A Robin Hood-style transfer of wealth from the rich to the poor through drastic tax changes is planned by Labour Party dream-mongers', before undercutting the item's newsworthiness by noting that TUC representatives were not interested in the plan, so that this proposal is likely to remain but a dream. A Saturday, 28 January 1978, story reports that Labour's Social Services Minister David Ennals has announced his intention to prioritise health and social services targeted at poor children: 'he said that he is to encourage a Robin Hood policy of "positive discrimination" favouring the transfer of cash and services to poor areas at the expense of better-off neighbourhoods'. A 16 February 1979 business article about Ireland's Industrial Development Agency (the Celtic tiger was then just emerging in its strength) contrasts this agency with Britain's (Labour government) politicians, who are accused of 'playing Robin Hood' rather than encouraging the creation of wealth. A news article of 2 October 1979 titled *Anger over Dole Tax* reports the unions' fury at the new Conservative government for secretly exploring the feasibility of taxing unemployment benefits; for the unions this was 'acting like Robin Hood in reverse by robbing the poor to pay the rich through their tax cuts'. This is rather different from the role the government was accused of playing back in February, but the difference is unsurprising, given the change of government. Besides, the *Mail* is not endorsing the union view they report – which leaves open the possibility that they regard the dole tax policy as, in fact, defensible.

Throughout the 1970s it seems to be accepted that *Robin Hood* represents an understandable attitude towards great wealth and power, albeit one that it would be economically risky, legally problematic and socially disruptive to adopt without qualification or if taken too far. A Robin Hood attitude was not devoid of all common sense. But as we shall see, at the close of the 1970s and throughout the 1980s the predominant understanding of *Robin Hood* even in *The Times* leaders and letters and news items becomes less tolerant, and more explicit as to the inappropriateness and even recklessness of 'playing' Robin Hood. Those in whom Robin Hood tendencies are detected now also tend to be characterised as extremist or unreasonably radical. The epithet formerly applied to a moderate Conservative such as Edward Heath in the early 1970s comes in the 1980s to be applied to committed left-wing figures such as Ken Livingstone.

6.6   *Robin Hood* in Mrs Thatcher's 1980s and John Major's 1990s

From around the time of Grunwick onwards, and certainly after the Winter of Discontent (the first months of 1979), *The Times* and the *Mail* editorially grow more openly intolerant of 'Robin Hood' tendencies, gestures or inclinations on the part of political leaders. They do so sometimes to the point of referring to fiscal developments that could be labelled 'Robin Hood in reverse' without the disapproval that was evident in the previous decade.

It is possible that a covert message was articulated by the winning side in the Grunwick dispute, and duly disseminated by *The Times* and the *Mail*, to the effect that there was to be 'no more Robin Hood!' – no more campaigns of action to express grievances or expose wrongdoing except by strictly constrained legal procedure. If there was some such resolve in the Conservative government and the right-wing press, then the first controversy in the 1980s to trigger an editorial mention of *Robin Hood* in *The Times* is interpretible as a continuation of that struggle.

This concerned a Granada Television 'World in Action' TV programme of February 1980 about the British Steel Corporation, whose workers were at that time striking for better pay. The programme relied extensively on leaked company documents that identified many of BSC's problems as stemming not from its workers' low productivity (as BSC publicly asserted), but poor management and inept government intervention (the latter again involving the Secretary of State for Industry, Sir Keith Joseph). When BSC demanded the names of those insiders who had supplied Granada with these damaging documents (to discourage further leaks with the threat of prosecution, presumably) a major legal dispute arose. Granada refused to provide names on press-freedom 'protection of sources' grounds. In the Court of Appeal, Lord Denning found in favour of BSC, controversially deciding that Granada had acted without due responsibility in their programme (he spoke of 'this damaging attack' on British Steel and the government, thereby arguably seriously misrepresenting matters). The case eventually reached the Law Lords, who ruled (on 30 July 1980; their arguments were published later) that journalists could not claim the same privilege as applied in lawyer–client and police–informer confidentiality. A *Times* leader of 31 July, 'A Charter for Wrongdoing', criticised the Law Lords' decision as 'restrictive, reactionary, and clearly against the public interest'. The supreme court's ruling threatened to curb press exposure of wrongdoing of public concern, until section 10 of the Contempt of Court Act 1981 was introduced. Prompted by article 10 of the European Convention on Human Rights, this stipulated that refusing to disclose was unlawful only if the disclosure was 'necessary' – for example, in the interests of national security.

All of this is in the framing background when *The Times* publishes a letter from a Mr Fotheringham on 7 August 1980, which invokes the name of Robin Hood in questioning passive submission to legal authority. The 31 July *Times* editorial had defended press protection of confidentiality-breaching information sources where a strong public interest existed, and that defence in turn triggered a number of letters (published on 2 August) critical of that position. Confronting those critics, Mr Fotheringham asserts in his letter that 'slavish obedience to the law is neither the hallmark of nor the pathway to a free society' and adds that 'our national folk hero, Robin Hood, is not some great patriotic

Alexander Nevsky figure, but one whose semi-mythical fame rests on his defiance of the authority of the law'. A letter two days later vehemently disagrees, addressing the editor directly:

Robin Hood, the SS soldier [sc., one who disobeys an order to carry out a massacre], the Tolpuddle Martyrs and the suffragettes were justified in defying the law. They had no say in its making. It was their oppressor. You, with Arthur Scargill and Granada, have no such justification.

The latter parties enjoy the legal right to vote and to publish, the writer argues, and therefore should themselves protect the law.

On one side we see Granada Television, the Grunwick workers, Mr Fotheringham and *The Times* leader writers implying that a 'Robin Hood' defiance of the laws or allegiance to its spirit rather than the letter is sometimes justified; on the other side we see the Grunwick owner and his Tory supporters (particularly Sir Keith Joseph), the British Steel Corporation and several of those whose letters appeared in *The Times* asserting an anti-Robin Hood line, essentially because all of us – even the little people – have the law to protect us, so that no one should resort to Hood-like illegality. Except that it was not clear to all observers that the law and the legal process, as made by successive governments and applied by judges of that era (on whom Griffith 1977 is the classic study), were entirely even-handed in the 1970s and 1980s, with cases such as that of the Grunwick women, the Birmingham Six and *Bromley LBC v. Greater London Council* [1983] among those cited as problematic.

On 30 April 1981 we see one of the earliest uses, in a British political context and in the period under study, of the precise phrase *Robin Hood in reverse*. Most noteworthy of the few earlier uses, before the period of interest, is in a *Times* story of 2 November 1970, which reports the phrase being used by Labour's former Education secretary, Edward Short, about the policies of the Conservative Education minister, one Margaret Thatcher. The 1981 usage comes in the headline and body text of a full-page *Times* article by Melvyn Westlake (for a few years an economics correspondent on the newspaper) entitled *How Robin Hood in Reverse Is Pushing the Poorest Worker into the Tax Trap*. This shows that the consequence of Geoffrey Howe's first three budgets in the Thatcher government has been both to increase the national tax burden by one-fifth, and to shift some of that tax burden from the richest workers to the poorest, extending the 'poverty trap' and exacerbating what Westlake calls the 'why work?' syndrome. The article was used by Labour leader Mr Foot in his challenges to a seemingly discomfited Mrs Thatcher at Prime Minister's Questions in the House of Commons the following day, fully reported in *The Times*. And a letter from Ruth Lister on 11 May, and two letters published on 12 May 1981, support Westlake's 'widening poverty trap' analysis and offer supplementary warnings. No refutations of his analysis appear.

Westlake dispassionately presents the inequality-exacerbating consequences of the early Thatcher taxation policies, and in adopting the phrase *Robin Hood in reverse* could be thought to signal a shift in sentiment from the 1970s, when governments risked criticism for 'playing Robin Hood'; now they are more likely to be challenged for doing the opposite.

But how vigorous is that challenge; how strongly is Westlake's article endorsed by *The Times* itself? Conversely, how unacceptable is it, in the discourse of *The Times* of the 1980s, for a 'Robin Hood in reverse' characterisation fitly to apply to government policy? The very presence of Westlake's article with its clear criticism of the government might lead one to think *The Times*'s typical representation of the new government's regressive tax moves was highly critical of them. But there is little evidence to support this supposition. Only taken up and supported by three letters published more than a week later, Westlake's article, I suggest, is an outlier, voicing a dissenting view rather than *The Times*'s consensus.

Westlake's key point is that the Conservative government's regressive tax changes have enlarged the 'poverty trap' – that is, the number of 'disincentivized' families for whom taxes applied to their low pay are so high that they are scarcely better off than families headed by unemployed parents and reliant upon benefits (thus inevitably living in poverty). If Westlake's 'Robin Hood in reverse' criticism is now the *Times*'s collective view, then we might expect more subsequent discussion of the 'poverty trap'. A simple search for mentions of *poverty trap* in *Times* editorials and commentary (including opinion pieces and letters) in the period April 1981 to May 1983 reveals a mere ten mentions, the earliest of these coming in December 1981, thus in no way prompt editorial support for Westlake's article of eight months earlier. The ten mentions comprise eight letters from diverse correspondents and two editorials. The first of the latter is a sceptical critique of the newly formed *Social Democratic Party's* proposals on how to tackle the poverty trap, and the second is a 16 March 1983 assessment of Geoffrey Howe's budget of the previous day, which notes that two of its measures will alleviate the poverty trap but that 'there is much more to be done here'.

As for writing about the poverty trap in its own voice, then, as distinct from publishing a very few letters from others, *The Times* appears to be silent. Despite the advocacy of its own Melvyn Westlake in one influential article, the *poverty trap* characterisation seems not be one the newspaper was inclined to include in its recurrent representation of life, work and prosperity in Britain in the early 1980s. Incidentally, a digital archive search for the phrase *poverty trap* in the *Mail* in the three years from 1980 to 1982, inclusive, reveals eleven mentions. The first of these, in an article summarising the research of an academic economist on the problem, actually pre-dates the first discussion in *The Times*. But by the time of Andrew Alexander's 6 April 1981 article about the high unemployment level, an unsympathetic line has emerged: 'The so-called poverty trap . . . makes it not worthwhile financially for large numbers of people to take work . . . [and through its over-generous benefits] . . . the State is to blame.' Alexander thus foregrounds the 'trap' and entirely disregards the poverty. Rather than seeing both the jobless and the taxed low-paid as poor, he implies that both groups are tolerably placed and that this is wrong: the state should grant the jobless fewer benefits than at present. Being worse off, they would be incentivised to work, while those in work, albeit low-paid, would be incentivised to stay in work. There is no mention of an alternative prescription involving a higher minimum wage and more tax relief for those in work: that, for Alexander, would be more state interference of the wrong kind.

From June 1977 there is a five-year silence with regard to uses of *Robin Hood* in the *Mail*'s leaders or letters, until 8 February 1982, in a comment which likens the exploits of the budget air travel entrepreneur Sir Freddie Laker, whose business was then facing bankruptcy, to 'some latter-day Robin Hood'. Somewhat irrelevantly the comment alleges that 'the Socialists' (presumably a reference to Labour MPs, at this time the Opposition party) are 'dancing with rancid quip' at the prospect of Laker's business empire collapsing, and failing to see that Laker Airways is 'a popular cause'. But the paper is troubled that Prime Minister Thatcher, who had so often cited Sir Freddie as an inspiring example, 'her champion, knight entrepreneur', is not willing 'to help up again' her 'fallen' knight. 'There is free market logic' in Mrs Thatcher's withholding of public money, it concedes, but it predicts that she won't be popular for doing so. This is clearly a conflicted commentary, uncertain about with whom to side, and this turbulence is perhaps reflected in the equation of Laker with Robin Hood and the contrived opposing of those two men to 'the Socialists'. Laker offered bargain flights but he was no Robin Hood, and the 'unreal dreamer' Robin Hood is more usually associated in the *Mail* with Socialist 'impracticality'.

On 11 March 1983 comes the editorial *Robin Hood Shore* (the unexplained reference is to Peter Shore, the shadow Chancellor of the Exchequer), whose opening paragraph vividly demonstrates the rhetorical work that the *Mail* has *Robin Hood* do. It serves to characterise actions and attitudes that it implies are 'well-intentioned, but ill-thought-out': 'Labour's latest budgetary scheme for putting the country to rights is a typical piece of Robin Hood economics offering largesse to the poor through plundering the rich.' The *Mail*'s ire is directed at a Labour proposal to phase out tax relief on mortgage interest payments, which would increase the income tax bills of those buying their homes, but would remove the more favourable treatment of them by comparison with those renting their homes. Characterising this as *largesse* to the poor and a *plundering* of the rich, the phrase '*Robin Hood* economics' involves a series of large exaggerations.

Implicit in these papers' deployment of the name is the assumption that unqualified application of the legendary hero's *modus operandi* is by broad agreement wrong, extreme, naïve and romantic folly, and dangerously extra-legal. But in the 1970s, *some* elements of interventions with a Robin Hood flavour to them could be reasonable, and even be applauded as revivals of a gallant old-English fighting on behalf of the poor and downtrodden. Therefore politicians in particular needed to avoid adopting attitudes or policies that appeared too sharply and visibly opposed to a Robin Hood stance – until the early 1980s at least. And in the press reporting of two-sided conflicts relating to wealth- or income-inequalities, neither opposed group wanted to be characterised as the one further away from Robin Hood values, as practising the opposite of Robin Hood principles. This, I suggest, may be why the 1981 Westlake article may have been troubling both for the Thatcher government and for the dominant political viewpoint of *The Times* newspaper in which it appeared. In subsequent Thatcher years both newspapers hardened in their dismissal of 'Robin Hoodism' – although the poll tax debacle of 1989–90 (see Section 6.7) was testing for them, since it prompted others to deploy damaging descriptions of the government as being *Robin Hood in reverse*.

6.7   Keynes, not Robin Hood

Keynes, Not Robin Hood is the title of a *Times* leader of 23 January 1984, which is critical of remarks made by the Queen in her Christmas Day television broadcast of the previous month (by 1984, watching the Queen's Christmas message was a hallowed tradition and an essential part of that holiday's routine for many in the United Kingdom). The leader is part of a multi-voiced discussion, extending over many days, and a telling demonstration of how, when these centre-right newspapers address the question of what should be done about economic inequality, Robin Hood is regularly invoked – as encapsulating a fleetingly attractive but disastrous response to the problem.

The editorial is not centrally an attack on the Queen herself – unlikely in a newspaper so much of the Establishment as *The Times* – but more a severe caution directed at those who let the Queen 'stray' into contentious political matters. In her broadcast, the Queen had alluded to the suggestion that the wealth gap between rich and poor countries might be narrowed by Commonwealth action. The Robin Hood rich-to-poor wealth transfer this seemed to propose was absolutely the wrong approach, according to the 1984 *Times* leader and its headline.

The 23 January editorial followed one from two days earlier, which questioned the Queen's urging of less attention to nationalism and more to international interdependence. Concerned now at the emergence of 'global egalitarian' and 'redistributionalist' interpretations of the Queen's comments,

The Times declares: 'The idea that the poor can be more than temporarily relieved of their poverty by a direct transfer of wealth from the better off is fundamentally incorrect.' *The Times* is adamant that a commendable desire to relieve poverty has no connection with egalitarianism and rich-to-poor redistributionalism. Other themes that are also familiar in discursive campaigns against redistribution follow, especially that equality of opportunity' will not bring equality of income because personal differences and motivations lead some to prosper and others not to. Applied to rich and poor countries, which was the Queen's topic, this is to assume that the gulf between median wealth in poor countries and that in rich countries was chiefly a matter of motivation and enterprise (the clear implication being that these are qualities those in the North have and those in the South do not). Income inequality should not prompt a moralising interpretation of 'what would otherwise be *natural economic diversity*' (emphasis added), *The Times* contends.

Once it is accepted that economic differences offend some moral code, it becomes morally permissible to attempt to eliminate them, even in defiance of market forces, by coercive methods involving the transfer of wealth, so that productive and economically active people are penalised while those who are not are favoured.

People 'operating in a free and open market will inevitably reach different levels of achievement' and in fact wealth-accumulation 'nearly always' advances economic enterprise more generally, and the trickling down of wealth and opportunity. We should avoid the folly of believing that wealth itself is 'improper', the *Times* contends. Any egalitarian-minded effort of redistribution would entail state control and the creation of monopolies, leading to waste, bureaucracy and market distortion. Egalitarian levelling is always a levelling down, the leader declares, moving on to the following extreme anti-state declaration: 'There is little evidence to suggest, in any economy, that the poor become richer when the rich are made poorer.' On any reasonable measure of 'richness', which allows it to include factors such as infant health, mass education and retirement pensions, it makes no sense to deny that the allocation of tax revenues gathered more from the rich than from the poor has significantly improved the quality of life of poorer citizens. The leader's assertion is close to an absolute rejection of the Robin Hood impulse, dismissing wealth transfers on two counts and concluding that everyone ends up poor. The leader's declaration relies on the reader not examining too closely the misrepresenting imprecision of the claim that redistributions 'make the rich *poorer*'. Rhetorically the leader draws persuasive power from its use of chiasmus (*rich poorer, poor – richer*), but this conceals what is a sharp asymmetry, since the 'richer' that the poor might become will still be far poorer than the 'poorer' that the rich might become. The editorial's stance is of a piece with Patience Wheatcroft's complaint, in 2001, about the 'impoverishing' £5 per week tax increase faced by families struggling to pay private school fees (see Section 6.9). If *The Times*'s claim were valid, there would be little justification ever to expect the rich to pay more for any service (police, defence, opera) than the poor did. In effect by 1984, for *The Times*, Robin Hood and his ilk can be rejected without qualification.

The following day (24 January 1984) comes a short letter in rebuttal of the editorial, which says in part, 'Regardless of what might have been said (or done) by Keynes, Robin Hood or yourself – I believe that I have a responsibility towards my less fortunate fellow humans.' A fuller and more forceful rejoinder only comes two weeks later (6 February 1984), in a letter from the Bishop of Worcester (Philip Goodrich). Neither for the first time nor the last in the period studied, we find a bishop lining up on the Robin Hood side of politics and opposing *The Times*'s views. The bishop criticises the newspaper for misrepresenting the Queen; he says her remarks, echoing the statement of the Commonwealth Heads of Government meeting in Delhi, were not about income redistribution but fairer terms of trade and a fairer market place for developing countries that export primary products. The bishop calls one phrase in *The Times*'s leader, 'natural economic diversity', a travesty of the truth. He adds that campaigners at the UNCTAD and GATT conferences are asking for 'a moderation of market forces'. In a letter published adjacently and also critical of *The Times*'s two editorials, Philip Snow deplores the '[l]et us help no one' isolationism of the leader article, suggesting that others too will regard it as a glimpse of 'a society going downhill, very fast indeed'.

On 19 July 1986 comes a *Mail* editorial on *Labour's plan for swingeing taxes*, accusing the opposition party of 'gleefully' devising 'schemes to help the poor by soaking the rich'; listing these schemes, the *Mail* comments: 'It all sounds very simple Robin Hood economics ... But who are the rich to be plundered in this way?' If implemented, the plans would create no new Jerusalem of social justice, but a 'wretched reality'. It is not only crazy Labour that the people need to beware of, the *Mail* warns; two months later in *Middle Classes Be Warned* (19 September 1986) comes an assessment of the Social Democrat Party's policy proposals, which are dismissed as 'Robin Hood schemes for redistributing income from the better-off to the poor' while promising no tax increases overall.

Winning Away and Losing at Home (3 December 1986) is a *Mail* Comment on the highest rate of tax (60%) and how this has prompted a departure of talent (here, a star footballer, but by implication other high earners too) to lower-tax countries such as Italy. Rather than criticising the status quo, the comment speculates that if Labour came to power and restored 80% as the top rate of tax, the talent drain would be immeasurably worse, to all our detriment. The villain in this imagined future is the Shadow Chancellor, Roy Hattersley: '[He] likes to pose as a latter-day Robin Hood, robbing the rich to help the poor.

In reality, he would be robbing this country of its talent, and making life more drab and impoverished for everybody else.' The word *drab* here is noteworthy, being one of a few recurrent vague but negative terms used in the unexplained evaluation of any policy change in a leftward or egalitarian direction; *dreary* is another such favourite. Also noticeable is the claim that 'everybody else' would be 'impoverished'. The phrasing cleverly implies three classes of people: those at the top, those at the bottom and a larger 'everybody else' (including *Mail* readers presumably) in the middle, who would be adversely affected alongside the rich. Hattersley is again targeted in a news article of 5 January 1987, *Labour's Big Tax Evasion*, which alleges that he is keeping secret, until after the approaching general election, his plans to tax the well-off, 'his Robin Hood scheme'.

A parliamentary sketch of Thursday, 20 July 1989, and aptly titled *Poll Tax Fall Guy*, says of Mr Nicholas Ridley, the Tory minister tasked with piloting the hated poll tax bill through Parliament, 'Labour MPs deem him a Robin Hood in reverse', while the sketch writer adds, '[H]e ends up robbing the rich instead of (or as well as) the poor. And see how Tory constituencies squeal!' As in a previous example, the *Mail* does not endorse this 'Robin Hood in reverse' evaluation of a Conservative minister, but simply reports the protesting reactions of Labour MPs and Tory constituencies.

In a 4 August, 1987 comment entitled *Wealth of Ideas*, the *Mail* welcomes Labour's Robin Cook, 'one of [Labour leader] Mr Kinnock's more cogent colleagues', for seeming to propose a Labour focus on managing prosperity rather than advocating 'inflationary spending plans by clobbering every wealth-maker'. The latter approach is identified with the older 'Socialists' such as, yet again, the then-portly Roy Hattersley:

Alack and alas for Hatters, the Friar Tuck of that unmerry band, neither he nor his Robin Hood economics are any longer in fashion with the Labour revisionists desperately trying to come to terms with popular capitalism in Thatcher's England.

Why Penalise the Thrifty? is the title of a *Mail* comment of 22 August 1989. It discusses the potentially damaging political consequences for the Conservatives of the 'transitional arrangements' covering the introduction of the controversial poll tax, in which lower-spending affluent Conservative local authorities were to cross-subsidise higher-spending and less affluent Labour regions ('robbing Bournemouth to pay Lambeth', as the editorial deftly puts it.) While conceding that 'you can argue that there is a primitive kind of Robin Hood justice in this', the *Mail* goes on to say they would not, since in practice this would probably be a 'repulsive' subsidising of spendthrifts by the prudent.

Throughout these years, *Robin Hood* is unambiguously associated with redistribution from the rich to the poor in ways that the *Mail* declares unjustified and unjust, the wasteful folly that socialist and egalitarian tendencies lead to. This is apparent in an editorial of 17 April 1991, *Labour's Signpost to the*

Meddle Way, which pours scorn on the party's election manifesto for amounting to 'the invitation to return to Robin Hood economics, based on the belief that you can squeeze the rich to succour the poor'. A long news item of 10 May 1991, just a few days before the general election, reports PM Major's denunciation of Labour leader Neil Kinnock's pledge to inject £20 billion into the public services; another Tory minister is reported saying '[h]e must have made that promise thinking he is Robin Hood. In fact, he is robbing everybody.'

In the event, Labour loses the general election, and Kinnock is replaced by John Smith as the new Leader of the Opposition. A 17 March 1992 leader ominously titled *You Have Been Warned* evaluates Smith's plan to remove the cap on National Insurance (enabling it more fully to become a secondary form of income tax). Labour 'remains more obsessed with redistribution than [economic] recovery', the *Mail* leader declares: 'At the best of times, such a relapse into Robin Hood Socialism could be dismissed as a romantic, if unrewarding, aberration. Now, it would be suicidal.'

6.8   Bishops More Progressive than Labour

In the later 1980s and early 1990s, the Conservative government's hold on power was secure, thanks to government victories in the Falklands war and the miners' strike. Neoliberal policies were taking firm hold. Perhaps as a consequence, mentions of *Robin Hood* in *Times* editorial material (including letters) are infrequent. One instance is a *Times* 'third leader' entitled *And a Penny on Peacocks*, which appeared on 16 March 1985, three days before Nigel Lawson's budget speech of 1985 (third leaders were an established site of humorous editorialising). This deploys heavy whimsy in imagining the imposition of special taxes on blatant luxuries such as over-long house driveways, private swimming pools, winter suntans and enormous yachts. But the leader adds that sharper forms of summary redistribution do not happen in the United Kingdom: 'It will not do for any Chancellor here to enrol Robin Hood in the Inland Revenue, but the temptation must be strong.' So absent from the political agenda is the idea of wealth redistribution that *Robin Hood* can be used in jokes. This continues through the early 1990s, when references to *Robin Hood* in editorials or letters are few and of slight consequence, using the phrase in ways that indicate his values are remote from the current political landscape.

But by the summer of 1995 a new phase in the uses of the name seems to be developing. First comes an opinion piece of 19 September, in which Janet Bush criticises then Chancellor Kenneth Clarke for continuing to promise tax cuts when the public borrowing requirement was predicted to overshoot the government target by £5 billion. Bush reports Britain's largest union, Unison, calling Clarke's promised tax cuts for the rich 'a case of Robin Hood in reverse' and adds: 'Why not play Robin Hood properly and impose a punitive windfall tax on the hated privatised water and electricity companies?' – an idea already proposed by the Shadow Chancellor, Gordon Brown. Against this comes a letter of 30 September, sceptical about politicians' promises and warning that '[i]f any political party decides to play Robin Hood against the utility companies the loser will still be the consumer'.

In 1997 a flurry of mentions of Robin Hood in a more serious politico-economic context occurs. The sequence begins on 28 January, when *The Times* reports the Bishop of Liverpool, David Sheppard, criticising the Labour party's tax proposals (announced in the run-up to the May general election which they were expected to win). Labour's decision not to raise the top rate of income tax was in his view a protecting of the comfortable at the expense of the vulnerable and needy. Sheppard also chaired the Christian Churches' inquiry into *Unemployment and the Future of Work*, which reported in April of that year and argued against acceptance in a globalised economy of long-term unem-ployment for some, and in favour of increased taxes to pay for new jobs in health care, education, child care, elder care, tourism and the environment. Responding to the *Times* report, a letter of 30 January under the title *Robin Hood Approach* challenges the bishop: 'The Bishop of Liverpool clearly believes that his Robin Hood approach to government is so self-evidently the only ethical one that he condemns politicians for deserting the poor in order to win votes … [But] governments cannot simply buy real, long-lasting jobs.' Countering this, another correspondent a few days later (4 February; also under the title *Robin Hood Approach*) declares: 'The Bishop of Liverpool speaks for many of us when he criticises the politicians for focusing the election on "comfortable Britain", leaving the vulnerable and needy without a voice.' Articulating a view that only became more widely recognised in later years, the writer adds: 'The additional wealth in our society over the past 20 years has gone mostly to those who were already the richest, leaving the poorest tenth actually poorer on average in real terms.' Not for the first time in this chapter, church leaders are criticised for 'interfering' in political matters (David Sheppard is the third bishop to grace this chapter; all received some oppro-brium in the press – but some support also – for their Robin Hood values).

The foregoing exchange is a good example of how, when used in serious political commentary, the phrase *Robin Hood* tends to appear as part of a reactive text, responding negatively to an initial statement or proposal where – unsurprisingly – the phrase does not appear. A public figure makes an observation or proposal about the economy which has some redistributive element to it. A response to this in *The Times* or the *Mail* then warns 'But this is (close to) Robin Hood economics!' with the clear implication that the idea is naïve, unrealistic, a flouting of the law and romantic folly, inappropriate to a complex modern economy. A further common implication is that the idea is a form of self-promoting grandstanding, with the person accused of 'casting themselves' in the role of Robin Hood.

Very much in this spirit is a story on 9 May 1998 from Andrew Pierce, about a wealth tax on London's corporate sector proposed by Ken Livingstone, then a candidate to become elected Mayor of London. The subheading runs *Ex-GLC Leader Casts Himself in Role of the Capital's Robin Hood*. There is something peculiarly shameful, according to British social mores, about casting oneself in any role; only others are supposed to do it, to you. The irony is that there is almost never an admitted self-casting as Robin Hood by public figures in Britain; the casting is done by the press or political opponents, with the intent of implying that the action is both unreal (playing a part) and unwarranted (*self-casting, not appointment by others).

6.9   Gordon Brown as (Nearly) Robin Hood: The New Labour Years (1997–2010)

Older readers may remember the general election of May 1997 as bringing the promise of a new dawn, an overdue change of government and the sense of a younger, more energetic, more cosmopolitan and more inclusive Britain led by a confident and youthful Tony Blair. Those on the political left were hopeful, even if those on the right were more doubtful. Many things seemed newly possible in the summer of 1997, even some version of 'Robin Hood economics', or so the early hostile uses of the phrase in *Mail* and *Times* editorial material might suggest. But these uses dwindle within two or three years – largely, it would seem, through lack of perceived need. In the New Labour years (1997–2010) when the phrase *Robin Hood* is used editorially in *The Times* concerning government policy, it is again an encapsulated evaluation of the policy as impractical or naïve redistributionalism, wrong not only in practice but even in principle – despite appearing noble and compassionate. This is also the spirit of a letter in the *Mail* on 4 July 1997, which complains that the new Labour government's 'windfall tax' will recover some of the profits made by privatised public utilities, but will spend this 'on its own objectives' rather than returning it to fleeced customers. Deploying the rhetoric of created oppositions, the writer suggests that in doing this Labour looks 'more like Al Capone than Robin Hood'. Five months later, a *Mail* comment of 3 December 1997 warns that while Gordon Brown has introduced new tax-free Individual Savings Accounts, he also 'plans to descend like an Old Labour reincarnation of Robin Hood on everyone who has managed to put by [in the previous PEPs and other tax-exempt instruments] more than £50,000 over the past decade' and denounces this as 'nothing less than a betrayal of public trust' and a 'fiscal con trick'. Brown later relaxed the upper limit on such tax-free savings transfers.

After the preceding 1997 comment, there are no truly relevant uses of *Robin Hood* in *Mail* editorials in the period 2005–2016; accordingly, most of the following paragraphs are devoted to *Robin Hood* in *The Times*. In particular, after 1998 no further *Mail* comments or letters equate Gordon Brown (or subsequent prime ministers or chancellors) with any kind of Robin Hood, even if others are so described. One of the latter is Peter Hain, the Northern Ireland minister, mocked on 13 February 2007 for having 'a Robin Hood moment' when he denounced London bankers' bonuses and advocated imposition of swingeing taxes or compulsory charitable donations on the financial industry super-rich. Written a year and more before the 2008 banking crash, the *Mail* article asserts that 'taxing City bonuses . . . is not the answer' to the bonus culture and inequality, and that the City of London is 'thriving as the world's new financial capital'.

By 8 July 1997, a week after Brown's first budget, the chancellor's policies are on the one hand reportedly criticised in the City of London for not taxing people sufficiently, but on the other hand denounced by the pensions industry for 'the most audacious daylight robbery since Robin Hood'. The description comes in the course of Anatole Kaletsky's largely positive assessment of the budget in the *Times*, even though he notes its foundation is not Keynesian but monetarist. And on Budget Day two years later (9 March 1999), Michael Gove predicts that Chancellor Brown will again increase the tax capture 'by stealth' or picking our pockets. Gove says these marginal real-terms tax increases are barely detectable: 'It is the redistribution not so much of Robin Hood as the Artful Dodger.' A business feature only two days later by Graham Searjeant disagrees, and tries to revive the Robin Hood descriptor, castigating Brown for using deliberately complex arrangements to mask his tax increases:

From the utility levy [aka windfall tax] onwards, Mr Brown has always sought to convert the mundane process of raising money from us to fund the public spending we voted for into a Robin Hood crusade. He will stamp out evil by taxing it and distribute the proceeds of social crime among worthy charitable causes.

Another feature article just two days after this agrees (*Times*, 13 March 1999), calling Gordon Brown 'the 'Robin Hood' Chancellor', for promising to name and shame those financial services companies that impose excessive charges on customers.

Two years pass before another flurry of identifications of Gordon Brown as Robin Hood occur (no other figure in these years is regularly so named). A feature by Patience Wheatcroft on 27 February 2001 with the title *When Will Gordon Brown Own Up to Being a Genuine Socialist?* assesses the chancellor's tax policies aimed at eradicating child poverty. 'Robin Hood Brown has been taking from the rich with the aim of giving to the poor', she reports, later referring to him as 'Robber Brown' (echoing the phrase *robber baron*). While conceding that this is a worthy ambition, she warns that if his 'Robin Hood tendencies' are given free rein there could be such heavy taxation that even 'those who are only moderately well off' will begin to suffer. She reports the Institute of Fiscal Studies calculation (from Andrew Dilnot, whose ideas are much used by the *Mail*, discussed later in this section) that the richest 10% of households will have a post-tax drop in income of two-thirds of 1%, and comments, 'While a weekly loss of £4-74 is not going to make the average investment banker weep, for a middle-class family striving to meet the school fees, every penny may count, and under Labour they will have fewer.' Whether readers agreed with Wheatcroft's contention that a tax increase of £250 per annum was a significant burden to families that could afford private school fees of £7,300 or more per child is doubtful.

On 23 May 2001, Mary Ann Sieghart reviews the silences and evasions in the election campaign declarations from both main parties. Neither of them is pledging major tax cuts or spending initiatives. The subhead declares: *Redistributing Wealth Robin Hood-Style Hardly Gets a Mention from Either Party*. Sieghart is I believe essentially correct, and these political circumstances constrained the opportunities for centre-right newspapers to deploy the *Robin Hood* epithet. It took these newspapers some time, however, to recognise that the gradualism of Brown's stealth taxes targeted the comfortable rather than the seriously rich, and that this could not easily be characterised as a 'Robin Hood' manoeuvre.

A *Times* leader of 19 September 2002, *Robin Hood Rides Again; But the Voters Are Turning Nervous*, notes, 'While most Britons enjoy the romance of the Robin Hood legend, they fear that modern-day Labour is more likely to label them as rich (to be stolen from) than poor (to be given to).' The leader suggests the windfall tax on utilities companies was 'politically popular and proved relatively painless', and thus a success. But (like its columnist Wheatcroft the previous year) it warns that yet more demands upon middle-class voters in the interests of redistribution risks 'stretching public tolerance to breaking point'. And in a business feature article of 4 February 2003, entitled *Beware the Chancellor's 'New Global Order'*, Rosemary Righter warns that while Gordon Brown's domestic spending initiatives are coming into question, his enthusiasm for international intervention, via a new International Finance Facility, is undimmed: '[H]e is more than ever bent on playing Robin Hood to the entire world', she complains. The article contrasts the left's uncritical reception of Brown's internationalist venture with the 'curmudgeonly left-wing response to Tony Blair's singular statesmanship over Iraq' (the Western allies' invasion of Iraq began on 20 March).

A couple of outlier uses of *Robin Hood* occur in June 2003 and January 2004. The first imagines Gordon Brown himself applying the Robin Hood label, in reverse, to the banks: an article describes his suspicions (later proved correct) of anti-competitive UK banking practices and links these to his reported conviction that 'banks left to their own devices behave like Robin Hood in reverse'. The second describes Tory party hostility towards Tony Blair as the essence of New Labour: 'He is, in their eyes, the combination of Robin Hood, Rasputin and Harry Houdini.' But on 10 March 2005 the emerging theme resumes, of Brown as a not-quite Robin Hood for taking from the middlingly affluent rather than the rich: another Anatole Kaletsky evaluation of Brown's economic strategy suggests that the chancellor has squeezed the middle classes (through stealth taxes) and left the rich unscathed (or even bolstered, by cutting capital gains tax from 40% to 10%), while aiding the poor: 'Mr Brown may have been a socialist towards the poor, but he has been no Robin Hood towards the rich.' Kaletsky's assessment is different and perhaps more insightful than Wheacroft's of February 2001, for whom Brown was both a socialist *and* Robin Hood. For Kaletsky, admittedly with four more years of his chancellorship and Labour policies to review, Brown is no Robin Hood at all, despite his investing in the poor.

Thus while Kaletsky is reassured by March 2005, his colleague Patience Wheatcroft remains suspicious. A month later (21 April 2005), a short article by her in the business pages is titled *Blair Doesn't Hit the Mark as Robin Hood* and begins by declaring that the then prime minister and the chancellor have been 'less upfront . . . than was Robin Hood' in robbing the rich to give to the poor. And a month earlier (17 March 2005) she criticised Chancellor Brown's preference (in his budget) for retention of discriminating pension tax credits over an indiscriminate improvement in the basic pension, saying that this reflected 'his efforts to be a modern-day Robin Hood'. She invokes Robin Hood a second time, in a strange *non sequitur*: 'Because the Robin Hood administration believes that it can spend our money so much better than we can ourselves, much of the cash that has been taken from the better-off has not found its way directly to those who are worse off.' It is unsurprising that much of the tax from the well-off, spent on such national concerns as health, defence and infrastructure, does not 'find its way directly' to the worse off. Things were simpler in Robin Hood's day, but the Wheatcroft sentence only confirms that no modern government can really operate 'just like Robin Hood'.

In the final years of the Labour government (2005–10) there are few uses of *Robin Hood*. The simplest explanation is that this is because *The Times*'s suspicions of radical redistributionist tendencies in New Labour had long been allayed. As a result *Robin Hood* can again be redeployed in flippant contexts: the few mentions in *Times* editorials of the last ten years are in comparatively frivolous leaders, about the modernising of old heroes to make them fit for the twenty-first century: 'Shakespeare as Internet Book Show Host? Robin Hood as Estate Agent?' (17 March 2006), or (5 May 2006) about Bill Gates wishing he were not so rich and oppressed [sic]. In the arena of government policy, it is again allegedly anti-Robin Hood actions which prompt use of the phrase, as expressive of something more criminal, a taking from the deprived and giving to the privileged, than Robin Hood's original action. Thus a leader on Monday, 7 April 2008, criticises Mr Brown, now prime minister, for abolishing the 10% income tax band for those on low incomes, in order to cut the standard rate from 22% to 20%:

[Brown is] robbing Peter in order to pay Paul ... Except in this instance Peter was notably poorer than Paul to start with ... Having wanted to be seen as some kind of Robin Hood, he [Brown] is about to be viewed as a new Sheriff of Nottingham.

And a 25 November 2008 economics feature on Alastair Darling's autumn budget reports that '[i]n a Robin Hood style budget statement, the Chancellor asked the 800,000 people who earn more than £100,000 a year to bear the brunt of a package of deferred tax rises designed to bring down borrowing'. The following year a letter of 16 December 2009 complains about the government's 'theft' of lottery funds to support the 2012 Olympics as an amoral diverting of money given for good causes to a jamboree for the elite and 'a total antithesis of Robin Hood' (but see Chapter 2 for discussion of a different view, in which playing the lottery is patriotically supporting Team GB).

Turning back to the *Mail*'s use of *Robin Hood* in political contexts over the past twenty years: as intimated most uses, even in letters and comments, are transient instances rather than anything detectably systematic. From close to the beginning of the Blair government, there are no comment editorials on New Labour in the *Mail* deploying the Robin Hood evaluation, and strikingly few news, letters or feature articles doing so. On 16 March 1998 there is a *Mail* preview of the following day's budget, which it calls *a 'Robin Hood' Budget* since it will reportedly target middle Britain to finance back-to-work measures for the worst off. Four days later, a 20 March 1998 commentary on Chancellor Brown's budget reports that 'Gordon Brown actually pulled off the biggest Robin Hood act of any Chancellor for 30 years, engineering a major switch of cash from the rich to the poor.' The budget is said to have 'hit' the middle class hard. The story is composed entirely of quotations from Andrew Dilnot, Director of the Institute for Fiscal Studies, who calls Brown's budget a redistributing one using 'taxes, reliefs and duties which fall hardest on the better-off.' Three months later, 29 June 1998, the *Mail* uses the same material, informing the reader that Dilnot 'told MPs recently that in his first two Budgets Gordon Brown had pulled off the biggest Robin Hood act of any Chancellor for 30 years'. Interestingly, Brown is not likened to Robin Hood nor is Dilnot named as an authoritative commentator in *The Times* in the years 1998 and 1999.

After these instances, the *Mail*'s naming of leading members of the government as *Robin Hood* adventurers drops away sharply. Other than the February 2007 story of Peter Hain having 'a Robin Hood moment' (noted earlier), there is the March 2007 report of an IFS economist's prediction that the public spending squeeze will adversely affect 'Mr Brown's capacity to play Robin Hood over the next few years' particularly with regard to slashing child poverty; and a year later (10 March 2008) a letter from a newly retired person complains that under revised arrangements she will be worse off: 'Gordon Brown is Robin Hood in reverse, robbing the poor to pay the rich.' But we have to jump forward to 25 March 2010 for the next substantive linking of *Robin Hood* and the economy, when London editor Alex Brummer criticises Alistair Darling's budget as spiteful and delaying of the economy's recovery: 'The 'Robin Hood' Chancellor's tax strategy may play well in Labour heart-lands but it is also an arrow pointed directly at the government's recovery hopes.'

What can be proposed, by way of tentative interpretation of the near-total absence of uses of *Robin Hood* in political commentary in the *Mail* in all but the earliest New Labour years (1997–2010), and their limited appearance in the *Times*? Throughout these years, the *Times* (especially) seems to have been keen to deploy the Robin Hood label as a way of negatively evaluating government policy, but found few opportunities where it could be appropriately applied. Some redistribution was being effected, its writers recognised; but – we may speculate – this was either so stealthy or reasonable (e.g., addressing child poverty) that the *Robin Hood* analogy was rarely felt fully to apply. The predicates 'naïve', 'romantic', 'fanciful', which use of *Robin Hood* was often intended to evoke, did not fit the public's impression of Gordon Brown, who was generally judged to be knowledgeable, hard-working, serious and prudent.

6.10   *Robin Hood* since 2010

In the years since the formation of the Conservative-led Coalition government in May 2010 and then the Conservative governments that returned in May 2015 and June 2017, it is perhaps unsurprising that no *Robin Hood* descriptors have been applied to government policies. In an article of 22 June 2010, previewing the first emergency budget of the Coalition government that was to be delivered that afternoon by George Osborne, Rachel Sylvester declares, 'The Liberal Democrats' Robin Hood instincts have tempered the Conservative Sheriffs of Notting Hill.' Sylvester predicts there will be some redistribution in the tax and spending plans, with 'fairness' at the heart of the mooted cuts programme. 'But everyone means different things by that word' she concludes, with Tory traditionalists wanting fair taxes for middle-class savers, while Liberal Democrat backbenchers seek fairness aimed at the poor. In the Coalition government years and after, in the government discourses reported largely uncritically in *The Times*, the *Robin Hood* epithet seems no longer fit for much purpose, and *fairness* is the preferred benchmark.

As noted at this chapter's opening, many recent uses of *Robin Hood* occur in discussion of the 'Robin Hood' tax on Australia's mining industry (proposed in 2010), and then in relation to a mooted EU-wide 'Robin Hood' financial transactions tax. The latter was proposed in 2010, rapidly vetoed for UK implementation by the British government, but pursued by eleven other EU countries until a further delay emerged in December 2014. Very often here the phrase *Robin Hood tax* either has scare quotes around *Robin Hood* or the whole phrase is prefaced by *so-called*: two devices with equivalent function. Strong opinions for and against the initiative are aired, with some arguing that it is unworkable, since it depends on an international tax harmonisation that is far from close to achievement. But a 29 April 2010 joint letter from a group of actors who support a Robin Hood tax, sees things differently:

> We believe that more must be done to repair the damage ordinary people around the world have suffered as a result of the financial crisis ... A Robin Hood tax is no pipe dream, as the IMF acknowledged last week ... the scale of need at home and abroad demands that our political leaders [agree to] fight for a bank tax that Robin Hood would have been proud of.

When the tax proposal is again in the news in November 2011, the chairman of a hedge fund vividly expresses his objections: 'A Tobin tax would primarily transfer wealth from hard-working savers to highly indebted Western sovereign states, from the prudent to the profligate. Somehow, this sounds more like the Sheriff of Nottingham than Robin Hood.' Probably most interesting of all is a *Times* editorial early in that month (3 November 2011), under this lengthy heading: *A Robin Hood Tax Is an Impractical and Unworkable Idea, but the Government must Take Steps to Show That Social Justice and Capitalism Run Best in Tandem.* The editorial reflects extensively on 'what is fair' and ends with the thought: 'Those with a sensible understanding of what fairness is and an agenda to advance it can and must shape the debate.' The editorial is intriguing since it bears some of the marks of pre-Thatcher or Heathite conservatism, and may well reflect conflicting views within the editorial department of *The Times* in late 2011. There might be some, such as Wheatcroft, holding strongly to 'small state' non-interventionism and to trusting to the nominally free market. Others, perhaps including Philip Collins, seem to be responding to changing public sentiment and growing concern about inequality that was reflected in the extra-parliamentary Robin Hood tax campaign, and sensing the beginnings of what this editorial calls *an anxious debate about fairness*.

As in *The Times*, many of the *Robin Hood* political references in the *Mail* in recent years are to the mooted Robin Hood transactions tax. The final mention of *Robin Hood* in the *Mail* in 2016 is in a speech by Mark Carney, governor of the Bank of England, defending its monetary policy committee's low interest rates: 'Has monetary policy robbed savers to pay borrowers? Has the MPC been Robin Hood in reverse? In a word, no.' Carney reminds his audience that in a recession the poorest are hit hardest, and that '[f]or free trade to benefit all requires some redistribution. We need to move towards more inclusive growth where everyone has a stake in globalisation.' It is interesting that the rebutted 'Robin Hood in reverse' phrase comes from Carney, rather than the *Mail's* editorial team, reflecting a general retreat in both newspapers over the last fifteen years or so, from chastising politicians for acting or playing Robin Hood or indeed being Robin Hood in reverse (the two extremes of censurable redistribution), this retreat being as apparent in *The Times* as in the *Mail*. The few twenty-first century uses tend to come in aggrieved readers' letters rather than from *The Times* or *Mail* editorial teams.

If this perception of *Robin Hood* avoidance is correct, it raises a further question. Have politico-economic mentions of *Robin Hood* dwindled simply because the epithet has become unfashionable or worn out? Or have they declined because redistributionalism itself has been pushed to the margins of attention or excluded from 'normal' political conversation over the last twenty years? The latter explanation seems more plausible. The very idea of Robin Hood economics has been shunted into an unused discursive siding, while upward wealth redistribution has continued. It might be thought that, in the interests of a nation-unifying moderating of inequality, more than at any other time in the past forty-five years a 'Robin Hood economics' could be applied to the top 1% for the benefit of the poorest 10%. But on such ideas, at least up to the end of 2016, *The Times* and the *Mail* remained silent.

6.11   Conclusion

What, then, can we finally say about *Robin Hood* as used in *The Times* and the *Mail* across the nearly fifty years since 1970? In the early 1970s, redistributive initiatives (whether by means of tax or a pay award) were not uncritically called *Robin Hood* actions. But the tone was moderated and the agent – Mr Heath or Denis Healey or the union representatives of workers in a pay dispute – was characterised as doing something potentially risky but understandable. These Robin Hoods, the newspapers conceded, had some moral justification even if their actions were weakened by naïvete or idealism. There might even be mockery in the commentary, but it was of a gentle kind: the 1970s centre-right newspapers, while disapproving of *Robin Hood* measures, did not want to be associated in readers' minds with the sheriff of Nottingham or anyone forcefully intent on opposing Robin Hood actions.

By the late 1980s and subsequently, the criticism and the objections are unequivocal, and the usage represents Robin Hood actions as culpably counter-productive. The chancellor or political party that flirts with Robin Hood redistributionalism is now cunning rather than naïve, dangerously interfering with the freedom of companies and individuals and their right to enjoy the wealth benefits of their own enterprise, the tide of growing wealth that will in time lift all boats.

Charting the shifting ways that the phrase *Robin Hood* has been used in these editorial news stories over the course of these decades helps us to see shifts in the mainstream and common-sense thinking of these powerful voices, concerning the rich and the poor, redistribution and fairness. For a phrase with such an entrenched array of talismanic meanings as *Robin Hood* carries, fifty years is too short a period to expect to see anything characterisable as 'meaning change'. But differences of use are extensively apparent, furthering the news editorial aim of emphasising one or another particular aspect of the phrase's meaning, and its applicability to a particular policy idea.

Most words, especially ones used to represent and evaluate, carry a broad penumbra of meanings from which interlocutors select on a particular occasion of use. This is most evident with metaphorical usage but is more general. In the situated use of any word or phrase, all sorts of background and contextual knowledge help to determine, on each specific occasion of use, just which qualities the addressee calculates the addresser may have in mind – and which among previously encountered features or meanings they presumably do not. The same goes for *Robin Hood*, in its various applications in political journalism. Accordingly its 'fantasy', 'children's story' connotations are sometimes implied but on other occasions not; its indexing of bravery, heroism, strength and defiance in the pursuit of justice are sometimes implied and sometimes not; sometimes the 'violent' and 'illegal' sememes are implicated and other times not.

In the editorial pages of *The Times* and the *Daily Mail* across the last half century, *Robin Hood* has been used as one of the more vivid epithets with which these newspapers have sought to police the very idea of redistributionalism in British politics and in relation to wealth inequality. Where newspapers judge that they cannot just come right out and declare it is wrong to require the rich and privileged to contribute from their wealth to help the poor, mentions of Robin Hood and allusions to his actions are a strategic framing. *Robin Hood* functions like a metaphor, and also insinuates that the person or action compared to Robin Hood is not reasonable, realistic, adult or normal in our complex, hi-tech, urban, globalised, modern world.

The lesson with regard to media representation for a British government actively in favour of a 'big state' mixed economy, progressive centre-left policies and committed to national provision of quality health, education, and care services, is that they should avoid and reject being characterised as offering *Robin Hood economics* or pursuing a comprehensive *Robin Hood solution*. For parties committed to taxing and spending so that the playing fields of health and education slope less, *Robin Hood* is a toxic brand. Rejecting *Robin Hood* as a characterisation of your entire set of policies or manifesto need not disqualify a very specific initiative, just one in a set of proposals, being so characterised with positive effect – for example, the Robin Hood tax, understood to apply just to the very rich, when they move their capital around. As for small-state centre-right political parties, they will only rarely attract the *Robin Hood* epithet, and then only for particular proposals, where it can serve as a warning that the right-wing press suspect 'soft' or 'wet' or centrist leanings; such parties have only to avoid being characterised as *Robin Hood in reverse*, lest this becomes linked in ordinary voters' minds not merely with 'toughness', but a dismissive lack of compassion for the poor and barely managing in society.

7   Conclusion

In this study I have tried to trace some of the ways *The Times* and the *Daily Mail* have changed their language over the past forty-five years, habituating readers to increased economic inequality. In news reporting of public discourse there are memorable moments and phrases, often misquoted, that resonate for decades: *a new Britain forged in the white heat of new technology; no change to the value of the pound in your pocket; the unacceptable face of capitalism; squeezing the rich for taxes until the pips squeak; this lady's not for turning; there's no such thing as society: there are individual men and women, and there are families; Education, education, education!* and *We are all in this together.* But it may be adjustments over time in the news media's use of more routine but still powerfully evaluative words that have a greater influence on readers' mindsets – and by extension national attitudes and identity. Such words and phrases might include *fair* and *unfair*, government *help, taxation* and *the burden of taxation, Luddite, Robin Hood, British, working class, luck, merit, deserving, hardworking* and *afford(able)*; all of these are found in editorial commentary on topics such as jobs, housing, taxes, health care, education and pensions. In those uses they are often narrative-bearing in the sense of alluding to or evoking a narrative explanation or judgement.

I have not studied readers' responses here, nor have I aimed to link adjustments in them to specific discursive patterns in the two selected newspapers. Rather I have attempted to complete a crucial, discourse-focussed first stage: showing that the terms in which wealth inequality is represented undergo change across the period from 1971 to 2016. Subsequent research is needed to explore whether and how older readers have reacted to those changes (younger readers will not have been exposed to the earlier *Mail* and *Times* discourses; they will know only the recent forms). But the evidence from many studies suggests that habitual ways of talking about a phenomenon – whether that talk is in the media or the primary school classroom or the family home – powerfully influence people's conception of that phenomenon. There are countless studies of children's acquisition and internalisation of sexist, racist or other discriminatory judgements from the media they consume, or from teachers or parents, which confirm that language choices (alongside images,

216

music, all forms of semiosis) have powerful effects – not to mention again Orwell's *1984*.

But are *Mail* and *Times* readers really like schoolchildren: vulnerable to having their minds filled and made up, without protest or resistance, by what the newspapers tell them? To some degree, and while acknowledging the myriad other sources of information they may be influenced by, I believe they are – particularly the habitual reader or loyal subscriber to a particular newspaper, whether this is one of the two newspapers studied here or ones such as *The Guardian* or the *Financial Times* for that matter. The habitual reader of a particular organ tends to trust that newspaper and its view of the world. The regular *Times* or *Mail* reader can be a sceptical one, but most of us most of the time lack the time and knowledge to formulate an entirely independent viewpoint, perhaps weighing up the reports and assessments of a variety of commentators. That is what we expect our newspaper to do for us. We look to them to confirm for us where we 'sit' in the local or national community, telling us how we are faring relative to everyone else (by many criteria in addition to the financial) and alerting us to the work, travel, health and education successes and difficulties of those around us, not to mention the incidents and histories of crime, terrorism, forced migration and war, which add to the representation. Extending out from these, a national newspaper will also 'cover' the arts, professional sport, holidays and travel, and it will include stories about pro-ducts in the marketplace along with advice on consumer spending, redress and savings; there may be room for columns on personal relationships, gardening and bridge. But crucially in all these are implied calibrations as to what is right, fair, reasonable or necessary – a host of ethical and political judgements; through its diverse contributors, a newspaper like the two studied here is a network of such judgements, linked through family resemblance.

I have explored how *The Times* and *Mail* seem to have adjusted to the changing world around them – in particular to the 'small state' low-regulated neoliberal market principles prominent in the United Kingdom since 1979 and the increased economic inequality that they inevitably entail. The adjustments appear to have been relatively smooth and unresisted, since the principles were largely congenial to these newspapers' editors and proprietors. Nevertheless they are detectable with close linguistic analysis: changes in ways of talking about the rich and the poor, employers and unionised labour and the unem-ployed, home-owners and those renting from councils or private landlords, private education and state education, the middle class and the working class, or Britain and the British as a nation and people with a distinct history and identity. Some of the discursive change – around what is now *fair* and *unfair*, around merit and who deserves what rewards, and about luck and lotteries – is easier to display, but often the shifts in the uses of a phrase such as *Luddite* or *Robin Hood* require a good deal of contextualisation to be comprehensible.

I see no way of avoiding this extensive contextualising or thickening of the description, in a historicised critical discourse analysis. It stems from the fact that the story I am imputing to these newspapers is in many respects a submerged one, a subtext, whose inequality-fostering implications they might deny, dismissing my analysis as misinterpretation. To meet that objection, I have tried to be constrained in interpretation, quoting keywords in their sentential contexts, and mostly relying on paraphrastic reformulation.

Clearly the *Daily Mail* and *The Times* are but one small part of the zeitgeist-shaping discourse on the United Kingdom and its values at any point in time, and with the information explosion effected by the internet and social media, the mass of discourse has grown unimaginably huge. It by no means follows, however, that 'everybody has a voice' now. True, anyone and everyone can maintain a blog and a twitter account, but mostly, few or none are reading these. The expansion of means of communication has not radically compromised the importance, to the national conversation, the national narrative of freedoms and obligations, and people's understanding of their own role in them, of news and editorial commentary in *The Times*, the *Mail*, the *Sun*, the *BBC* and *ITN* and *SkyNews*.

Twenty years ago I argued that our myriad uses of language and our remaking of language in new situations were central to democracy and political participation (Toolan 1997). Thanks in part to a widened suffrage, wider participation in tertiary education and wider acceptance of principles of equality without regard to sex, race, class, beliefs or physical ability, more people were more attentive to their own and others' usage, in ways that reached far beyond reactionary gibes about 'political correctness', than ever before. This spreading awareness came with wider recognition that language is not fixed and codelike, but is continually revised and adapted, the better to fit changing circumstances. Old representations may no longer suit new realities. The flexibility of language can take revised representation in any direction, and when a 'voice' that has a readership in the millions speaks, day after day, their account will be particularly influential, as those of *The Times* and *Mail* have been, in normalizing economic inequality.

In the opening section of Chapter 2 on what is fair and unfair, I briefly mentioned the idea of literal and figurative walls and barriers, and related concepts of containment, inclusion, membership – and their sometimes problematic inevitable corollaries: exclusion, removal, distancing, invisibility, an engineered unknowing. Acute wealth inequality creates a wall or separation, an affordability/unaffordability divide, dangerous to democracy, as Sandel noted:

At a time of rising inequality, the marketing of everything means that people of affluence and people of modest means lead increasingly separate lives ... Democracy does not require perfect equality, but it does require that citizens share a common life. What matters is that people of different backgrounds and social positions encounter one another, and bump up against one another, in the course of ordinary life. (2012: 203)

A thinning and impoverishment of shared experience, encounter, a decline in the possibilities of all kinds of people in a polis bumping up against each other, are among the consequences of a deeply embedded system of inequality. The thinning or decline is not accidental but systematic and engineered and, this book contends, in part sustained and reinforced by discursive representations in centre-right national newspapers such as *The Times,* the *Daily Telegraph, Daily Mail, Sun* and *Express*. Collectively they have naturalised ways of talking about work, unemployment, pay, housing, pensions, health care and taxes that prioritise private retention of wealth and income, a balanced budget and a reducing budget, low inflation and a strong currency, near-full employment and competitive interest rates. These are represented as the 'vital signs' of life in Britain; they are routinely and invariably cited as having to 'come first', as the objectives to which the entire machinery of politics should be oriented.

Putting these market-economic factors first entails marginalising, even to the point of rendering them invisible and 'undiscussable', many other primary goals of living well in the United Kingdom of today: good health and good health care, security of bodily integrity, a good diet and freedom from hunger, access to good education, opportunities to be creative in a variety of fields, freedom of expression (including religion), freedom of assembly, equality of respectful treatment without regard to differences of race, belief, gender or sexuality. Many of these underpin the 'capabilities' approach propounded by Sen and Nussbaum, and others. Many of them also amount to taking happiness (or good mental health, as we might term it today) seriously: the happiness of the individual and the happiness of the groups to which individuals may choose to belong.

Acute economic inequality means that, in all the areas of life where having money makes a difference, we are emphatically not all in this together. An income and wealth gulf enables an absolutely general separation, in all areas of life. Accordingly the very rich live in exclusive developments among their own kind, behind gates and security guards, travelling in smoked-glass cars and private jets. Their wealth largely immune, by avoidance, from taxation, they live very largely apart from ordinary Britons. They meet the average English person nowhere, except when the latter works for them (hence, not a meeting, and not between equals). By and large they have different pursuits, go to different schools, different hospitals, different clubs and different social gatherings. The very rich, the 1% (even more so the 0.1%), have no interest in the lives of ordinary people, nor any identification with them. Having no shared identity with Britons of ordinary wealth, why should this British plutocracy, the richest 1%, care about or make any contribution to the transport, education, health care, employment, defence or pension needs of those ordinary Britons? The emergence of the 'difference' of the very rich has been noted in various ways for some considerable time [see, e.g, Christopher Lasch's *The Revolt of the Elites: And the Betrayal of Democracy* (1994)], but in the United Kingdom the effects have been more noticeable in the last two decades than previously.

The 'everyone's better off' rejoinder ignores the fact that for the poor things have only improved marginally and in some respects, while for the top 20% things have improved wealth-wise, more markedly for the top 10%, and massively so for the top 1%, as reported in, for example, Dorling's *Inequality and the 1%*. My argument is not for 'national unity' with any great emphasis on the word *national*; but it is a warning that sharp separateness within a society, here particularly with regard to the affordances of income and wealth, where the separation into groups comes with an implicit hierarchy of more powerful and less powerful groups, is hugely damaging.

Despite the comparatively strong support for Labour's redistributive proposals in the June 2017 general election, and the recent commentaries suggesting that globalised market economics 'aren't working' for a growing proportion of Britons and that change is in the air, the immediate Brexit-distracted future gives few indications of a progressive turn in societal arrangements. In 2017 there were continued low levels of business investment in research, development and innovation; wages for most people have been stagnant since 2003 or have even lost ground in real terms; personal credit debt is at a perilously high level; home-ownership is at a thirty-year low, and seemingly out of reach for many young people who are living less comfortably than their parents; an age-related affluence gap is apparent in the middle-class especially, between twenty-somethings struggling to pay London living costs while their retired grandparents leave their comfortable mortgage-free home several times a year to enjoy expensive holidays; seven years of austerity cuts have worsened living conditions for the disadvantaged and are likely to have only added to the inequality that has caused the longevity or life-expectancy measure unexpectedly to plateau. The June 2017 report of the Social Mobility Commission found that the gap in development and school-readiness between children from deprived and non-deprived areas was narrowing between 2006 and 2011 but has not improved since. Tellingly, this agency was formerly called the Social Mobility and Child Poverty Commission, but was renamed in July 2015 when, *inter alia*, the Conservative government scrapped the New Labour child poverty reduction target for 2020, knowing that they would not meet it. Equally tellingly, since the first drafting of this paragraph the Chair of the Commission, Alan Milburn, has resigned from his post (in December 2017) complaining that the May government is failing in its pledge to reduce social inequality and immobility.

Twenty and more years ago, people in poverty were mostly unemployed, whereas today they are more often in work, but lowly paid. And there is currently no prospect of eliminating the attainment gap between poorer and wealthier children in the public examinations at ages 16 and 18 (GCSE and A-level, respectively). Even more acute is the underfunding of the National Health Service, where an industrial action by so-called junior hospital doctors, though unsuccessful in the face of an intransigent government and Health Minister (the latter castigated in August 2017 for his misrepresentation of the evidence by Britain's most famous physicist, the late Stephen Hawking), was backed by a remarkable 90% of doctors.

Taken together, all these suggest that there ought to be widespread dissatisfaction among ordinary Britons with aspects of the prevailing terms of Britain's neoliberal, 'small state', free-market economy, with its insufficient government investment in health care, education, and pre-school child care and ensuring the 'school readiness' of poorer children. But reading the *Mail* or *The Times*, much of the time, this would not be apparent. As the chair of the Social Mobility Commission commented in June 2017: 'Whole tracts of Britain feel left behind . . . Whole sections of society feel they are not getting a fair chance to succeed . . . The growing sense that we have become an us-and-them society is deeply corrosive of our cohesion as a nation.' In these circumstances, the present study is just one very small contribution to an ongoing holding to critical-discursive account of British newspapers and the policies and politics they report and refract. There is ample scope for further research, on the same or other newspapers, on broadcast media and the new social media platforms – all the routes by which ideas and actions are framed and disseminated to the many from a few but, with the impact of new media, a now widening few.

Many other 'key' words and phrases besides those I have concentrated upon can be tracked down the years. Those on my own present to-do list include *afford, affordable (sustainable), sharing, fair share, reward, (real) property, investing, greed(y), subsidy* and *subsidizing, tax, tax avoidance, inheritance planning*. The list could certainly be extended. Sometimes these words can be found working in combination to further a particular argument, as when a *Daily Mail* comment of 2 July 2011 declared: *It is grotesquely unfair to expect private sector workers to continue subsidising the final-salary pensions they themselves can no longer afford.*

A future study could usefully narrow the focus, within health and education, to an early indicator of wealth-based inequality: the 'school-readiness' of five-year-olds. It is well documented that even at the age of five, an inequality gap has opened up and is already holding back some children of kindergarten age. An unlevel playing field is already in place: children growing up in poverty are more likely to be disadvantaged in body (already habituated to an unhealthy diet which may lead to obesity and eating disorders later, poor participation in sports and exercise, lowered self-esteem, etc.) and in mind (delayed literacy skills; poor powers of concentration; lower self-confidence, empathy, imagination and realistic ambition, etc.). If these are some of the comparative disadvantages with which poorer five-year-olds enter school, putting them already behind their better-off contemporaries, what does the *Mail* or *The Times* or the *Telegraph* have to say about these important inequalities?

According to Dorling (2015), social and economic inequality persists in the United Kingdom (and elsewhere, e.g., the United States) because on the whole, in our discourses and our institutions, we have accepted rather than contested five 'socially evil' propositions. These Dorling summarises bluntly as follows: 'elitism is efficient; exclusion is necessary; prejudice is natural; greed is good; and despair is inevitable' (2015: 2). Some of these sound shocking and extreme until explained further, when they become disturbingly plausible. Consider the last of these. By 'despair' Dorling alludes to the levels of mental ill-health, depression, stress, loneliness, alienation, and simple unhappiness that people in Britain today report: high by comparison with most comparable countries, and rising by comparison with reported rates in the United Kingdom of two and three decades ago. Dorling's point is that people in Britain are generally accepting of this, as what we must 'put up with', in return for the material benefits that our constant work rewards us with or, failing those, just in order to get by.

Can the validity of Dorling's 'socially evil' propositions be tested? Proponents of the neoliberal status quo cannot be expected openly to admit their commitment to some version of them. Can these 'socially evil' propositions, or parts of them, nevertheless be found woven into the discourses of centre-right newspapers? A few of the predicates in Dorling's injustice theses have featured in the foregoing chapters, such as the attention to efficiency, and, in copious mentions of the talented and meritorious, an elite. That is the CDA challenge: to demonstrate what *The Times* or the *Mail* is really committed to. In the case of Dorling's theses, for example, an impartial discourse analysis would aim to determine whether the linguistic evidence did or did not suggest that these newspapers accepted or even endorsed elitism, stress, greed and poverty as natural, necessary and inevitable.

It is worth briefly reflecting on a domain where inequality and discrimination have diminished since 1971: sexist stereotyping in assumptions about the 'suitability' of men and women for most jobs. To be a barrister or a GP in 1971 meant – with a few exceptions that proved the norm – to be a man, as if it were in the nature of and part of the identity of a barrister or GP to be male. By the 2010s postulating such an identification would be absurd, hugely at variance with the facts. There has been a shifting and a revision of the identity of British lawyers and doctors over the past forty years. How has that revision been effected? By countless social acts, ranging from decisions about equality of consideration of male and female candidates for legal and medical training, to state provisions that make it easier for women to develop a career even if for a few years they curtail this in order to have and raise children. Also by legal means, in part, such as the anti-discrimination laws of the 1970s, the Human Rights Act of 2000, and the Equality Act of 2010, among many others, but also, underpinning and often preceding everything else, by discourses at every level. Such equality-advancing discourses include all 'verbal hygienic' interventions where the inequality-affirming assumptions within another person's discourse are challenged and contested.

In large part relations between women and men are more equal in the United Kingdom today than in 1971 because our discourses about the relations between women and men are different and more equality-mindful than they were. The same principles – with evidently a different outcome – apply in relation to our discourses about appropriate levels of wealth equality and fairness, and the degrees of actual fairness and equality that then obtain. Not that the discourses are a mere labelling, a mere description of 'that which is the case': they are also performative and promissory. We tend to get the social terms and conditions that our discourses – especially our public discourses with their huge reach – have assumed, specified or prepared us for. A reflexive awareness of these terms and discoursal choices can be preliminary to larger adjustments; slowly and often by indirect means, alternative discoursal prefer-ences can be introduced, defended, reinforced, made 'natural', reasonable and commonsense. By talk, argument, reconsideration, and persuasion, discourses can change, and conditions can change with them.

The year 1971 was one of much misery and violence in Northern Ireland (not part of Britain, but joined to it in the UK), where there had been deep discrimination and inequality in employment and housing and social justice. But overall, UK society in 1971 was demonstrably less unequal with regards to wealth and wealth-based opportunity then than it was by 2011. One often noted contrast concerns the relations between the individual and the state that existed in 1970 and individual–state relations that apply today. It is said that the person who had been a subject and had recently become a citizen (in the immediate postwar period, arguably, circa 1950) was in the course of the final decades of the twentieth century turned into a consumer. We were citizens of the United Kingdom, and indeed of the European Union, but we seemed to care less about this and more about the fact that we were consumers with consumers' rights, as if these were more important than citizens' rights.

As consumers, we were tasked with making choices as to what to buy (literally or metaphorically) in the market, and rather less under any obligation to participate in a social system, for collective benefit. In the words of Teubert (personal communication):

Decisions concerning the 'common good' are no longer based on democratic discussions but on the necessities of the markets … The markets themselves give us freedom of choice … What we choose [in education for our children, as our own employment, healthcare, pension arrangements, etc.] is, however, entirely our responsibility … Our inequality today [is presented in right-wing news discourses as] the result of our having made the right or wrong [but free] choices as individuals; it is not the fault of the system.

Teubert's assessment of contemporary Britain (shared by many others critical of the neoliberal status quo) seems confirmed, albeit for a different western European country, in Nafstad et al.'s (2007) diachronic study of media discourse in Norway, from 1984 to 2005. They found an increasing use of lexis associated with neoliberalism, such as the Norwegian words for *rights, entitlement, optional, freedom* and *choose*, and a declining use of words for *duty, equality, solidarity* and *obligation*. They attribute these trends to a developing 'ideological climate' in which a sense of collective responsibility for the welfare of all has declined considerably, and is therefore the less discussed. In McKenna's summary:

Responding to capitalism's growth imperative (Jameson, 1991), where consumption is presented as an act of choice (Rose, 1992), workers shed their class role and become actors maximizing quality of life through choosing goods and services that determine a lifestyle and cultural signification (Bourdieu, 1984; DuGay, 1996a,b; Featherstone, 1991). Consequently class identity as a worker and solidarity in collective organizations such as unions are supplanted by the self-orientation of consumption. (2004: 21)

I have tried to show how over the past half-century the way that *The Times* and *Daily* have used a number of keywords bearing on wealth inequality has both reflected and effected a change in the zeitgeist, that is, in the attitudes and views now regarded as normal, reasonable and mainstream. As a result, both the acceptance of inequality as 'natural' and inevitable, and the rejection of egalitarian policies and redistribution as unreasonable and unjustified, became considerably more discursively entrenched. There are many politicians and policy makers on both the left and the right who recognise and deplore the huge extent of inequality of opportunity in contemporary Britain. But arguably one consequence of the historic inequality-normalising shift in centre-right newspapers is that the body politic is further hampered in its attempts to articulate a more egalitarian revision of conditions – at least, that part of the body politic influenced by the discourses they absorb from *The Times* and the *Daily Mail*.

Bibliography

Aston, G. (1997) 'Small and Large Corpora in Language Learning', in B. Lewandowska-Tomaszczyk and P. Melia (eds.) *Practical Applications in Language Corpora*, pp. 51–62. Lodz, Poland: Lodz University Press.

Atkinson, Anthony (2015) *Inequality: What Can Be Done?* Boston, MA: Harvard University Press.

Atkinson, A. and T. Piketty, eds. (2010) *Top Incomes: A Global Perspective*. Oxford: Oxford University Press.

Atkinson, Will, Steven Roberts and Michael Savage, eds. (2012) *Class Inequality in Austerity Britain: Power, Difference and Suffering*. London: Palgrave.

Baker, P. (2004) 'Querying Keywords: Questions of Difference, Frequency, and Sense in Keywords Analysis', *Journal of English Linguistics* 32(4): 346–59.

(2005) *Public Discourses of Gay Men*. London: Routledge.

(2006) *Using Corpora in Discourse Analysis*. London: Continuum.

(2012) 'Acceptable Bias? Using Corpus Linguistics Methods with Critical Discourse Analysis', *Critical Discourse Studies* 9(3): 247–56.

(2015) 'Does Britain Need Any More Foreign Doctors? Inter-analyst Consistency and Corpus-Assisted (Critical) Discourse Analysis', in N. Groom, M. Charles and S. John (eds.), *Corpora, Grammar and Discourse: In Honour of Susan Hunston*, pp. 283–300. Amsterdam: John Benjamins.

Baker, P., C. Gabrielatos, M. Khosravinik, M. Krzyzanowski, T. McEnery and R. Wodak (2008) 'A Useful Methodological Synergy? Combining Critical Discourse Analysis and Corpus Linguistics to Examine Discourses of Refugees and Asylum Seekers in the UK Press', *Discourse and Society* 19(3): 273–306.

Baker, Paul, Costas Gabrielatos and Tony McEnery (2013) *Discourse Analysis and Media Attitudes: The Representation of Islam in the British* Press. Cambridge: Cambridge University Press.

Baker, P. and T. McEnery (2005) 'A Corpus-based Approach to Discourses of Refugees and Asylum Seekers in UN and Newspaper Texts', *Journal of Language and Politics* 4(2): 197–226.

Baker, P., T. McEnery and C. Gabrielatos (2007) 'Using Collocation Analysis to Reveal the Construction of Minority Groups: The Case of Refugees, Asylum Seekers and Immigrants in the UK Press', paper given at Corpus Linguistics 2007, University of Birmingham, 28–30 July 2007. Available at: http://eprints.lancs.ac.uk/602.

Ball, James (2012) 'From Silver to Diamond Jubilee, Are We Really Better Off?' Guardian Online, 5 June. Available at: www.guardian.co.uk/commentisfree/2012/jun/05/silver-diamond-jubilee-better-off.

Bauer, L. and P. Nation (1993) 'Word Families', *International Journal of Lexicography* 6(4): 253–79.

Beckett, Andy (2017) 'How Britain Fell Out of Love with the Free Market'. *The Guardian*, 4 August. Available at: www.theguardian.com/news/2017/aug/04/how-britain-fell-out-of-love-with-the-free-market. Last accessed 20 July 2018.

Bednarek, Monika (2006) *Evaluation in Media Discourse: Analysis of a Newspaper Corpus*. London: Bloomsbury.

Bednarek, Monika and Helen Caple (2012) *News Discourse*. London: Bloomsbury.
    (2014) 'Why Do News Values Matter? Towards a New Methodological Framework for Analysing News Discourse in Critical Discourse Analysis and Beyond', *Discourse and Society* 25(2): 135–58.

Bell, Alan (1991) *The Language of News Media*. Oxford: Blackwell.

Benn Michaels, Walter (2006) *The Trouble with Diversity: How We Learned to Love Identity and Ignore Inequality*. New York, NY: Metropolitan Books.

Bennett, Joe (2013) 'Moralising Class: A Discourse Analysis of the Mainstream Political Response to Occupy and the August 2011 British Riots', *Discourse and Society* 24(1): 27–45.

Biber, D. and S. Conrad (2001) 'Quantitative Corpus-based Research: Much More than Bean Counting', *TESOL Quarterly* 35(2): 331–36.

Biber, D. and B. Gray (2013) 'Being Specific about Historical Change: The Influence of Sub-register', *Journal of English Linguistics* 41(2): 104–34.

Billig, Michael (2002a) 'The Language of Critical Discourse Analysis: The Case of Nominalization', *Discourse and Society* 19(6): 783–800.
    (2002b) 'Critical Discourse Analysis and the Rhetoric of Critique', in G. Weiss and R. Wodak (eds.) *Critical Discourse Analysis: Theory and Interdisciplinarity*, pp. 35–46. Houndsmill: Palgrave Macmillan.

Binfield, Kevin, ed. (2004) *Writings of the Luddites*. Baltimore, MD: Johns Hopkins University Press.

Black, Peter (1972) *The Biggest Aspidistra in the World: A Personal Celebration of 50 years of the BBC*. London: BBC.
    (1973) *The Mirror in the Corner: The People's Television*. London: Hutchinson.

Blackledge, A. (2005) *Discourse and Power in a Multilingual World*. Amsterdam: John Benjamins.

Block, David (2014) *Social Class in Applied Linguistics*. London: Routledge.

Blommaert, J. (2005) *Discourse: A Critical Introduction*. Cambridge: Cambridge University Press.

Bondi, M. (2007) 'Key-words and Emotions: A Case Study of the Bloody Sunday Enquiry', in N. Fairclough, G. Cortese and P. Ardizzone (eds.) *Discourse and Contemporary Social Change*, pp. 407–32. Bern: Peter Lang.

Brien, Alan (1960) 'Four Plays (review)', *Sight and Sound* 29(2 Spring): 100–01.

Brown, G. and G. Yule (1983) *Discourse Analysis*. Cambridge: Cambridge University Press.

Bulmer, Martin (1980) 'The Royal Commission on the Distribution of Incomes and Wealth', in M. Bulmer (ed.) *Social Research and Royal Commissions*, pp. 158–79. London: Routledge.

Cameron, D. (1993) *Verbal Hygiene*. New York, NY: Routledge.
  (2003) 'Gender Issues in Language Change', *Annual Review of Applied Linguistics* 23: 187–201.
Cameron, L. (2011) *Metaphor and Reconciliation*. New York, NY: Routledge.
Cammaerts, Bart (2012) 'The Strategic Use of Metaphors by Political and Media Elites: The 2007–11 Belgian Constitutional Crisis', *International Journal of Media and Cultural Politics* 8(2/3): 229–49.
Charteris-Black, Jonathan (2013) *Analysing Political Speeches: Rhetoric, Discourse and Metaphor*. Basingstoke: Palgrave Macmillan.
Chen, L. (2005) 'Transitivity in Media Texts: Negative Verbal Process Sub-functions and Narrator Bias', *International Review of Applied Linguistics in Language Teaching* 43: 33–51.
Chilton, P. (2004) *Analysing Political Discourse*. London: Routledge.
Clark, C. (2007) 'A War of Words: A Linguistic Analysis of BBC Embedded Reports during the Iraq Conflict', in N. Fairclough, G. Cortese and P. Ardizzone (eds.) *Discourse and Contemporary Social Change*, pp. 119–40. Bern: Peter Lang.
Clark, Tom, with Anthony Heath (2015) *Hard Times: Inequality, Recession, Aftermath*. New Haven, CT: Yale University Press.
Cmnd 3968 (1998) *Fairness at Work*. London: HMSO.
Cmnd 4755 (1971) *Strategy for Pensions*. London: HMSO.
Conboy, M. (2006) *Tabloid Britain:Constructing a Community through Language*. London: Routledge.
Corner, John (1999) *Critical Ideas in Television Studies*. Oxford: Oxford University Press.
Cotter, C. (2010) *News Talk: Investigating the Language of Journalism*. Cambridge: Cambridge University Press.
Coulthard, Malcolm (1994) 'On Analysing and Evaluating Written Text', in M. Coulthard (ed.) *Advances in Written Text Analysis*, pp. 1–11. London: Routledge.
Cribb, Jonathan, et al. (2012) 'Jubilees Compared: Incomes, Spending and Work in the Late 1970s and Early 2010s'. Institute of Fiscal Studies Briefing Note 128. Available at: www.ifs.org.uk/bns/bn128.pdf.
Curran, James and Jean Seaton (1997) *Power without Responsibility*, 5th edn. London: Routledge.
Curran, James, Ivor Gaber and Julian Petley (2005) *Culture Wars: The Media and the British* Left. Edinburgh: Edinburgh University Press.
Da Fina, Anna and Alexandra Georgakopoulou, 2012. *Analyzing Narrative: Discourse and Sociolinguistic Perspectives*. Cambridge: Cambridge University Press.
D'Arcy, Conor and Laura Gardiner. 2017. The Generation of Wealth: Asset Accumulation Across and within Cohorts. London: Resolution Foundation. Available at: www.resolutionfoundation.org/publications/the-generation-of-wealt h-asset-accumulation-across-and-within-cohorts.
Davidse, K., L. Brems, P. Willemse, E. Doyen, J. Kiermeer and E. Thoelen (2013) 'A Comparative Study of the Grammaticalized Uses of English *sort of* and French *genre de* in Teenage Forum Data'. To appear in Proceedings of 'Languages Go Web'. Available at: https://limo.libis.be/primo-explore/fulldisplay?docid=LIRIA S1820493&context=L&vid=Lirias&search_scope=Lirias&tab=default_tab&lan g=en_US&fromSitemap=1.

Davies, Matt (2012) *Oppositions and Ideology in News Discourse*. London: Bloomsbury.

— (2014) 'Militancy or Manipulation: Demonization of Trade Unions in the UK Press', *Babel* 6(Feb. 2014): 19–24.

Davies, Matt and Olga Mudraya-Whitehouse (2011) 'Class Struggle Denied? How the UK Press Demonize Workers on Strike'. *Spectres of Class* Conference, University of Chester, July 2011.

Day-Lewis, Sean. (1993) 'The Best Years: Review of Philip Purser's *Done Viewing*, Quartet Books', *Sight and Sound* 3(2): 36–37.

Deignan, Alice, Jeannette Littlemore and Elena Semino (2013) *Figurative Language, Genre and Register*. Cambridge: Cambridge University Press.

Dickman, S.L., D. Himmelstein and S. Woolhandler, MD (2017) 'Inequality and the Health-Care System in the USA', *The Lancet* 389(10077): 1431–41.

Dilts, Philip (2010) 'Good Nouns, Bad Nouns: What the Corpus Says and What Native Speakers Think', in S. Gries, S. Wulff and M. Davies (eds.) *Corpus-Linguistic Applications: Current Studies, New Directions*, pp. 102–17. Amsterdam: Rodopi.

Dorling, Danny (2012) A Conversion on the Road from the Barbican. *Renewal: A Journal of Labour Politics* 20(2/3): 130–33.

— (2014) *Inequality and the 1%*. London: Verso.

— (2015) *Injustice: Why Social Inequality Still Persists*. Bristol: Policy Press.

Dorling, Danny (2016) *A Better Politics: How Government Can Make Us Happier*. London: London Publishing Partnership.

— (2017) *The Equality Effect: Improving Life for Everyone*. London: New Internationalist.

Dorst, A.G. (2015) 'More or Different Metaphors in Fiction? A Quantitative Cross-Register Comparison', *Language and Literature* 24(1): 3–22.

Dowell, Ben (2011) 'Casting a Critical Eye over the TV Critics', Guardian TV and radio blog. Available at: www.theguardian.com/TV-and-radio/TVandradioblog/2011/ju l/20/TV-critics-biggest-mistakes.

Eldridge, John, ed. (1995) *The Glasgow Media Group Reader, Vol. I: News Content, Language and Visuals*. London: Routledge.

Elliott, P. (1977) 'Reporting Northern Ireland', in UNESCO (ed.) *Ethnicity and the Media: An Analysis of Media Reporting in the United Kingdom, Canada and Ireland*, pp. 263–376. Paris: UNESCO.

Ellis, John (2008) 'TV Pages', in Bob Franklin (ed.) *Pulling Newspapers Apart: Analysing Print Journalism*, pp. 231–38. London:Routledge.

Evans, Matthew and Lesley Jeffries (2015) 'The Rise of Choice as an Absolute "Good": A Study of British Manifestos (1900–2010)', *Journal of Language and Politics* 14 (6): 751–77.

Ewing, K. D. and J. Hendy (2012) 'Unfair Dismissal Changes – Unfair?', *Industrial Law Journal* 41(1): 115–21.

Fairclough, Isabela and Norman Fairclough (2012) *Political Discourse Analysis: A Method for Advanced Students*. London: Routledge.

Fairclough, Norman (1995) *Critical Discourse Analysis*. London: Longman.

— (2000) *New Labour, New Language?* London: Routledge.

— (2001) [1989] *Language and Power*. London: Longman.

— (2003) *Analyzing Discourse*. London: Routledge.

(2010) *Critical Discourse Analysis*, 2nd edn. London: Routledge.

Fairclough, N. (2014) *Language and Power*, 3rd edn. London: Longman.

Fairclough, N., G. Cortese and P. Ardizzone, eds. (2007) *Discourse and Contemporary Social Change*. Bern: Peter Lang.

Fairclough, Norman, Jane Mulderrig and Ruth Wodak (2011) 'Critical Discourse Analysis', In T.A. van Dijk (ed.) *Discourse Studies: A Multidisciplinary Introduction*, pp. 357–78. London: SAGE.

Fairclough, N. and R. Wodak (1997) 'Critical Discourse Analysis', in T.A. van Dijk (ed.) *Discourse as Social Interaction*, pp. 258–84. London: SAGE.

(2008) 'The Bologna Process and the Knowledge-based Economy: A Critical Discourse Analysis Approach', in R. Jessop, N. Fairclough and R. Wodak (eds.) *Education and the Knowledge-based Economy in Europe*, pp. 109–26. Rotterdam: Sense Publishers.

Fengler, Susanne (2003) 'Holding the News Media Accountable: A Study of Media Reporters and Media Critics in the United States', *Journalism and Mass Communication Quarterly* 80(4): 818–32.

Ferrari, Federica (2007) 'Metaphor at Work in the Analysis of Political Discourse: Investigating a "Preventive War" Persuasion Strategy', *Discourse and Society* 18 (5): 603–25.

Firth, J.R. (1957) *Papers in Linguistics 1934–1951*. London: Oxford University Press.

Flowerdew, J. (1997) 'The Discourse of Colonial Withdrawal: A Case Study in the Creation of Mythic Discourse', *Discourse and Society* 8(4): 453–77.

Forsey, Andrew (2017) Hungry Holidays: A Report on Hunger amongst Children during School Holidays. An APPR Report. Available at: https://feedingbritain.files.word press.com/2015/02/hungry-holidays.pdf.

Fowler, Roger (1991) *Language in the News: Discourse and Ideology in the Press*. London: Routledge.

Fowler, Roger, Bob Hodge, Gunther Kress and Tony Trew (1979) *Language and Control*. London: Routledge.

Frank, Robert (2016) *Success and Luck: Good Fortune and the Myth of Meritocracy*. Princeton, NJ: Princeton University Press.

Gabrielatos, C. (2006) 'Towards Quantifying "Quality" in the Press: Comparing the Stance of UK Broadsheets and Tabloids towards Refugees, Asylum Seekers and Immigrants', Joint meeting of the Corpus Research Group and the Language, Ideology and Power Research Group, Department of Linguistics and English Language, Lancaster University, 13 June 2006. Available at: http://eprints.lancs .ac.uk/231.

(2007) 'Selecting Query Terms to Build a Specialised Corpus from a Restricted Access Database', *ICAME Journal* 31: 5–43.

Gabrielatos, C. and P. Baker (2008) 'Fleeing, Sneaking, Flooding: A Corpus Analysis of Discursive Constructions of Refugees and Asylum Seekers in the UK Press 1996–2005', *Journal of English Linguistics* 36(1): 5–38.

Gale (firm). (1896) *Daily Mail Historical Archive, 1896–2004*. Available at: gdc.gale .com/products/daily-mailhistorical-archive-1896–2004.

Galtung, Johan and Mari Holmboe Ruge (1965) 'The Structure of Foreign News', *Journal of Peace Research* 2(1): 64–91.

Gavioli, L. (2005) *Exploring Corpora for ESP Learning*. Amsterdam: John Benjamins.

Goatly, Andrew (2007) *Washing the Brain – Metaphor and Hidden Ideology.* Amsterdam: John Benjamins.

(2011 [1977]) *The Language of Metaphors.* London: Routledge.

Gomez-Jimenez, Eva (forthcoming) '"An Insufferable Burden on Businesses?" On Changing Attitudes to Maternity Leave and the Idea of Affordability in the *Times* and *Daily Mail*', *Discourse, Context and Media.*

Greenslade, Roy (2003) *Press Gang: How Newspapers Make Profits from Propaganda.* London: Macmillan.

Griffith, J.A.G. 1977. *The Politics of the Judiciary.* London: Fontana.

Habermas, J. (1967) *Theorie und Praxis.* Neuwied am Rhein: Luchterland.

Hall, Stuart, Chas Critcher, Tony Jefferson, John Clarke and Brian Roberts (1978) 'The Social Production of News', in Stuart Hall et al., *Policing the Crisis: Mugging, the State, and Law and Order*, pp. 53–60. London: Macmillan.

Halliday, M.A.K. (1978) *Language as Social Semiotic: The Social Interpretation of Language and Meaning.* London: Arnold.

(1994) *An Introduction to Functional Grammar*, 2nd edn. London: Arnold.

Halliday, M.A.K. and C.M.I.M. Matthiessen (2004) *An Introduction to Functional Grammar*, 3rd edn. Oxford: Oxford University Press.

(2014) *An Introduction to Functional Grammar*, 4th edn. London: Arnold.

Hardt-Mautner, Gerlinde (1995) 'Only Connect.' Critical Discourse Analysis and Corpus Linguistics. UCREL Technical Paper 6. Lancaster, UK: Lancaster University. Available at: ucrel.lancs.ac.uk/papers/techpaper/vol6.pdf (last accessed 14 December 2015).

Hart, Christopher and Piotr Cap, eds. (2014) *Contemporary Critical Discourse Studies.* London: Continuum.

Hartley, J. (1982) *Understanding News.* London: Methuen.

Hasan, Ruqaiya (1999) 'The Disempowerment Game: Bourdieu and Language in Literacy', *Linguistics and Education* 10(1): 25–87.

Hastings, Max (2011) 'A Nation Divided', Saturday essay. *Daily Mail*, 2 April.

Hendy, J. (2014) 'The Forensic Lottery of Unfair Dismissal', in N. Busby, M. McDermont, E. Rose and A. Sales (eds.), *Access to Justice in the Employment Tribunal.* Liverpool: Institute of Employment Rights.

Hills, John (2015) *Good Times, Bad Times: The Welfare Myth of Them and Us.* Bristol: Policy Press.

Hills, John and Francesca Bastagli (2015) *Wealth in the UK: Distribution, Accumulation, and Policy.* Oxford: Oxford University Press.

Hills, J. and K. Stewart (eds.) (2005) *A More Equal Society? New Labour, Poverty, Inequality and Exclusion.* Bristol: Policy Press.

Hilton, Boyd (2006) *A Mad, Bad, and Dangerous People? England 1783–1846.* Oxford: Oxford University Press.

Hodge, R. (1979) 'Newspapers and Communities', in R. Fowler, B. Hodge, G. Kress and T. Trew (eds.) *Language and Control*, pp. 157–74. London: Routledge and Kegan Paul.

Hunston, S. (2002) *Corpora in Applied Linguistics.* Cambridge: Cambridge University Press.

Hutton, Will (2011) *Hutton Review of Fair Pay.* London: HM Treasury.

(2014) 'Its Inequality, Stupid', *The Observer*, 19 January. Available at: www.theguar dian.com/commentisfree/2014/jan/19/inequality-threat-recovery-poverty-pay.

(2015a) *How Good We Can Be*. London: Little, Brown.

(2015b) 'Inequality Has Become a Challenge to Us as Moral Beings', *The Observer*, 25 January. Available at: www.theguardian.com/books/2015/jan/25/inequality-ha s-become-challenge-how-good-we-can-be-extract-will-hutton.

Iedema, R. (2003) *The Discourses of Post-bureaucratic Organization*. Amsterdam: John Benjamins.

Jäger, S. (2001) *Kritische Diskursanalyse*. Duisberg: DISS.

James, Clive (1977) *Visions before Midnight*. London: Jonathan Cape.

Jeffries, Lesley (2010a) *Opposition in Discourse: The Construction of Oppositional Meaning*. London: Continuum.

(2010b) *Critical Stylistics: The Power of English*. Basingstoke: Palgrave Macmillan.

Jeffries, Lesley and Matthew Evans (2013) 'The Rise of Choice as an Absolute "Good": A Study of British Manifestos (1900–2010)', *SRC Working Papers* 5: 1–24.

Jeffries, Lesley and Brian Walker (2017) *Keywords in the Press: The New Labour Years*. London: Bloomsbury.

Jessop, Bob (2003) 'From Thatcherism to New Labour: Neo-Liberalism, Workfarism, and Labour Market Regulation', in H. Overbeek (ed.) *The Political Economy of European Employment: European Integration and the Transnationalization of the (Un)employment Question*, pp. 137–153. London: Routledge. Also available from the Department of Sociology, Lancaster University at: www.comp.lancs.ac.uk/so ciology/soc131rj.pdf.

Jones, Owen (2014) *The Establishment: And How They Get Away with It*. London: Penguin.

Jones, Steven E. (2006) *Against Technology: From the Luddites to Neo-Luddism*. London: Routledge.

Kapadia, Anush (2016) Brexit Is What a Dark Age Feels Like: Here's Why, 27 June. Available at: www.ndtv.com/opinion/why-brexit-is-just-the-first-earthquake-of-it s-kind-1423847.

Kelsey, Darren (2015) 'Defining the "Sick Society": Discourses of Class and Morality in British Right-Wing Newspapers during the 2011 England Riots', *Capital and Class* 39(2): 1–22.

Kerswill, Paul (2007) 'Socio-economic Class', in Carmen Llamas, Louise Mullany and Peter Stockwell (eds.) *The Routledge Companion to Sociolinguistics*, pp. 51–61. London: Routledge.

Khosravinik, Majid (2009) 'The Representation of Refugees, Asylum Seekers and Immigrants in British Newspapers during the Balkan Conflict (1999) and the British General Election (2005)', *Discourse and Society* 20(4): 477–98.

(2010) 'The Representation of Refugees, Asylum Seekers and Immigrants in British Newspapers: A Critical Discourse Analysis', *Journal of Language and Politics* 9 (1): 1–28.

Kitis, Eliza and Michalis Milapides (1997) 'Read It and Believe It: How Metaphor Constructs Ideology in News Discourse. A case study', *Journal of Pragmatics* 28 (5): 557–90.

Knowles, G.M. and R. Moon (2006) *Introducing Metaphor*. London: Routledge.

Koller, V. and G. Mautner (2004) 'Computer Applications in Critical Discourse Analysis', in C. Coffin, A. Hewings and K. O'Halloran (eds.) *Applying English Grammar: Corpus and Functional Approaches*, pp. 216–28. London: Arnold.

Kovács, A. and R. Wodak (eds.) (2003) *NATO, Neutrality and National Identity*. Vienna: Böhlau.

Kovecses, Z. (2010) *Metaphor: A Practical Introduction*. New York: Oxford University Press.

Kress, G. and R. Hodge (1979) *Language as Ideology*. London: Routledge and Kegan Paul.

Kress, G. and T. Van Leeuwen (2001) *Multimodal Discourse: The Modes and Media of Contemporary Communication*. London: Arnold.

Krishnamurthy, R. (1996) 'Ethnic, Racial and Tribal: The Language of Racism?', in C. R. Caldas-Coulthard and M. Coulthard (eds.) *Texts and Practices: Readings in Critical Discourse Analysis*, pp. 129–49. London: Routledge.

Krzyz'anowski, M. and F. Oberhuber (2007) *(Un)Doing Europe: Discourses and Practices of Negotiating the EU Constitution*. Brussels: P.I.E.-Peter Lang.

Krzyz'anowski, M. and R. Wodak (2007) 'Multiple Identities, Migration and Belonging: "Voices of Migrants"', in C.R. Caldas-Coulthard and R. Iedema (eds.) *Critical Discourse and Contested Identities*, pp. 95–119. Basingstoke: Palgrave Macmillan.

Lakoff, G. and M. Johnson (1980) *Metaphors We Live By*. Chicago, IL: University of Chicago Press.

Lansley, Stewart (2012) *The Cost of Inequality: Why Economic Equality Is Essential for Recovery*. London: Gibson Square.

Lansley, Stewart and Howard Reed (2013) *How to Boost the Wage Share*. Touchstone pamphlet #13. Trade Union Congress. Available at: www.tuc.org.uk/sites/default/files/tucfiles/How%20to%20Boost%20the%20Wage%20Share.pdf.

Leech, Geoffrey (1983) *Principles of Pragmatics*. London: Longman.

(1992) 'Corpora and Theories of Linguistic Performance', in J. Svartvik (ed.) *Directions in Corpus Linguistics: Proceedings of the Nobel Symposium 82, Stockholm, 4–8 August 1991*, pp. 105–22. Berlin: Mouton de Gruyter.

Leech, Geoffrey, Paul Rayson and Andrew Wilson (2001) *Word Frequencies in Written and Spoken English: Based on the British National Corpus*. London: Longman.

Louw, B. (1993) 'Irony in the Text or Insincerity in the Writer? The Diagnostic Potential of Semantic Prosodies', in M. Baker, G. Francis and E. Tognini-Bonelli (eds.) *Text and Technology: In Honour of John Sinclair*, pp. 157–76. Philadelphia: John Benjamins.

Machin, D. and Mayr, A. (2012) *Critical Discourse Analysis*. London: SAGE.

Magalhaes, C.M. (2006) 'A Critical Discourse Analysis Approach to News Discourses and Social Practices on Race in Brazil', *DELTA* 22(2): 275–301.

Mauranen, Anna (1997) *Hedging in Language Revisers' Hands*. In R. Markkanen and H. Schröder (eds.) *Hedging and Discourse*, pp. 115–33. Berlin: de Gruyter.

Mautner, Gerlinde (2007) 'Mining Large Corpora for Social Information: The Case of *Elderly*', *Language in Society* 36(1): 51–72.

(2009) 'Checks and Balances: How Corpus Linguistics can Contribute to CDA', in R. Wodak and M. Meyer (eds.) *Methods for Critical Discourse Analysis*, 2nd edn., pp. 122–43. London: SAGE.

Mayr, Andrea and David Machin (2012) *The Language of Crime and Deviance.* London: A and C Black.

McEnery, T. (2005) *Swearing in English: Bad Language, Purity and Power from 1586 to the Present.* London: Routledge.

McEnery, T. and C. Gabrielatos (2006) 'English Corpus Linguistics', in B. Aarts and A. McMahon (eds.) *The Handbook of English Linguistics*, pp. 33–71. Oxford: Blackwell.

McKenna, Bernard (2004) 'Critical Discourse Studies: Where to from Here?', *Critical Discourse Studies*, 1:1, 9–39.

Meinhof, U.H. and K. Richardson (eds.) (1994) *Text, Discourse and Context: Representations of Poverty in Britain.* London: Longman.

Meyer, M. (2001) 'Between Theory, Method, and Politics: Positioning of the Approaches to CDA', in R. Wodak and M. Meyer (eds.) *Methods of Critical Discourse Analysis*, pp. 14–31. London: SAGE.

Miall, Leonard (1984) 'Review of Bernard Sendall, *Independent Television in Britain* (Macmillan, 1982)', *Business History* 26(1, Mar 1984): 100–01.

Moon, Rosamund (2004) 'On Specifying Metaphor: An Idea and Its Implementation', *International Journal of Lexicography* 17(2): 195–222.

(2014) 'From Gorgeous to Grumpy: Adjectives, Age, and Gender', *Gender and Language* 8(1): 5–41.

Moon, Rosamund and Carmen Caldas-Coulthard (2010) 'Curvy, Hunky, Kinky: Using Corpora as Tools in Critical Analysis', *Discourse and Society* 21(2): 1–35.

Moran, Joe (2013a) *Armchair Nation: An Intimate History of Britain in Front of the TV.* London: Profile Books.

(2013b) 'The Fall and Rise of the TV Critic', *Financial Times*, 23 August. Available at: www.ft.com/cms/s/2/5af41f88-0a65-11e3-aeab-00144feabdc0.html#axzz3nOeDfZIo.

Morley, J. and P. Bayley (eds.) (2009) *Corpus-assisted Discourse Studies on the Iraq Conflict: Wording the War.* New York: Routledge.

Mount, Ferdinand (2012) *The New Few: Or a Very British* Oligarchy. London: Simon and Schuster.

Mulderrig, Jane (2009) *The Language of Education Policy: From Thatcher to Blair.* Saarbrücken, Germany: Verlag Dr Müller.

(2012) 'The Hegemony of Inclusion: A Corpus-based Critical Discourse Analysis of Deixis in Education Policy', *Discourse and Society* 23(6): 1–28.

(2015) 'Enabling Participatory Governance in Education: A Corpus-based Critical Analysis of Policy in the United Kingdom', in P. Smeyers, D. Bridges, N. Burbules and M. Griffiths (eds.) *International Handbook of Interpretation in Educational Research*, pp. 441–70. London: Springer.

Muntigl, P., G. Weiss and R. Wodak (2000) *European Union Discourses on Unemployment.* Amsterdam: John Benjamins.

Murphy, M. Lynne (2003) *Semantic Relations and the Lexicon: Antonymy, Synonymy, and Other Paradigms.* Cambridge: Cambridge University Press.

Musolff, Andreas (2012) 'The Study of Metaphor as Part of Critical Discourse Analysis', *Critical Discourse Studies* 9(3): 301–10.

(2015) 'Dehumanizing Metaphors in UK Immigrant Debates in Press and Online Media', *Journal of Language Aggression and Conflict* 3(1): 41–56.

(2016) *Political Metaphor Analysis: Discourse and Scenarios*. London: Bloomsbury.

Nafstad, H., R. Blakar, E. Carlquist, J. Phelps and K. Rard-Hendriksen (2007) 'Ideology and Power: The Influence of Current Neo-liberalism in Society', *Journal of Community and Applied Social Psychology* 17(4): 313–32.

Nattinger, J.R. and J.S. DeCarrico (1992) *Lexical Phrases and Language Teaching*. Oxford: Oxford University Press.

Negrine, Ralph (1998) *Television and the Press Since 1945*. Manchester: Manchester University Press.

Newman, Nic, Richard Fletcher, David A.L. Levy and Rasmus Kleis Nielsen (2016) *_Digital News Report*. Oxford: Reuters Institute.

Nexis database (2012/3) *Daily Mail* stories.

Nikula, Tarja (1997) 'Interlanguage View on hedging', in R. Markkanen and H. Schröder (eds.) *Hedging and Discourse*, pp. 188–207. Berlin: de Gruyter.

Nussbaum, M. and A. Sen (1993) *The Quality of Life*. Oxford: Clarendon Press.

O'Halloran, K. and C. Coffin (2004) 'Checking Overinterpretation and Underinterpretation: Help from Corpora in Critical Linguistics', in C. Coffin, A. Hewings and K. O'Halloran (eds.) *Applying English Grammar: Corpus and Functional Approaches*, pp. 275–97. London: Arnold.

Ooi, V. (2001) 'Investigating and Teaching Genres Using the World Wide Web', in M. Ghadessy, A. Henry and R.L. Roseberry (eds.) *Small Corpus Studies and ELT*, pp. 175–203. Amsterdam: John Benjamins.

Orpin, Deborah (2005) 'Corpus Linguistics and Critical Discourse Analysis', *International Journal of Corpus Linguistics* 10(1): 37–61.

(2015) Discussing Science in the Public Sphere: A Corpus-assisted Study of Web-based Interaction Concerning the Measles, Mumps and Rubella (MMR) Triple Vaccine. Unpublished PhD dissertation, University of Birmingham.

Orwell, George (1949) *1984*. New York, NY: Harcourt.

Partington, A. (2003) *The Linguistics of Political Argumentation: The Spin-doctor and the Wolf-pack at the White House*. London: Routledge.

(2004) 'Corpora and Discourse, a Most Congruous Beast', in A. Partington, J. Morley and L. Haarman (eds.) *Corpora and Discourse*, pp. 11–20. Bern: Peter Lang.

(2006) 'Metaphors, Motifs and Similes across Discourse Types: Corpus-assisted Discourse Studies (CADS) at Work', in A. Stefanowitsch and S. Gries (eds.) *Corpus-based Approaches to Metaphor and Metonymy*, pp. 267–304. Berlin: Mouton de Gruyter.

(2009) 'Evaluating Evaluation and Some Concluding Thoughts on CADS', in J. Morley and P. Bayley (eds.) *Corpus-assisted Discourse Studies on the Iraq Conflict: Wording the War*, pp. 261–304. New York, NY: Routledge.

(2010) 'Modern Diachronic Corpus-assisted Discourse Studies (CD-CADS) on UK Newspapers: An Overview of the Project'. *Corpora* 5(2): 83–108.

Partington, Alan, Alison Duguid and Charlotte Taylor (2013) *Patterns and Meanings in Discourse Theory and Practice in Corpus-assisted Discourse Studies (CADS)*. Amsterdam: John Benjamins.

Philo, Greg, Emma Briant and Pauline Donald (2013) *Bad News for Refugees*. Cambridge: Pluto Press.

Piketty, T. (2014) *Capital in the Twenty-First Century*. Boston, MA: Harvard University Press.

Piper, A. (2000) 'Some Have Credit Cards and Others Have Giro Cheques: "Individuals" and "People" as Lifelong Learners in Late Modernity', *Discourse and Society* 11(3): 515–42.

Pragglejaz Group (2007) 'MIP: A Method for Identifying Metaphorically Used Words in Discourse', *Metaphor and Symbol* 22(1): 1–39.

Prince, Ellen, J. Frader and C. Bosk (1982) 'On Hedging in Physician-Physician discourse', in J. di Pietro (ed.) *Linguistics and the Professions*, pp. 83–97. Norwood, NJ: Ablex.

Propp, Vladimir (1971) *Morphology of the Russian Folktale*. Austin, TX: University of Texas Press.

Purser, Philip (1992) *Done Viewing*. London: Quartet Books.

Randall, Adrian (1986) 'The Philosophy of Luddism: The Case of the West of England Woolen Workers, ca. 1790–1809', *Technology and Culture* 27(1): 1–17.

Raven, J. (2016) 'Debating the Lottery in Britain c. 1750–1830', in Manfred Zollinger (ed.) *Random Riches: Gambling Past and Present*, pp. 87–104. Abingdon: Routledge.

Rayson, P. (2009) Wmatrix: A Web-based Corpus Processing Environment, Computing Department, Lancaster University. Available at: ucrel.lancs.ac.uk/wmatrix.

Reisigl, M. and Wodak, R. (2001) *Discourse and Discrimination: Rhetorics of Racism and Anti-Semitism*. London: Routledge.

Renkema, J. (2004) *Introduction to Discourse Studies*. Amsterdam: John Benjamins.

Richardson, J. (2004) *(Mis)representing Islam: The Racism and Rhetoric of British Broadsheet Newspapers*. Amsterdam: John Benjamins.

(2006) *Analysing Newspapers: An Approach from CDA*. London: Palgrave.

Rixon, Paul (2011) *TV Critics and Popular Culture: A History of British Television*. Criticism International Library of Cultural Studies 16. London: I.B.Tauris.

(2014) Popular Newspaper Discourse: The Case of UK TV Criticism from the 1950s to the 1980s, *Journal of Historical Pragmatics* 15(2): 314–30. Available at: https://benjamins.com/# catalog/journals/jhp.15.2.08rix/details.

Robinson, David (2016) 'Review of Fairclough, *Language and Power*, 3rd edition', *Journal of Language and Politics* 15(1): 116–19.

Rowlingson, Karen (2012) *Wealth Inequality: Key Facts*. Birmingham: University of Birmingham Policy Commission on the Distribution of Wealth.

Sandel, Michael (2012) *What Money Can't Buy*. New York, NY: Farrar Strauss Giroux.

Sandford, Cedric (1980) 'The Diamond Commission and the Redistribution of Wealth', *British Journal of Law and Society* 7(2): 286–96.

Santa Ana, Otto (1990) '"Like an Animal I Was treated": Anti-immigrant Metaphor in US Public Discourse', *Discourse and Society* 10(2): 191–224.

Sapir, E. (1983), *Selected Writings of Edward Sapir in Language, Culture, and Personality*, ed. D.G. Mandelbaum. Berkeley, CA: University of California Press.

Scott, M. (1999) *WordSmith Tools Help Manual, Version 3.0*. Oxford: Mike Scott/ Oxford University Press.

(2007) *Oxford WordSmith Tools Version 4.0*. Available at: www.lexically. net/down loads/version4/wordsmith.pdf.

Sedlak, M. (2000) 'You Really Do Make an Unrespectable Foreign Policy', in R. Wodak and T.A. van Dijk (eds.) *Racism at the Top: Parliamentary Discourses on Ethnic Issues in Six European States*, pp. 107–68. Klagenfurt, Austria: Drava-Verlag.

Semino, E., Z. Demjén and J. Demmen (2016) 'An Integrated Approach to Metaphor and Framing in Cognition, Discourse and Practice, with an Application to Metaphors for Cancer', *Applied Linguistics*, https://doi.org/10.1093/applin/amw028.

Semino, E. and M.H. Short (2004) *Corpus Stylistics*. London: Routledge.

Simpson, P. (1993) *Language, Ideology and Point of View*. London: Routledge.

Simpson, P., ed. (2004) *Stylistics: A Resource Book for Students*. London: Routledge

Simpson, P. and A. Mayr (2010) *Language and Power*. London: Routledge.

Sinclair, J. (1991) *Corpus, Concordance, Collocation*. Oxford: Oxford University Press.

(2001) 'Preface', in M. Ghadessy, A. Henry and R.L. Roseberry (eds.) *Small Corpus Studies and ELT*, pp. vii–xv. Amsterdam: John Benjamins.

(2004) *Trust the Text: Language, Corpus and Discourse*. London: Routledge.

Sotillo, S.M. and J. Wang-Gempp (2004) 'Using Corpus Linguistics to Investigate Class, Ideology, and Discursive Practices in Online Political Discussions: Pedagogical Applications of Corpora', in U. Connor and T.A. Upton (eds.) *Applied Corpus Linguistics*, pp. 91–122. Amsterdam: Rodopi.

Stallybrass, Peter (1989) 'Drunk with the Cup of Liberty': Robin Hood, the Carnivalesque, and the Rhetoric of Violence in Early Modern England', in Nancy Armstrong and Leonard Tennenhouse (eds.) *The Violence of Representation*, pp. 45–76. London: Routledge.

Steen, Gerard J., Ewa Biernacka, Aletta G. Dorst, Anna A. Kaal, Irene Lopez-Rodriguez and Trijntje Pasma (2010) 'Pragglejaz in Practice: Finding Metaphorically Used Words in Natural Discourse', in Graham Low, Zazie Todd, Alice Deignan and Lynne Cameron (eds.) *Researching and Applying Metaphor in the Real World*, pp. 165–84. Amsterdam: John Benjamins.

Steen, Gerard J., Aletta Dorst, Berenike Herrmann, Anna Kaal, Tina Krennmayr and Trijntje Pasma (2010) *A Method for Linguistic Metaphor Identification: From MIP to MIPVU*. Amsterdam: John Benjamins.

Stiglitz, Joseph (2012a) 'The Price of Inequality', *Guardian Online*, 5 June. Available at: www.guardian.co.uk/business/2012/jun/05/price-of-inequality-united-states.

(2012b) *The Price of Inequality: How Today's Divided Society Endangers our Future*. New York, NY: Norton.

Stubbs, M. (1994) 'Grammar, Text, and Ideology: Computer-assisted Methods in the Linguistics of Representation', *Applied Linguistics* 15(2): 201–23.

(1995) Collocations and Semantic Profiles: On the Cause of the Trouble with Quantitative Studies. *Functions of Language* 2(1):23–55.

(1996) *Text and Corpus Analysis*. Oxford: Blackwell.

(1997) 'Whorf's Children: Critical Comments on Critical Discourse Analysis', in A. Wray and A. Ryan (eds.) *Evolving Models of Language*, pp. 100–16. Clevedon: Multilingual Matters.

(2001) *Words and Phrases: Corpus Studies of Lexical Semantics*. Oxford: Blackwell.

Temple, Mick (2008) *The British Press*. Maidenhead: Open University Press.

Teubert, Wolfgang (2010) *Meaning, Discourse and Society*. Cambridge: Cambridge University Press.

Thompson, E. P. (1963) *The Making of the English Working Class*. London: Penguin.

Titscher, S., M. Meyer, R. Wodak and E. Vetter (2000) *Methods of Text and Discourse Analysis*. London: SAGE.

Tognini-Bonelli, E. (2001) *Corpus Linguistics at Work*. Amsterdam: John Benjamins.

Toolan, Michael (1997) Language, English Studies, and Democracy: Inaugural Lecture, University of Birmingham, 29 April.
(1998) *Language in Literature: An Introduction to Stylistics*. London: Arnold.
(2015) *Making Sense of Narrative Text: Situation, Repetition, and Picturing*. New York, NY: Routledge.
Toynbee, Polly and David Walker (2008) *Unjust Rewards: Ending the Greed that is Bankrupting Britain*. London: Granta Publications.
Van der Valk, I. (2000) 'Parliamentary Discourse on Immigration and Nationality in France', in R. Wodak and T.A. van Dijk (eds.) *Racism at the Top: Parliamentary Discourses on Ethnic Issues in Six European States*, pp. 221–60. Klagenfurt: Drava.
Van Dijk, T.A. (1988) *News as Discourse*. Hillsdale, NJ: Lawrence Erlbaum.
(1991) *Racism and the Press*. London: Routledge.
(1993) *Elite Discourse and Racism*. Thousand Oaks, CA: SAGE.
(1998a) *Ideology*. London: SAGE.
(1998b) *Ideology: A Multidisciplinary Approach*. London: SAGE.
(1998c) 'Opinions and Ideologies in the Press', in A. Bell and P. Garrett (ed.) *Approaches to Media Discourse*, pp. 21–63. Oxford: Blackwell.
(2000a) 'New(s) Racism: A Discourse Analytical Approach', in Cottle, S. (ed.) *Ethnic Minorities and the Media: Changing Cultural Boundaries*, pp. 33–49. Buckingham: Open University Press.
(2000b) 'Parliamentary Debates', in R. Wodak and T.A. van Dijk (eds.) *Racism at the Top: Parliamentary Discourses on Ethnic Issues*, pp. 45–79. Klagenfurt: Drava.
(2001) 'Critical Discourse Analysis', in D. Schiffrin, D. Tannen and H. Hamilton (eds.) *The Handbook of Discourse Analysis*, pp. 352–71. Blackwell, Oxford.
(2005) *Discourse and Racism in Spain and Latin America*. Amsterdam: John Benjamins.
(2006) 'Ideology and Discourse Analysis', *Journal of Political Ideologies* 11(2): 115–40.
(2008a) *Discourse and Context: A Socio-cognitive Approach*. Cambridge: Cambridge University Press.
(2008b) *Discourse Reader*. London: SAGE.
(2011) *News Analysis: Case Studies of International and National News in the Press*. London: Routledge.
(2014) *Discourse and Knowledge: A Sociocognitive Approach*. Cambridge: Cambridge University Press.
Van Leeuwen, Theo (1995) 'Representing Social Action', *Discourse and Society* 6(1): 81–106.
(1996) 'The Representation of Social Actors', In M. Coulthard and C.R. Caldas-Coulthard (eds.) *Texts and Practices: Readings in Critical Discourse Analysis*, pp. 32–70. London: Routledge.
(2008) *Discourse and Practice: New Tools for Critical Discourse Analysis*. Oxford: Oxford University Press.
Verschueren, Jef (2013) *Ideology in Texts*. Cambridge: Cambridge University Press.
Vessey, R. (2016) 'Language Ideologies in Social Media: The Case of Pastagate', *Journal of Language and Politics* 15(1): 1–24.
Weiss, G. and R. Wodak, eds. (2003) *Critical Discourse Analysis: Theory and Interdisciplinary*. Basingstoke: Palgrave.

Westergaard, John (1995) *Who Gets What: The Hardening of Class Inequality in the Late Twentieth Century.* Cambridge: Polity Press.

Whorf, B.L. (1956) *Language, Thought, and Reality: Selected Writings of Benjamin Lee Whorf,* ed. J.B. Carroll. Cambridge, MA: MIT Press.

Widdowson, H.G. (2000) 'On the Limitations of Linguistics Applied', *Applied Linguistics* 21(1): 3–25.

Wilkinson, R. (2005) *The Impact of Inequality: How to Make Sick Societies Healthier.* London: Routledge.

Wilkinson, R. and Pickette, K. (2009) *The Spirit Level: Why More Equal Societies Almost Always Do Better.* London: Penguin.

Williams, Raymond (1976) *Keywords.* London: Fontana.

Wodak, R. (1986) *Language Behavior in Therapy Groups.* Los Angeles, CA: University of California Press.

(1996) *Disorders of Discourse.* London: Longman.

(2001) 'The Discourse Historical Approach', in R. Wodak and M. Meyer (eds.) *Methods of Critical Discourse Analysis*, pp. 63–94. London: SAGE.

(2004) 'Critical Discourse Analysis', in C. Seale, G. Gobo, J.F. Gubrium and D. Silverman (eds.) *Qualitative Research Practice*, pp. 197–213. London: SAGE.

(2006) 'Review Article: Boundaries in Discourse Analysis', *Journal of Language in Society* 35(4): 595–611.

(2007) 'Pragmatics and Critical Discourse Analysis: A Cross-disciplinary Inquiry', *Journal of Pragmatics and Cognition* 15(1): 203–27.

(2008) 'Introduction', in R. Wodak and M. Kryz·anowski (eds.) *Qualitative Discourse Analysis in the Social Sciences*, pp. 1–29. Basingstoke: Palgrave Macmillan.

Wodak, R. and P. Chilton, eds. (2007) *A New Agenda in Critical Discourse Analysis*, 2nd edn. Amsterdam: John Benjamins.

Wodak, R. and M. Krzyz·anowski, eds. (2008) *Qualitative Discourse Analysis in the Social Sciences.* Basingstoke: Palgrave Macmillan.

Wodak, R. and M. Meyer, eds. (2001) *Methods of Critical Discourse Analysis.* London: SAGE.

Wodak, R. and T.A. van Dijk, eds. (2000) *Racism at the Top: Parliamentary Discourses on Ethnic Issues in Six European States.* Klagenfurt, Austria: Drava-Verlag.

Young, M. (1958 [1967]) *The Rise of the Meritocracy.* London: Penguin.

Zucman, Gabriel (2015) Inequality: Are We Really 'All in This Together'? Available at: http://blogs.lse.ac.uk/politicsandpolicy/inequality-are-we-really-all-in-this-together.

Index

Milton Keynes UK
Ingram Content Group UK Ltd.
UKHW020836110324
439289UK00017B/86

9 781108 464208